STEVEN SPURRIER
A LIFE IN WINE

To Bella, and to Wine

STEVEN SPURRIER
A LIFE IN WINE

ACADEMIE DU VIN LIBRARY

Published 2020 by
Académie du Vin Library Ltd
academieduvinlibrary.com

Publisher: Simon McMurtrie
Editor in Chief: Susan Keevil
Editor: Diane Pengelly
Art Director: Tim Foster
Index: Hilary Bird
Commissioned photography: Lucy Pope

First published in 2018 by Adelphi Publishers

ISBN: 978-1-913141-07-3

Printed and bound in Italy by Elcograf, Verona

CONTENTS

A FEW WORDS ABOUT STEVEN

How to explain Steven Spurrier? Wine merchant, world traveller, explorer of cellar and vineyard. His Paris career saw him turn teacher, taster, wine educator and enthusiast. A third incarnation as author, columnist and communicator firmly established him on the world stage. Then lately (septuagenarian status notwithstanding) he has become a grower, wine-maker and pioneer of Bride Valley Dorset sparkling wine. As reading these memoirs will attest, Steven's contribution to the wine world has been phenomenal. But perhaps he is too modest to tell the full story.

Simon McMurtrie

(Publisher, Académie du Vin Library)

Steven Spurrier remains as important a figure in the wine world today, aged 79, as he has been since 1976, when the Judgement of Paris not only put California wines on the map but also propelled him into wine's global spotlight. In the last five years alone, Steven has been named *Decanter* Man of the Year (2017), IWSC (International Wine & Spirits Competition) Honorary Chair (2019) and Honorary President of the WSET (Wine & Spirit Education Trust) (2017 to 2020). I have also worked closely with him on the creation of his brainchild, the Académie du Vin Library, which was launched in 2019 with a new edition of Michael Broadbent's groundbreaking *Wine Tasting*, shortly before Michael's 92nd birthday. Steven's *A Life in Wine* is the eighth title for the Académie du Vin Library.

These recent accomplishments have coincided with what perhaps may prove to be his most enduring venture yet: the nurturing of Bride Valley Vineyard in Dorset, now pitching its excellent Brut Reserve, Blanc de Blancs, high-end Chardonnay and – importantly, in a new departure for English wines – its Crémant, into the top flight of English wines.

Indeed, it is Steven's achievements in recent years that have motivated me to refresh and republish his memoirs, this time with the benefit of personal tributes from some of the notable wine-world figures who are proud to call him their friend, advisor and inspiration. They reflect on Steven's impact on their own lives, and his immense influence on wine globally.

Hugh Johnson
(Friend and fellow Rugbeian)

Master of brainwaves and bubbly

Were we really at school together? Surely I'd have followed such an elegant figure, even taking notes, but at Rugby we were three years apart. No, I first heard of Steven when he had already had the brainwave of teaching Paris about wine. How had he realized that Paris knew even less about wine than London did? Ostensibly his wine shop, Cave de la Madeleine, was aimed at an ex-pat clientele, largely American. In fact its impudent elegance had a deep appeal to proper Parisians, however chauvinist (a trait not unknown in France). When Steven coined the inspired title of L'Académie du Vin it was not only Americans who showed up. Sadly I never did. Paris was never big on my itinerary.

I even missed the seismic Judgement of Paris tasting on May 24th 1976. He kindly invited me, but I was on other duties at the Chelsea Flower Show that day.

It was when Steven came home to England, and he and Bella settled in their idyllic Dorset village, that we really met. The sight of his cellar is a vivid memory. To a seriously afflicted wine man, certain labels shine like gemstones – and there were a lot of those.

Steven's ventures, always brainwaves, rather reminded me of Ukridge, Wodehouse's character who was always on the point of making a fortune, but who always needed a fiver to get the scheme off the ground. Steven didn't need the fiver (nor did he call you 'laddie', thank goodness). Some of his ideas sounded so exciting I would gladly have bid for a small share if there had been one going.

School came back into the picture when Steven, Ben Howkins (another Rugbeian) and I were asked to help with fund-raising for the school's admirable bursary scheme. We came up with a *Call My Bluff*-style wine tasting. Well-wishers paid for tables with friends, where they were given a series of wines to taste. The three of us, Steven, Ben and I, took turns to persuade them that the Sancerre came from Marlborough, the Tempranillo was Pinot Noir and the Sonoma Cab was from Pessac-Léognan, totally contradicting one another. None of us is a practised liar, but after a few sips we seemed to succeed. The winning table got a prize and the evening ended with blushes and supper.

We all followed Steven's recommendations in *Decanter*, and *Decanter* for years followed his lead to regions and growers worth exploring. Not surprisingly, a relatively recent enthusiasm of his (and mine) has been English wine.

The hills near Steven and Bella's house (hills where Bella the Shepherdess grazed her flock) suddenly looked to them like unplanted vineyards. Not for long. To Steven the little river Bride (it emerges at Bridport) is the future Marne, and his bubbly (the initial batch a touch too bubbly) started to become a picture of his palate: precise, intense, sophisticated, acute. What could be more satisfying in a critic's life than to write the masterpiece he has been pursuing for so long?

Marcel Guigal
(Renowned Rhône winemaker and
ambassador for organic viticulture)

Egalitarian to the letter

At the beginning of the 1970s, I had the great pleasure of presenting my wines at Cave de la Madeleine in Paris. Steven and I were so young… I was struck by his interest and his involvement in the great wines of the Rhône at a time when our region evoked a lot less interest than it does now. It was my first and greatest memory, and the start of a long friendship marked by a profound admiration.

Jasper Morris MW
(Burgundy specialist, merchant,
author and critic)

Going bravely into the world

Sometimes I think of Steven as Voltaire's hero *Candide*, going bravely out into the world, albeit with a certain naivety. Characteristically, he has found his own tweak to the famous advice, *Il faut cultiver notre jardin*, by turning his attention to planting a vineyard on the chalky Dorset hillsides of his home.

Steven has all the ideas. Many are ahead of their time, some have worked triumphantly – most notably, of course, those around his masterminding of the famous 1976 Judgement of Paris – and while others may have dented the Spurrier finances, they have never daunted Steven's enthusiasm, which he shares so widely with all who know him.

Steven has been unfailingly helpful throughout my career in wine. He is one of the most generous and supportive individuals I have come across. He also has perfect manners. Years ago, when Steven always wore a tie, he came to a very informal party at our house in Burgundy, where he knew the dress code would be casual. His solution? Still to wear a tie but to cover it up with a roll-neck sweater. Elegance personified!

Steven is a living paradox. In some ways the quintessential English gentleman, he nonetheless rose to fame abroad in Paris; he is rightfully esteemed in Japan where his Académie du Vin has been thriving since he founded it in 1987, and in India (which perhaps was not quite ready for the same approach, but as always Steven was the first to see its vast potential as a market).

I have never heard the slightest negative word about Steven – apart from some stories he has told against himself, not all of which are suitable for print. He is so full of energy it is hard to believe he is about to enter his 80th year. We will hear more from him in his ninth decade, for sure.

John Livingstone-Learmonth
(Fellow wine writer)

A man of elegance and durability

The obvious starting place for *mon cher ami Stéphan* is pedigree. He has pedigree in bucket-loads. His parents conducted the sort of lifestyle that would have featured in Anthony Powell's epic 12-book series *A Dance to the Music of Time*, set in the inter- and post-war years, descending from Derbyshire to the gilded lights and glamour of fine dining in London, Paris, the Côte d'Azur. Elegance was very much on the menu.

The young Steven wasn't at all a country lad, and would take to walking the five-and-a-half miles into Derby 'to buy comics and variety magazines; I would then take the bus back home. It's amazing what you do when you're bored. If I'd had a bicycle, I would have been much more adventurous'. Missed a trick there, Steven.

As soon as he could, he escaped his bucolic surroundings. 'The utter boredom drove me to London; I haven't had a moment's boredom since.'

I first came across Steven in the early 1970s, when he was the British maestro of the Parisian wine scene. I was living in Aix-en-Provence, teaching English to the deep-sea divers of Jacques Cousteau's company, Comex. I had started to research a book on the wines of the Rhône a project suggested by my sponsor Melvyn Master, an old friend of Steven's. I heard tales of Steven's exploits with tastings, teaching, retailing, and reckoned he had the north of France pretty well covered.

It was sometime in the mid-1970s that I first experienced Steven's penchant for elegance. We had tasted together at the Mâcon Wine Fair and were about to dine at the grassroots one-star Restaurant Robin in Chénas, which had a lovely terrace looking across the vineyards. I was a substitute for Georges Duboeuf (a long story), and Timothy Johnston was also present. Tim and I were dressed pretty casually, long hair and all, but there was Steven in a sharp suit, immaculately pressed trousers – and a moustache. Dressed for a film set, perhaps…

Little did we know what was about to occur. There was an advertising shoot for the heavily marketed Le Piat de Beaujolais brand at the restaurant. One of the male actors failed to arrive at the luncheon table (all hair-tossing girls and *beau monde*), so the producers looked around at the other diners and selected the dapper Monsieur Spurrier to stand in.

There was one hitch for our hero: association with such a wine as Piat Beaujolais. Steven struck a hard bargain. 'I demanded that my dog Digby would accompany me at the end of the table [where the impeccable crease in his trousers would be visible].' Digby was a large Briard sheepdog from southwest France, not easy to control. Canine antics duly delayed the shoot even further, but once some calm was managed, the photos were taken.

Steven's trump card was revealed later. 'I refused to have my hand on a bottle of Le Piat de Beaujolais, or on a glass of it, so the ad showed me with my hand on Digby.' Pure Spurrier.

I have always regarded Steven as a mentor and close friend; we have managed trips to the Rhône naturally enough, but also to California, where to see the esteem in which he is held by leading lights such as Paul Draper of Ridge and Warren Winiarski of Stag's Leap, is truly impressive.

However, the Judgement of Paris, shocking as it was for the French, hasn't clouded the respect of the Bordelais for him, either. Whether his portrayal in one of the resulting films was anywhere near the truth, I leave others to decide. Note to filmmakers: beyond the foppish exterior lies great durability. To be knocked off his bicycle on the way to lunch at his club, Boodle's, and still manage to get the message from the inside of an ambulance that his guests should continue without him, is more pure Spurrier.

As are the ideas. Out they pour, with seasoned Spurrier-watchers taking bets on which ones will float or sink, indeed how well or how badly – often a pretty close equation. Would I be Steven's bank manager? No. But I remember the Smirnoff vodka ad decades ago – 'he was an accountant until he drank Smirnoff vodka' – showing a Spurrier-like dude in a large hat. Maybe Steven has inspired a long line of such officials over the years?

So I tip my hat to this *révolutionnaire*, this *créateur et homme de grande élégance*. *Allez* Spurrier!

Charles Lea
(Wine merchant, Lea & Sandeman)

A sartorial role model

In some ways Steven's presence in my life has been fleeting, and yet he has had a profound influence. My interest in wine was kindled through the dregs of samples left over from Académie du Vin tastings brought back to our Paris flat by George Leggatt (now Lord Leggatt PC), who told us what he could remember about them from the Académie lectures.

Gradually, through George's stories of his work as Cave de la Madeleine's delivery driver (which sounded a lot more fun than the photocopying room of the lawyers' offices where I spent my days), I learned about Steven, eventually meeting him. He often seemed to be on the way to a tasting, or returning from one, wearing a pale linen Tommy Nutter suit, a pink shirt and a wide Mr Fish unbleached silk tie, looking as crisp and elegant on his return as he did when he set out, and radiating smiles of enthusiasm. I even saw him in his famous silk-faced kingfisher-blue velvet dinner jacket with the tight and then flared sleeves (and seven covered buttons on each). I have long tried to emulate his skill in long-distance and precision spitting, but also wondered that he went to tastings where he seemed in no danger from other 'looser cannons'.

Pursuing the kindled interest, I too went to work for Steven at the Cave, and learnt much about the producers he was working with. Later, when I began to work for Graham Chidgey at Laytons, there was Steven too, involved with the Malmaison Wine Club, and Graham had also taken over Cave de la Madeleine UK, in which he put Patrick Sandeman to run as a standalone merchant.

As Steven's third career of wine writing blossomed at *Decanter*, we began to see more of each other at press tastings or in our shop, and he would occasionally suggest to me that I look at this or that winery and who to contact. Surprisingly (or not) these contacts were never men – and Patrick's first question was always '...and how pretty is she, Steven?'

Sarah Kemp

(Former managing director of *Decanter* magazine)

Respected commentator and wine judge

I remember clearly the evening I first met Steven Spurrier. It was at the wine industry trade ball, he was walking off the dance floor, head held high, immaculately dressed as always. I enquired how his new job at Harrods was going and with typical Steven frankness he replied: 'I've been fired.' I knew instantly that he would be a huge asset to *Decanter* and asked him to join us as the magazine's consultant editor. So began a great partnership and a new era for us all.

We worked together for a quarter of a century, but work seems the wrong word for it. Discussing anything with Steven was a total pleasure as he was enthusiastic, open to new ideas and always happy to connect his extraordinary network of wine industry friends to ensure the best possible outcome for any venture.

Steven was for many years *Decanter*'s leading Bordeaux taster, and was always welcome in the region, despite the 1976 Paris Tasting in which the California wines he brought in trounced those of its top châteaux. This tasting made him world-famous – although his wife, Bella, quipped at the time: 'There goes his Légion d'Honneur.'

Steven and I travelled together to all corners of the globe. I have happy memories of him at a conference in Seattle telling the astonished audience that a good bottle of wine is one you want to have a second of right away. He opened *Decanter*'s first Wine Encounter in Shanghai by presenting the best Chinese wines with Professor Li Demei. Here he showed what I really valued about working with him: his egalitarian approach to wine. Steven is as excited about an unknown wine from an obscure region as he is about one of the great classics. What he looks for in each is its intrinsic quality, and his objectivity, openness and honesty as a judge has cemented his international reputation as one of the world's great wine commentators. Steven's influence on the way *Decanter* magazine became a world-wide brand was considerable.

There is also no one I know who is more generous with his knowledge than Steven. One of the reasons that the *Decanter* World Wine Awards became the world's largest wine competition – at its peak featuring 17,000 wines – was in no small part due to judges wanting to work under his guidance. Whenever there was a dispute about a wine, it was Steven they wanted to arbitrate and to learn from. The respect he commanded from the world's judges was total.

But beyond all this, he is a true and loyal friend, there to celebrate the highs and to commiserate in the lows. Erudite, elegant, generous, cultured, with a delightfully dry sense of humour, his objectivity and fairness in recognizing quality wherever it comes from has made him one of the true wine industry legends.

Eduardo Chadwick
(Winemaker and ambassador for Chilean wine)

**A revolutionary and
a gentleman**

Steven Spurrier has been a real disrupter in the world of fine wines, championing the recognition of quality beyond preconceived ideas, origin or history. He masterminded the 1976 Paris blind tasting for California wines. He then repeated this impeccable template with the Berlin Tasting in 2004, bringing instant recognition and awareness for Chilean wines, showing them to be among the great wines of the world.

I am honoured and thankful to have had the opportunity to travel the globe with Steven since, conducting countless masterclasses and learning from his vast knowledge and experience.

He is the very best ambassador for genuinely world-class wines. And more importantly, he is a great man of immense generosity and a true gentleman.

Andrew Caillard MW

(Australia-based specialist wine auctioneer
and author)

Around the wine world in (nearly) 80 years

Steven Spurrier is an unforgettable force in the cause of fine wine. His boyish enthusiasm and brilliant optimism outshine every silver *tastevin*. Few wine professionals have soared above the clouds, battled against headwinds and retained so graciously their humility, generosity of spirit and sense of perspective. He is a role model of the ages and one of the most memorable of all those great English wine identities who have lived on the wide cusp of the 20th/21st century.

Although his reputation is anchored in the Judgement of Paris tasting held in 1976, Steven's catalogue of achievements is a far greater volume of work. The themes of trial and error, failure and success, risk and reward are all intertwined with that golden thread of resilience. His experience in the world of wine has a dream-like quality, especially when seen through the rear-view mirror.

I first met Steven Spurrier in London on one of my occasional visits to England in the 1990s, when representing Wine Australia and the auction house Langton's. During the 2000s he was chairing the Japan Wine Challenge in Tokyo, where his dapper Englishness and open-minded curiosity promoted a sense of rigour and daring. There was no technical straitjacketing typical of Australian wine shows and so the results always reflected a marvellous diversity of style and regional character. Steven's natural presence, authority, underlying eccentricity and charm captivated and inspired the Japanese. His iconic gravitas gave this annual event a specialness that endeared him to everyone including the honorary patron, Princess Takamado.

When we all went to China together for the inaugural China Wine Challenge (organized by polyglot wine entrepreneur Ron Brown), Steven transformed from mortal-being to god-like figure. Then in his late 60s he possessed the aura of a legendary scholar. Combined with his charming English patrician manner he magnetized the Chinese. Queues of wine professionals and hangers-on, wherever we would go, politely requested a shared photograph. '*Spurriermania*' was a genuine phenomenon, reflecting his international standing and ability to connect effortlessly with people.

When He Lan Qing Xue's 'Jia bei lan' won a significant *Decanter* trophy in 2019 it showed progressive thinking, no doubt steered to some extent by chairman Steven Spurrier's perceptive and worldly attitude to wine. Unusually for his generation, he is far less entrenched in old-world narratives, hierarchies and mythologies. Steven has done much to break down the 'Emperor's New Clothes' syndrome and the snobbish barriers that feature in the fine wine scene. Nonetheless I can never remember him undermining the experiential value of beautiful wines of any type or cost – whether from a modest or legendary producer.

Steven's quixotic venture into English sparkling wine is typical of his enlightened imagination, love for wine and extraordinary optimism. A 'numbers man' would simply walk away, yet such ambitions are the essence of leadership. The rhythm of agriculture transcends a human lifetime. And Steven's Bride Valley Vineyard underscores a type of thinking that inspires progress and purpose for future generations.

That beaming confident smile, enquiring interest in humanity, the arts and love of everything to do with wine are the essence of his character. He personifies the classic Englishman, ripped from the pages of Victorian enlightenment and charged with modern-day visions. Few people have so profoundly informed, guided and inspired generations, including mine, through their journeys in wine. Steven Spurrier is one of England's great modern renaissance figures and a colossus in the world of fine wine.

Bartholomew Broadbent

(Specialist wine importer, son of Michael Broadbent)

Long-time friend and confidant

Steven Spurrier has always been incredibly kind to me. When I was 15 years of age he gave me a summer job at Cave de la Madeleine, his wine shop in Cité Berryer, Paris. I arrived clutching a suitcase and a bottle of Pimm's and he put me up in my own apartment. The accommodation was basic but the times were memorable in so many ways. Quite often, one of his restaurant friends would ring up and ask for help, needing to borrow an employee from Steven. I can claim that I have worked as a restaurant dishwasher, having been sent to fill in for lunchtime no-shows.

One day, the manager of Steven's shop, Mark Williamson – who later became famous for Willi's Wine Bar – asked me to make a wine delivery. There was a lot of snickering and I was unclear as to why I was being sent to deliver to this regular. What was so funny? I trundled off with a few cases on a hand cart and found the building. Upon ringing the door-bell, I was summoned by intercom to deliver the wine up a few floors. The door to the apartment was open and I deposited the cases of wine in the front hall, calling out for the lady, who had to sign the receipt. She shouted back, summoning me down the hallway. I am not sure who was more surprised, her seeing that a child had replaced her usual manly deliveryman, or me seeing that she was in the bath, expecting to give more than a signature.

Of course, Steven was a close family friend. My father called him the Peter Pan of the wine trade, and would often regale us with the famous Spurrier legends. Steven called my father his mentor. We saw each other frequently at family events, trade tastings, Vinexpo dinners and London Wine Fairs but my first career association with him was when I was working for Schenley Distilleries in Toronto. Steven agreed that I could open a branch of L'Académie du Vin there and he came over for the inauguration of this new chapter. He already had a branch in Montreal. I learned everything I needed to know to teach wine classes from Steven's excellent Académie du Vin wine course books, and basically taught the syllabus verbatim from those. We also arranged amazing tastings, such as a vertical of Château d'Yquem, which was written up in *Wine Spectator* in 1986.

To mark the 10th Anniversary of Steven's 1976 Judgement of Paris tasting, he arranged a repeat event in New York City; I was asked to be a judge. This was a wonderful opportunity and I was very thankful to Steven, although at the time I didn't fully realize the significance of his choice. The California wines beat the French again and the French press were scathing to say the least, picking apart every detail to make excuses. One French newspaper questioned the legitimacy of the judges, saying that since one of them was just a 24 year old who couldn't possibly have the experience to know what makes a wine good, the results proved nothing. But Steven had respect for my palate and knew that I had been tasting fine wines since before the age of seven.

I have had the pleasure, more recently, of judging with Steven for the Governor's Cup, which takes place each year in Richmond, Virginia or Washington DC. We taste through the best Virginia wines, picking 12 for the Governor's Case and awarding one the overall trophy. Some very jolly dinners ensue and he is always tremendous fun.

Steven has been an enormous influence in my life and over the years our friendship has grown. Where once he was a friend of my parents I now sense, after the easiest of transitions, that I am his friend in my own right. And this makes me very proud.

Miguel Torres

(Leading Spanish winemaker)

A fine judge in the winery

I met Steven many years ago in London, at one of those gatherings that wine people used to have, when celebrations and meetings in person were possible… On one of these occasions I asked him – and he accepted immediately – to come every year and taste our wines with us in Vilafranca del Penedès (Barcelona).

So, for several years we welcomed Steven at our winery, and we tasted morning and afternoon all our wines from Spain, Chile and California. I still keep all the notes of the tastings, and I was impressed by the precision and the quality of the remarks Steven used to make. Thanks to him we managed, on many occasions, to change the direction of our winemaking and by doing so, have improved the quality of our wines.

My daughter Mireia also has good memories of the tastings, for instance before launching our Vardon Kennett sparkling wine in 2016, she asked Steven what kind of 'dosage' would be ideal at disgorgement. He recommended that we keep the wine as pure and fresh as possible, so we rejected alternatives with different draft liqueurs. The approach he suggested could not have been more successful.

Mireia also remembers a tasting in 2017 where we got to taste Steven's rosé sparkling wine, Cuvée Bella, from Bride Valley. We all loved it, and she still remembers his expression of pride and satisfaction very fondly. But what Mireia highlights the most is that we all have learned a lot from Steven. After the tastings we used to have dinner together and we had long conversations about the vineyards and the wines. I keep great memories of these occasions.

I think Steven has made a fantastic contribution to the world of wine, and my son Miguel also joins me in hoping that in many years from now we will continue to enjoy his company and his friendship.

David Zambra

(School friend and fellow wine explorer)

From Rugby to recklessness…

I have sometimes wondered whether Steven's predilection for wearing suits on every possible occasion, and his choice of bicycling recklessly through London's lethal streets, sprang from his lack of affection for the school, where we met. In those days, Rugby was inhabited by the sons of country squires, clergymen and army officers, who wore dull tweed jackets and grey flannels and epitomized a world that was a far cry from the more glamorous and bohemian one Steven's soul hankered for. I was more conventional by nature but I must have shared this hankering as I joined him in forming the 'Architectural Society', which was founded entirely on the wish to avoid the misery of 'sports' and gain entry into any grand local house that we could reach on our bikes.

We would pedal down country lanes and up endless drives to be met by long-suffering and amiable hosts, complete with black Labradors at heel. Captivated by Steven's enthusiasm, our hosts would give us tours of mainly dilapidated but beautiful houses, followed by tea in draughty drawing rooms, before we wobbled down the pot-holed drives and back to semi-captivity.

For a while, after escaping from school, we remained in close proximity as we shared 'digs' in Paddington. These were run, as was so often the case at that time, by an ancient (to us – probably only middle-aged in reality) member of the upper classes known as The Baroness, who had fallen on hard times and was forced to take in 'nice young things' to make ends meet.

We were then thrown into a social whirl of parties and debs' delights but Steven was more suited to this than I, and besides, he was a carefree student whilst I toiled at an unexciting job. Our paths gradually parted and there followed a dormant period in our relationship, which was not really picked up again until he and Bella moved to France.

I was almost certainly introduced to wine by Steven (it was definitely a no-show in my childhood days) and my succumbing to its charms was in no small part due to my fascination with his wine shop in Paris. Somewhat late in the day – but, I have to say, extremely willingly – I abandoned my successful but dreary career in order to open the English offshoot of the Cave de la Madeleine in the Fulham Road. Initially, Steven chose the wines we stocked and his imaginative selection of growers allowed us to branch out beyond the usual Bordeaux and burgundies. One of the greatest perks of the job was the opportunity to visit vignerons. There were many happy occasions when Steven, sundry others (mainly now notable characters in the wine trade) and I had a fantastic time tasting and drinking (usually far too many) unusual and often delicious glasses of wine.

Our friendship survived the closure of both businesses and over the last 30 (help!) years my wife Phoebe and I have continued to have wonderful times with Steven and Bella. Apart from many visits to their house in Dorset, to be met by a scuffle of dogs, delicious food and amazing wine, we have spent numerous holidays with them in Italy. These have often been at Peter Femfert's immaculate wine estate outside Castellina in Chianti or at the ridiculously romantic Castello di Argiano, with its five-star view and even more stellar cast of inhabitants. There, Steven settles immediately into his routine of 10 lengths of the swimming pool followed by coffee and tapping away on his laptop until it's time to pull the cork before lunch.

Carefully organized vineyard visits are the only change to this pattern. Without exception, these are to staggeringly beautiful wine estates, almost always owned by immaculately dressed and utterly charming Italian aristocrats who are always thrilled to see Steven, and polite enough to make the rest of us welcome. Bella and Phoebe sometimes fall at the final hurdle of another bottling plant, but they have never yet failed to turn up at the finishing post to enjoy the superb lunches that follow.

All in all, meeting Steven at Rugby was the luckiest of encounters and has led to some of the most enjoyable, albeit sometimes bibulous, moments of my life.

Mark Williamson
(Founder of Willi's Wine Bar, Paris)

Volcanic ideas and unending enthusiasm

I have known Steven since 1976, a time when he was much scorned in certain circles for his famously disruptive wine tasting, and when his future in France was anything but assured. But the Judgement of Paris turned out to be a defining moment in the making of a rock star. Steven proved to be a man of Etna-like qualities – always smoking quietly in the distance, glowing attractively after dark and occasionally erupting spectacularly with a new ground-breaking idea to inspire and enthuse…

His inspirational ventures have ranged from the Cave de la Madeleine (where Steven was an early promoter of small producer, hand-crafted single-vineyard selections) to the Académie du Vin, which was to expand its educational reach across the globe; from decades of consultancy – where he helped to vastly improve the travel experience of the first-class passengers on Singapore Airlines – to a regular column in *Decanter* which saw him co-founding and nurturing the hugely successful Decanter World Wine Awards programme, to a not-so-small, daringly planted vineyard on the coast in Dorset – albeit at the expense of some rather delicious lamb chops.

Through all this, Steven was, as he still is, a terrifically generous sharer of friends, and an ever-willing participant in exciting ideas. His contribution to wine has been unending as well as unendingly varied.

James Lawther MW
(Wine writer and Bordeaux specialist)

My mentor and inspiration

I entered the world of wine via Cave de la Madeleine in Paris in 1983 and wasn't sure how it was all going to pan out. A foot on the lowest rung of the ladder wasn't a problem, but along with cellar work and deliveries I needed the stimulus to confirm this was my calling. Steven was the one who generated the spark and fanned the flame. It wasn't a specific event or incident that did it; more his enormous enthusiasm and passion for wine, whether it be grand cru or *petit vin*. All vied for his interest, and therefore kindled mine too.

And then there were the excursions into vineyards and the vivid memories retained: tasting in some of the greatest (but coldest) cellars in the world in Burgundy, Steven impeccable in suit and tie with just a raincoat to denote the chill; the eye-opening experience of drinking good, aged Chablis (Raveneau, as it happens) in the town bistro; the yearly pilgrimage to select our cuvée of Beaujolais Nouveau chez Pierre Ferraud (and the litres we would sell afterwards); capping a circuit of visits in the Southern Rhône (Beaucastel and Rayas included, of course) with lunch at Hiély Lucullus in Avignon, white Châteauneuf poured by the jug, before sprinting for the station and train back to Paris. On these experiences and more was my own career built and for this I am indebted to Steven.

Patricia Gastaud-Gallagher

(Fellow pioneer in Paris)

The Englishman who
sold wine to the French

Steven acknowledges two mentors in his wine life, Alexis Lichine and Michael Broadbent. I had one: Steven.

We met in Paris. Steven was living with Bella and infant Christian on a barge near Alexander III bridge, one year into his chosen trade of *caviste* in a tradition-bound 'City of Light' that held tightly to its prejudices on almost every subject, including wine. I was a young American with a BA in political science, an editorial assistant job at the *International Herald Tribune*, a column in my hometown newspaper, and a growing passion for wine.

On November 15th 1971, Steven was intent on selling Beaujolais Nouveau before anyone else, and I was researching an article on the immensely popular young wine for the *Wilmington Morning News*. Steven left Pierre Ferraud's winery in Belleville-en-Beaujolais at midnight, when the wine was officially released, and drove all night to arrive in Paris before shops opened. I had seen a classified ad in the '*Trib*' announcing 'Beaujolais Nouveau 8.30am at the Cave de la Madeleine in the Cité Berryer', near the American Embassy and across from Hermès; which was, luckily for me, only a few minutes from my small flat. I arrived on the dot expecting a French *caviste*, probably in overalls and quite possibly gruff. Instead I met Steven, a personable, handsome Englishman, unloading wine in front of his shop. I had my article on Beaujolais Nouveau but, clearly, Steven was a more interesting story.

An Englishman selling wine to the French? Could he possibly succeed? Steven obviously thought so, and he was right. By the time we met, he was building up a solid international clientele in the chic eighth *arrondissement* of embassies, fashion houses and international companies, sometimes delivering the wines himself.

As a client, I appreciated his approach to sales. It seemed to me that Steven did not actually 'sell' wine, he took the time to 'educate' clients by explaining the wines and describing the winemakers. Once clients had a glimpse behind the label, how could they resist taking a few bottles home? This teaching approach was especially well suited to the excellent, lesser known estate-bottled regional wines that had become Steven's specialty and stood shoulder to shoulder on his shelves with the great wines of Burgundy, Bordeaux and the Rhône Valley.

Wine-lovers, especially English speakers, began to gather at Cave de la Madeleine in the hope of tasting a wine or two at the end of the day. They were eager to know more and would soon be gratified with a dedicated space for structured tastings. In less than two years Steven was not only successfully selling wine to the French, he was also teaching them about it. In beautifully restored premises next door to the wine shop, he opened L'Académie du Vin, the first wine school in Paris, and perhaps the world. It had such potential, I thought Steven might need help. Fortunately, he agreed with me, and in September 1973 I left the *Trib* and began an exhilarating decade as Steven's assistant director, then director, of L'Académie du Vin.

By 1976 we were on a roll, with fully-booked courses in English and French most evenings in one or both tasting rooms, vertical and horizontal tastings with well-known château and estate owners on Monday evenings, wine-tasting lunches, day trips to Sancerre, Chablis and Champagne, weekends in Burgundy and Bordeaux, and a contract with the French restaurant association to train sommeliers. The first courses for sommeliers were taught by Jean-Luc Pouteau, *Meilleur Sommelier de France*, and later *Meilleur Sommelier du Monde*. Black-tie dinners came later.

Steven's invaluable contacts in every region of France, also in Italy and Spain, colleagues who respected him and were amused by the idea of Anglo-Saxons running a wine school in Paris, readily accepted invitations to present their wines at L'Académie du Vin.

The impact of the tasting in 1976 was most unexpected. Steven and I had gathered together a selection of boutique California wines to share with respected French colleagues in commemoration of the 200th anniversary of the Declaration of Independence of the American colonies. Our 'Bicentennial Tasting' became 'The Judgement of Paris' in *Time* magazine a few days later and 'the wine tasting that changed the world' in *Decanter* magazine. Steven credits me with the idea because, as he says, 'the English do not celebrate American independence', and I did make the exploratory trip to Napa. But I credit my incredible boss with making the tasting a landmark event with the friends and colleagues he invited, the benchmark French wines he chose – and for telling our friend and ex-student, journalist George Taber, that the tasting was taking place. Not only did George's article in *Time* set the event down in history, George also joined Steven for innumerable repeat tastings on at least two continents that confirmed the original scores. Steven's true genius was asking his *chère épouse* to stop by and take some photos. Bella Spurrier's photos have been published around the world, the only tangible evidence that the event actually happened.

In the 1980s, when Steven returned to England for the next chapters of his wine life, I continued in France as a columnist for *Cuisine & Vins de France*, editorial director of the *Who's Who International in Wine & Spirits*, and wine department director and academic director for Le Cordon Bleu Paris. This was thanks to my background at L'Académie du Vin, with Steven to guide me in wine tasting, his kindness, patience and incredible generosity in sharing his knowledge and contacts – all enhanced daily, of course, by his witty story-telling and the eternal Spurrier optimism.

For the record, his impact extended beyond wine. Steven also set the standard for elegance in the French retail world. He was the first *caviste* to wear a tie to work.

Reva K Singh

(Founder and editor of India's first
wine magazine, *Sommelier India*)

My friend and guide in wine

I first met Steven Spurrier in Bombay at a gathering of The Wine Society of India. The Society was started by David Banford in 2006 and Steven, always happy to promote wine in a new region, agreed to join as chairman of the board of wine advisors. This was a time when very little was known about wine in India, and our Wine Society did an immense amount to change this, providing information, education, specialized events and wine tastings, in which Steven played a pivotal role.

I was lucky to have met Steven so early on when the magazine I founded, *Sommelier India*, was still in its infancy. He has been a great supporter and a regular contributor. It was Steven who came to me with the idea of a Sommelier India Wine Competition, and Steven who persisted when I hesitated. I thought ours was still a very young industry and it was too early for the wines to be judged and rated. I was wrong.

As it turned out, the Sommelier India Wine Competition in 2009, organized in association with The Wine Society of India, was the first wine competition 'created by Indians and judged by the best Indian palates for the benefit of the Indian consumer' and was an extraordinary success. Subsequently, I was approached by several organizations to partner with them, but after working with Steven I was reluctant. I sensed in him a certain genuineness and authenticity that is rare to find. I believed in him.

In India, Steven was genuinely interested in sharing his love for wine with a people who were primarily whisky drinkers. He is generous to a fault and gives so much of himself, patiently answering even the most basic questions. It's a pity our Wine Society didn't last. It could have been a great force for good, but it was an idea ahead of its time. And since our Sommelier India Wine Competition is no longer feasible, Steven suggests we instead stage a special wine tasting and call it 'The Judgement of Delhi'!

Steven still regularly visits us. He is ever ready to taste another Indian wine and find something positive to say about it, helping many a concerned winemaker to stay the course. His confidence in the future of Indian wine hasn't waned and is reflected in his collaboration with Tuscan winemaker Piero Masi to produce three excellent Indian wines – MS Red, MS White and MS Rosé, with the 'M' and 'S' standing for their surnames as well as Master Selection. His faith in Indian wine is justified by the fact that our wines are now exported around the world.

I am delighted that Steven is bringing out this second edition of his memoirs and wish him every success with what is perhaps his greatest project, Bride Valley Vineyard. I look forward to the time when Bride Valley sparkling wines appear on wine lists in India.

Michel Bettane
(Leading French critic and fellow lover of vinous controversy)

Decisive, bold and the best of friends

At the end of the 1970s, I was a young teacher in Paris who did not know what to do on a Thursday evening. I was a beginner in the matter of wine appreciation and decided to enter the famous wine school opened by Steven Spurrier near the Place de la Madeleine. I did not know at the time, but this was to be the departure point for a long friendship that did not end when Steven returned to England – not even when he started to make 'champagne' there!

I owe my second life as wine taster to everything I learned at the Académie du Vin, where I met the best French growers and shared with Steven and his students their best wines. Bold as ever, Steven appointed me teacher there after only two years as a student. Chantal Lecouty, who had just bought the *Revue du vin de France*, was one of my first pupils, leading me to my third life, building a modern *Revue*.

I well know how charismatic Steven is and how important his influence on the international wine trade. I am eager to read his memories!

Ben Howkins
(Wine marketing specialist and author)

The most elegant of hosts

Steven does seem to carry the air of a magician about him. His Beau Brummel elegance combined with a steely resilience always makes for an interesting encounter. If he is explaining his next creative move, he will happily end with that contagious smile and pronounce '*et voilà*!' with an elegant flourish of his hand.

Although he breathes ideas as others breathe oxygen, Steven is someone who gets things done. His whole wine career is built on a series of innovations that his creative gene ensures are all trailblazers, some iconic, some may have an element of the helter-skelter, but all have the dedicated purpose of furthering the enjoyment of wine through education.

Hugh Johnson, Steven and I just overlapped at Rugby. They were both more senior than me – in every way – and our paths did not really cross. It was not until Steven married Bella, a delightful girl who haled, like me, from Northamptonshire, that our friendship was struck.

I hasten to May 1976. My diary for the week commencing May 17th says that I had dinner with Steven and Bella in Paris at their charming apartment in Rue de la Cerisaie. I think it must have been after that meal that Steven announced, after treating us to several delicious 1961 clarets, that he needed a decent glass of port. He dashed downstairs with the faithful Digby at his side, jumped on his bicycle and shot off to his splendid wine shop in the Cité Berryer, retrieved a bottle of Croft Old Particular 30-year old tawny port and triumphantly brought it back to the apartment. Such style.

Midweek I had dinner with the legendary Martin Bamford MW of Château Loudenne, then swooped down to Monte Carlo, as one does, to see my father, then back to Paris to spend Sunday night with the Spurriers. The following morning, May 24th, outside the apartment building, Steven and I bade each other farewell. He casually asking, as old friends do, what

I was doing that day. I explained that I was visiting Croft's French agents Rémy Martin; in return, I asked him the same question. 'Oh,' he said in a gentle matter-of-fact voice: 'I've got a tasting arranged. Bit worried about it. Hope it will work. I want to show the French that other people can also make wine.'

That event on May 24th 1976, 'as any fule kno', turned out to be the Judgement of Paris, possibly the most game-changing tasting the wine world has ever seen. As ever, Steven was diligent, far-sighted and modest.

Thirty years on, the plan was to hold a rerun at the Rothschild's place in Buckinghamshire, Waddesdon Manor. With less than two months to go, Philippine de Rothschild, no doubt still narked that 30 years ago Mouton (now a first growth) had come second, made it difficult for us to go ahead at Waddesdon. As I was the go-between, I made a few frantic calls to friends for an alternate venue. Simon Berry immediately volunteered Berry Brothers' enchanting wine cellars opposite St James's Palace.

First, the blind tasting was held, behind closed doors, for a chosen panel tasting the same wines as in 1976. The California wines wiped the floor with the French selection. Then, immediately afterwards, there was a 'non blind' tasting of the same wines from the 2000 vintage, for about 40 invited guests. I sat opposite Steven as the votes came in. It was nail-biting to say the least, but this time the Bordeaux reds triumphed.

Steven is the most generous of men. He thrives on sharing, whether it is his encyclopaedic knowledge or a bottle or three with friends. As we chatted one day about sport, which does not feature large in Steven's life, he proposed that his sport was 'lunching'. We often happily engage in this most convivial of sports at our respective clubs across the road from each other in St James's Street.

Steven is also a born host and organizer. Staying with him and Bella at home in Dorset is always a joy, and his pride in their Bride Valley vineyard very evident. His birthday celebrations, whether in Dorset, at the late Ransome's Dock in Battersea, or at the Arts Club, and other shared lunches at Le Gavroche to celebrate being *Decanter*'s Man of the Year or our annual shortest-day longest-lunch at the Garrick Club, are always immense fun, echoing Steven's contagious and exhilarating joie de vivre.

Our trio of Old Rugbeians has also convened to host the occasional *Call my Bluff* evening for charity events. We were perfect foils for each other, fibbing through our teeth about the provenance of each of the wines. Steven once remarked that of course the table at which Hugh's and my wife sat won because they knew when their husbands were lying.

Over the years, we became involved in several ventures together, such as the time when Steven generously passed me the Nicolas consultancy role, as he was 'too busy'. Then we spent months lugging 'sweat equity' around the extraordinary Vinopolis project.

The one venture we are both now happily involved in is the Académie du Vin Library. Its antecedent, the trail-blazing wine school, L'Académie du Vin, forged in the tasting room of Steven's innovative wine shop in Paris in 1972, came full circle on July 25th 2018 when Hugh, Steven and I had lunch at Brooks's to discuss how best we could resurrect this brilliant concept in today's world. As always, Steven led the way. '*Et voilà!*'

Marc Nadeau
(President and co-founder, with Steven, of Académie du Vin Canada)

My friend Steven

There are so many reasons why I feel that moving to France in 1981 in order to study at the Institut Européen des Affaires led to many of the best things that ever happened to me. Soon after I arrived, in October, I met Elizabeth who would become my fiancée in 1985 and is still my wife after 34 years together. I also met Steven Spurrier as a result of a lunchtime stroll from the private bank I was working for to finally explore the goings-on in the Cité Berryer.

A chalkboard sign outside the Cave de la Madeleine wine shop announcing both English and French wine courses compelled me to walk right in, as this was surely the door to wine heaven. I signed up for everything available, of course, but then I wanted to know who was in charge of this fine place. An elegant, courteous and well-dressed Englishman came down a spiral staircase (the Académie du Vin office then was upstairs) and offered to buy me a coffee at a restaurant a few metres away. He asked me who I was and what I was doing, but did not tell me a thing about himself. I told him that I had worked in restaurants and for a Formula One team a few years back while working my way through school, and that I got to see and try some very fine wines but wanted to learn much more about them.

Steven invited me to a small dinner party at his Paris home where he introduced me to his friends and opened a Guigal La Mouline 1976. That was it for me. I knew then that there was something generous and very special about this man. He also seemed to like me as I much as I liked him, in spite of our completely different backgrounds and upbringings.

The two of us would go on to have many tête-à-tête meals together over the next few years in Paris, and we have continued to do so in the many cities that we have visited as a team since, representing our respective businesses or the Académie du Vin around the world. One memorable lunch cancellation (by me) happened on February 17th 1988. We had planned to have a *déjeuner* at his bistro near St-Germain which was quite close to Elizabeth's doctor who wanted to see how her first pregnancy was coming along. I was told, instead, to rush to the clinic where my son Steven Nadeau was born a few hours later.

Steven Spurrier only once told me what to do. It was at a very prestigious wine tasting organized by Georg Riedl at Château Cheval Blanc during Vinexpo 1989. I was about to get up and offer comments to this small crowd of professionals. Steven put his hand on my arm and whispered: 'Just watch and listen, Marc.' I have never forgotten this, my finest lesson from the man who taught me – and continues to show me – more than anyone else about wine appreciation.

Warren Winiarski

(Napa Valley winemaker and founder of
Stag's Leap Wine Cellars)

The spur to new horizons

It is both an honour and a pleasure to make some public reflections on the life and works of Steven Spurrier. Our two paths have been entwined for quite a few years going back to that fateful year for both of us – 1976 – and the tasting that occurred in Paris. But these reflections will not, of course, reach out to encompass all of his works, because Steven continues to enrich the contemporary wine universe with his fertile presence.

I mention the year 1976 because that is when my path became to a degree bound together with his. We then both moved along in a direction that I certainly did not imagine or anticipate, and, I'm guessing, Steven himself did not fully foresee beforehand.

But, again I'm also guessing, perhaps Steven did imagine the *possibility* of the outcome of the Paris tasting more fully than anyone else associated with that event. Somewhere in the shadowy recesses of the boundary-land between thought and imagination, and the nameless something which asks 'what if?', he must have divined that the structure of his tasting created the possibility of the outcome that actually occurred. For, in the past, no one else had provided for such a possibility.

Over time, that tasting came to be seen by some as an image, in the world of wine, of the Copernican Revolution that altered the way of looking at the heavenly bodies. The tasting was eventually viewed by many as a Copernican moment for the world of wine. And, because it raised the aspirations for many winemakers around the globe, it had the same effect of shaking things up a bit. Steven was then viewed, in a limited way, as another 'spur', with a similar name: 'spurrier'.

It is curious that my name, which in Polish is originally tethered to wine, became even more bound to it by the tasting of 1976 – devised by a man who never appears to have had an ear for a dispiriting Muse.

Jancis Robinson OBE MW
(Wine writer, author and critic)

The champion of French wines

Listeners to the BBC's landmark morning news programme *Today* on a Thursday morning in May 2006 were told that France's top wine producers might be 'rather miffed' by the results of the major taste-off of mature California Cabernets versus mature first growth red Bordeaux, in which California unexpectedly swept the board. 'Miffed'? Pure Spurrier.

In many ways the man who organized the re-run of the famous California vs France tasting in London, and the original in Paris in 1976, is more interesting than the taste-offs themselves – and ironically he could hardly be more pro-French wine.

Perhaps every area of activity has its puzzlingly under-celebrated pioneer and Steven Spurrier is certainly the unsung hero of wine. He has quite exceptional wine knowledge, particularly but not exclusively of France, has fingers in vinous pies in six countries, and has had all manner of brilliant wine ideas that other people have managed to spin into gold.

Fortunately he began life with a fortune and seems to have been happy enough to spend his 42 years in the wine business gently frittering it away in various agreeable wine-related pursuits. Not that he is indolent. Far from it. At the Christie's Wine Course which he set up in 1982, it is more often than not Spurrier who carries the boxes and opens the bottles. His prolific wine writing output includes three very solid books, of which *The Clarke & Spurrier Fine Wine Guide* really stands out. When a group of us British wine writers need to fix up our programme of visits to taste the Bordeaux *primeurs* each spring, it is Steven who does all the hard work of writing to the châteaux and co-ordinating our split-second timetable.

Steven has enriched the wine world considerably, and played a key part in the wine education of such luminaries as France's top wine writer Michel Bettane, Tim Johnston and Mark Williamson of Willi's Wine Bar in Paris, Britain's most fastidious wine importer Roy Richards of Richards

Walford, Charles Lea of Lea & Sandeman fine wine shops around London, Paul Bowker (who was so cute he was known as '*le petit ange*' by Cave de la Madeleine customers and went on to run Christie's wine department) and Jenny Dobson, whom Spurrier met when she was an au pair for the Seysses family at Burgundy's Domaine Dujac and, touchpaper lit by Spurrier, has gone on to make great wine at Château Sénéjac in Bordeaux and Te Awa in New Zealand. If he has a fault, it is hardly the most serious: an excess of enthusiasm about even the most humdrum of wines.

Count John Umberto Salvi MW
(Wine writer)

A wonderful man and dear friend

I am exceedingly proud of the fact that Steven is my closest friend. We have known each other since the 1960s. Although I live in the Médoc and Steven lives in London and Dorset, we find that we meet regularly, wherever we are in the world, usually on wine related business. He has stayed at my houses in Soussans and in Ujue, in Navarra, and I have stayed at his flat in Barons Court and his house in Litton Cheney. He differs in that he has reached heights of fame (to which I can never aspire) and deserves every moment of it.

We have drunk many great wines together. From serendipitous discoveries at Vinexpo receptions to the 1900 Château Margaux at my office in London in 1967 to celebrate the birth of the first of my six children. We have eaten white truffles together in Alba and caviar at Domaine de Chevalier. He has been my guest at dinner in Vintners' Hall and I was a guest at his 70th birthday party at the farm in Dorset.

In his preface to my book, *The Count of Wine*, he calls me 'his treasured friend'. I take this opportunity to reciprocate with warmth and gratitude. Steven, you have done a great deal for the wine trade over many years. May you and Bella, together with your children, be happy in the knowledge of your many remarkable achievements.

Fiona Morrison MW
(Winemaker and fellow wine writer)

An eye for Bordeaux' finest

Like many people in the wine business, I find it hard to remember the first time I met Steven. His dapper presence, his interest, his enthusiasm and his enchantingly polite, old-world manner charms those he meets for the first time into thinking they have known him forever. There is a *Dorian Grey* magic about Steven; he always looks the same. I have always known him wearing if not a well-tailored suit, at least a bespoke blazer; if he is eschewing a collar and tie for a more informal look, there will always be a silk handkerchief nonchalantly tucked into his breast pocket. I have pulled an all-nighter with Steven (on a Virgin Atlantic direct flight to Japan) where he, myself and the late, beloved, John Avery brought select wines and old champagnes on board and talked and tasted as the world went by: Steven emerged smooth and unruffled in Tokyo while John and I slouched behind him.

That ability of his to absorb a lack of sleep and excess of wine makes all those who travel with Steven deeply envious. This skill was particularly evident at the gruelling annual En Primeur week in Bordeaux, where each year for almost two decades '*la groupe Spurrier*' travelled around the top châteaux in Bordeaux tasting the newly born vintage in neatly arranged 30-minute slots in a sort of vinous speed dating as he wrote up his tasting notes for *Decanter*. We had to greet, slurp, spit and write while all the time maintaining the decorum expected in the greatest tasting rooms of the Gironde.

Our group comprised some of Britain's most famous palates – Michael Broadbent and Jancis Robinson MW being the most illustrious – and there were times when, early on a cold March morning, without coffee or croissant to revive us as we waited to be let into a freezing cellar, the only solace was Steven's wonderfully cheerful banter. He reminded us how previous vintages had tasted; how a certain rather unpromising vintage has opened up, and he would be the first to bravely comment on the wine in hand while the rest of us desperately twirled our glasses around in the hope of prying some fruit and perfume out of a cold, tannic and stubbornly taciturn wine. We will be forever grateful for his enthusiasm and optimism as he beamed at the winemaker with such phrases as 'what a lovely way to start the day'; 'how pleased you must be with this vintage'; 'this wine has such marvellous density'; commentary that none of the rest of us could manage to articulate. We'd gently snigger into our coat collars and woollen scarves when the best Steven could produce was: 'How interesting this wine is.' That phrase became the politest put-down in our repertory.

Our En Primeur group expanded and contracted as Steven found new, bright, interesting journalists, wine critics or Masters of Wine to join us. It added a sense of spice and intrigue to our annual meetings with the producers – who would be part of Monsieur Spurrier's group this year? That generosity of his to nurture and foster new talent ran through all ages and countries so eventually the age range must have run from 20-something to 80-something and encompassed several continents. Steven organized the entire programme, carefully sending out emails to the different Bordeaux estates shortly after Christmas, gently informing them when he was going to pay them a visit. No one refused him, and few were those who dared to question his appointed time. One year, a group of us tried to give Steven a token of our gratitude and presented him with what we all considered to be a very fetching purple silk tie. For years, we waited in vain to see him wearing it.

Oz Clarke

(Wine writer, author and critic)

An opener of closed doors…

What was I doing on Monday the 24th of May 1976? I know what I *wasn't* doing, and that was tasting wines at the Intercontinental Hotel in Paris. In fact I was performing street theatre in the very grubby schoolyards of Inner Manchester.

But what was happening in the elegant surrounds of a smart Paris hotel was to have an enormous impact on my future life as a wine man. And the ringmaster in Paris that day was an equally elegant young Englishman called Steven Spurrier.

Steven's now-famous Judgement of Paris blind wine tasting which pitted the young pretenders from California against the cream of the French elite really did change our world of wine. Burgundy and Bordeaux had lived in the belief that only they possessed a God-given right to produce the world's greatest wines on sites hallowed by time. California had modelled its wines on the French classics, and in less than a generation, less than a decade, even, had taken on and vanquished its idols.

The wine universe revolved around France. It was an incontrovertible truth. Until Steven Spurrier turned such certainty on its head in just three hours on a fine Paris morning in the springtime of 1976. So when I began to get involved in wine during the 1980s, and got swept along in the intoxication of a Brave New World of wine able to match anything that France could offer, it was the door that Steven had prised open in Paris that I hurtled through. And when I finally met the man, well, he wasn't quite what I was expecting – urbane, impeccably turned-out and appearing to be every inch a member of the Establishment, not a rebel.

But this is what makes Steven so special. He is completely at ease in the established world of wine. But he has always had the heart of a radical beating in his breast. It was only because he knew France so well that he could set up and carry off the Judgement of Paris. Yet his inquisitive nature and open mind understood instinctively the excitement that brewed in California as a result.

And he's never changed. Although we do now happily debate the great classics of France and purr at each other as mature vintages slip down our throats, I am just as likely to meet him at a poorly attended try-out tasting of wines from some barely recognized corner of the wine world.

There is *no* corner of the wine world that doesn't interest Steven. He's shared with me his enthusiasm for Georgia and Croatia, Lebanon, India and Virginia, just as keenly as he's enthused about Pauillac or Saint-Julien. And it's led me to realize that one of the reasons I enjoy spending time with him is that he believes in thinking the best of people, in giving a wine and a producer a second chance, in seeing the potential in grapes and regions that are still rough and unpolished but which could one day shine.

And what's he doing now? Smoothing and burnishing the rough-cut brilliance of his chalky Dorset hillside at Bride Valley into supremely elegant wine that precisely reflects the character of its owner.

Steven's range of Bride Valley wines, nurtured in the same chalk-soil conditions as the great wines of Champagne.

From vintage-hand to wine explorer, then pioneer Paris merchant, educator, author, critic and *Decanter* columnist. Steven's work now comes full circle in a return to the vineyard, this time his own, Bride Valley in the chalk hills of Dorset.

PREFACE

It was Christmas Eve 1954, and I was 13 years old. At the end of dinner at Marston Hall, my family home in Derbyshire, my grandfather said that he thought I was old enough to try the port, and asked the butler to bring me a glass. The decanter was moved in my direction. The wine, Cockburn's 1908, was quite extraordinary, and the impression it left has lasted a lifetime. That was my Damascene moment, the moment when the seed was firmly planted for my life in wine.

My parents used to take my elder brother and me with them on trips to France and Italy, introducing us while we were still young to the 'conviviality' of wine. As a student I joined the London School of Economics Wine Society, but even before that there was no doubt in my mind that I would make wine my career. Many decades later, the Symington family, having recently added the historic House of Cockburn to their portfolio of estates, held a tasting at the Factory House in Oporto to show vintages from 1977 down to 1874. The 1908, reckoned to be the finest of them all that day, was there. After we had heard the history of the vintage over its lifetime, Paul Symington asked the 60 or so of us present if we had any comments. I volunteered that the first and only time I had tasted this wine before was on Christmas Eve 1954, and I described the impression it had made. A couple of years later at another Cockburn's tasting where the 1908 was shown, Paul (not knowing I was in the room) recounted the tale, saying 'this is the vintage that inspired Steven Spurrier to go into the wine trade'.

It has made for a bumpy ride. My career's trajectory has not disproved the theory that the way to make a small fortune in the wine trade is to start with a large one… but it has been worth it. I am still totally and utterly in love with wine, the places where it is produced and the people who produce it; it has given me more pleasure, excitement and satisfaction than I could ever have imagined.

CHAPTER ONE
EARLY DAYS AND LEARNING THE TRADE

I was born on 5th October 1941 in Cambridge. I was supposed to have been born a day or two later in the Royal Infirmary in Derby, nearer to our family home, but my mother was visiting friends in Cambridge and delayed the trip back to join a game of poker – playing for matchsticks rather than for money – which my arrival cut short. I was also supposed to have been a girl named Sarah.

Family circumstances were secure and comfortable. On my father's side, a great-great uncle had founded an engineering enterprise in Leyland, Lancashire, which in the late-19th century became Leyland Motors. Grandpa Spurrier was a hunting, shooting, fishing country squire who had built up a sand and gravel business. My mother's family lived more on the east side of the county, spending the summer and the shooting and stalking season on their estate on Scotland's Loch Linnhe.

Early in World War II the family decamped from London to 'Brills' in Aston Clinton, a village near Aylesbury in Buckinghamshire, and my first memories are of our timbered cottage there. My father served in the Derbyshire Yeomanry, part of Britain's Eighth Army under General Montgomery, first in North Africa and later in Italy. To me he was a person of mysterious glamour. My mother was always there – so was in no way mysterious – but she certainly was glamorous: tall, fair, slim and always beautifully turned out.

In 1947 we moved to Derbyshire, where my father joined his father's business. I went to school in Derby and then, from aged eight years old, to boarding school, following my older brother Nicky. Summerfields, our prep school on the outskirts of Hastings, had simply everything. Here I learnt to swim and play tennis, squash, golf, cricket (which I loved) and football. The terrace, where we regularly took our morning exercises, ran the length of the house; the gardens and grounds were seemingly endless, and the weather at the seaside was better than it was in Derbyshire. Subjects were well taught and the library had every sort of book an inquisitive boy could wish for.

At Rugby, where my father had also been at school, the teaching stepped up a gear or two. I did quite well, enjoying the summer terms for the cricket, but by the end was ready to move on and take up my place at the London School of Economics, where I felt I would 'grow up'.

From the start, I couldn't have been happier. Nicky was also in London at the time and there was everything to explore, from cinemas to coffee bars, restaurants and pubs (for the first time on my own). I went back to Derbyshire for regular visits, but living – at first in 'digs' – in the centre of the big city was a different life entirely.

Girls were still a closed book to me. When a charming young French woman named Marie-Claire moved into the room across the landing from mine, we shared the bathroom with mutual respect. None of the others in the house seemed to pay her much attention, so I asked her out to the occasional party in my schoolboy French, '*Il y a un parti ce weekend…*' and before she left to go home for Christmas, bought some nice wines for her last dinner at the house. A good time was had by all. Later that evening, sitting at my desk and checking through stuff for the next day's lectures, I heard a knock at my door. Marie-Claire, in her nightdress, stood in the doorway. 'I just wanted to thank you properly for tonight', she said.

'My pleasure, Marie-Claire,' I replied. 'See you tomorrow at breakfast.' I had a lot to learn.

I moved on from digs to sharing flats, revelling in having everything on my doorstep. The Portobello Road antiques market was nearby, there were all kinds of museums to visit and galleries, particularly Zwemmer's in the Charing Cross Road and St George's Gallery Prints in Cork Street, where on my father's advice I sought out lithographs from 20th-century British artists. I went for three: Julian Trevelyan (1910–88), Michael Ayrton (1921–75) and even acquired a

Left: Steven and Tadpole at Brills, our cottage in the little village of Aston Clinton in Buckinghamshire, 1945.

Below: My brother Nicky's christening at Marston in October 1939. Seated in front: Pamela Spurrier; Standing (*left to right*): Jack Spurrier, Bernard Neame, John Spurrier, Margery Spurrier, Agnes Neame.

John Piper (1903–92). I had a financial allowance from the family trust and lived inexpensively, so at very reasonable prices these appeared affordable.

My passion for art had grown from an early age alongside my interest in wine; in my lifetime I have spent much, much more on the former than on the latter. It was my second idea for a profession; I have surrounded myself with the stuff wherever I have lived, and regret only what I've had to sell. When Nicky and I travelled abroad with our parents, they used to take us to galleries, churches and museums. Back at home, books on art were readily at hand and we would often go to the 'half-crown houses', a half-crown (two shillings and sixpence) being the price of admission to National Trust properties. These stately homes and other architectural gems were stuffed with splendid furniture and works of art that had been amassed by aristocratic families over centuries.

The flat in London, my first experience of independence, soon became a social gathering place, and friends sometimes asked if they could borrow it for romantic interludes while I was away. One such guest was Willy Feilding, who was even then already known as a painter of murals. Willy and his beautiful girlfriend Clare often stayed there, and by way of thanks he suggested painting a mural on part of my sitting-room wall. I gave him carte blanche and he created a Grecian-themed composition, a discreetly naked Clare on a Mediterranean shore leaning against a pillar, her feet being caressed by gentle waves. It was much admired... but then Clare left him. Willy called round late one night for a drink, and once there he made a 'roux' from tomato ketchup, Worcestershire sauce and flour and finger-painted spiders and scorpions crawling all over Clare's naked body. Of course I washed these off the following morning, returning the mural to its pristine glory. Some months after moving out I was passing the front door and saw a young woman with her key in the lock. I asked if by any chance she lived on the top floor, which she did, and said how nice it was. 'Do you like the mural?' I asked.

'That revolting thing,' she replied, 'we painted over it as soon as we moved in.' An original Feilding gone for good. Luckily, I still have a couple of his water-colours in my Dorset collection.

My next place, a top-floor flat in South Kensington's Courtfield Gardens, had a large sitting-room with fine views over the gardens, and a smaller third room that became my first-ever dining room. I bought a set of Georgian candlesticks and a canteen of Victorian silver for my dinner parties as well as other odds and ends at The London Silver Vaults, Holborn's answer to the jewellers in nearby Hatton Garden, which was a short walk from the LSE in Chancery Lane.

My career plan had been inspired early on by the magical glass of Cockburn 1908 that Grandpa Spurrier had offered me in 1954. When I later mentioned to my parents that I was planning to go into the wine trade, my mother told me she had once worked briefly for someone named Tommy Layton at what was London's first true wine bar. I knew Tommy to be a complete wine man and creative author of a series of *Wine Primers*. It so happened that some years later I was at Château Pontet-Canet, about to be inducted into the Commanderie du Bontemps de Médoc et des Graves, when I found myself standing beside Tommy. I introduced myself saying that I had read his books, adding that perhaps one of the reasons for my being in the wine trade was the fact that my mother had once worked for him. When I mentioned her name, he reflected for a moment before replying thoughtfully: 'Pammy Neame, of course I remember her. Awful lot of rich boyfriends!'

My father's reaction to my career choice was slightly less sanguine. He was not immune to the pleasure of drink himself, but on insurance questionnaires could truthfully answer 'NSI' (Normal Social Intake). I would have had to enter 'ASI' (Abnormal Social Intake). 'You're quite mad', he said, 'at the rate you're going you'll be dead within 10 years!' It's true, I had not always shown exemplary restraint. I did not cover myself in glory when on my 21st birthday my parents threw a party for me, a dinner-dance in Derbyshire. I had planned a breakfast party at my flat in London on the same day, not with champagne since I couldn't afford it, but with a lethal 'champagne cocktail' based on Merrydown Cider (a brand then noted for its strength). I had been dancing the night before, but felt that the few hours' sleep in between would leave me refreshed enough to welcome the 50-odd friends who turned up, as invited, at 8am. (Who on earth would go to a drinks party, even a birthday party, at 8am these days?) Some food was served, but the Merrydown took hold, and even before everyone had left I was in such bad shape that my plan to take the train from St Pancras to Derby looked very doubtful. I wouldn't even have made it to the Underground station. Adrian Cooper-Key, a great friend and one of my former flatmates, kindly agreed to drive me to Derby and off we went, but I was still pretty much out of it when we arrived. Strong coffee and a cold shower helped a bit, and while I made it through the dinner, I retired much the worse for wear before the birthday cake, candles aglow, made its appearance. Grandpa Spurrier summed it up while I was trying to make some sense of the evening: 'My boy, you are what we in these parts call "smock-raddled".' Over my parents' lifetimes I know that I surprised them often, both positively and negatively, but this was one of the rare times I knew that I had let them down. Smock-raddled, totally and utterly.

Contrary to my father's predictions, however, it was probably the wine trade that saved me from an early demise, for although I never minded losing my inhibitions socially, relying on charm to smooth over the consequences, I soon realized that I could not do this professionally.

Nicky and I, he elegant in Grandpa Neame's morning coat, make our way to his wedding in Kensington in December 1963.

After university I was a bit stumped as to how to launch my proposed career, employment agencies not then offering much help for young aspirants to the wine trade. I was voicing my frustration to Nicky one evening over dinner when a suave and handsome young man on the next table leant over and said: 'If you're looking to go into the wine trade, here's my card. Call me tomorrow.' This was Malcolm Gage, who worked for Christopher's in Jermyn Street, one of the big three merchants alongside Berry Bros & Rudd and Justerini & Brooks, both of which were located a stone's throw away in grander St James's Street. I made an appointment to meet the MD the following morning. The interview comprised a single question: 'Where were you at school?'

'Rubgy, Sir.'

'Oh dear; we normally only employ Etonians. But since you will have been a fag [a junior boy obliged to act as personal servant to a senior 'fag-master'] at Rugby, you will know what a trainee's position with a company of our reputation will be like. You can start on Monday.' And so, in early February 1964, I began a year of hard learning in the firm's Hollen Street cellars under the dual rods of Mr Taylor and his son Malcolm.

The London Wine Trade in 1964 was a two-tier system, much of which is still recognizable today. There were importers, known as shippers, who sold to the merchants, who in turn sold both wholesale to universities and clubs, and retail to the public. There were also regional wholesalers who bought from shippers and sold to local merchants. There were some smart restaurants, mostly in the West End and mostly French, that had extensive wine lists, and a growing number of Italian trattorias, beginning in Soho and spreading out to fashionable Knightsbridge, Kensington and Chelsea, that had their own Italian suppliers. Pubs were almost entirely in the hands of the brewers, who sold beer, spirits and apéritifs, but not wine. Off-licenses were popular for all sorts of alcoholic drinks, but there were very few retail wine shops until licensing laws were relaxed after the 1960s. This led to the 'democratisation' of wine drinking in the following decade, and competition for customers resulted in a wider choice of product and better-priced offers.

Christopher's, which liked to boast that its historical documents had been destroyed in the Great Fire of 1666, claimed to be the oldest wine merchant in

London, established 30 years before what became Berry Bros & Rudd was founded as a coffee shop. Christopher's was not interested in wine democracy, neither were their St James's Street neighbours. If bottles were displayed at all, they were ancient and dusty and carried no price tag. In such establishments clients were received by an elegantly dressed young man at a polished mahogany desk; shown a comfortable chair, and invited to discuss their needs. In those days wine was a male-only preoccupation: gentlemen had their own wine merchant just as they had their own tailor, shirt-maker and barber, and money seldom changed hands. Everything was purchased on account.

Christopher's was a true working cellar. We bottled claret from Bordeaux's greatest châteaux – two barrels of the 1962 Cheval Blanc, the last St-Emilion *premier grand cru classé* vintage to be shipped in bulk, passed through my hands. Vast quantities of wine and spirits were boxed up to be dispatched all over London and the country – some to the palaces, as Christopher's proudly held the Royal Warrant. Most of the time there were three trainees, a permanent staff of four who were old hands, and the two Taylors. Taylor Snr was a tough, old-school manager, reminiscent of a seasoned sergeant-major dealing with junior officer-quality recruits, who commanded our respect and in return respected us. I was paid £10 a week – a fair wage – plus 'luncheon vouchers', which I used to save up for a once-a-month splurge in Soho's Italian restaurants.

I enjoyed the bottling above all. Wine was poured directly from the cask through a two-spout spigot into bottles, which were then taken away in a 24-bottle wheelbarrow affair to be corked. The huge barrels of Bordeaux and bur-gundy, and barrels known as 'pipes' of port, were allowed to rest until they 'fell bright'. Victorian fathers used to lay down a full pipe (720 bottles) of port for their sons or godsons. When my nephew Edward was born in 1964, I bought him a full barrel of first growth St-Emilion Château Beauséjour-Dr-Fagouet, bottled at the château; but by the time *his* first son was born, all I could manage was a case of the second growth St-Julien Château Ducru-Beaucaillou – a comment as much on the rising price of Bordeaux as on my declining fortune.

English bottling was of the highest quality, in most cases superior to the Bordeaux châteaux's own efforts. Château Lafite Rothschild 1953, for example, was bottled over a nine-month period, the workers turning to the task only when there was no work for them in the vineyards. At Christopher's the corks, bought directly from Portugal, were superb, the best being the 'full long' (two-and-a-half inches). We triple-washed them: once in hot water, again in cold and once again in wine. Corking was by hand, the better, smoother end of the cork being selected to be in touch with the wine. The care and precision of the bottling and corking regime stayed with me a long time.

Christopher's reputation for the claret they bottled was good, but perhaps not up to that of their St James's neighbours. In the City of London, W Coates & Co and Corney & Barrow were highly regarded, and a friend of my father's introduced me to Mr Harcourt of the Army & Navy Stores in Victoria from whom, once I began to collect wine seriously from 1966, I bought several cases of 1959s and '61s. Bristol, the port to which barrels of Bordeaux had been being shipped since the 1300s, was famous for Averys and Harveys. Then there was The Wine Society (my maternal grandmother had given me membership as a birthday gift) or to give it its full name The International Exhibition Cooperative Wine Society. This was founded in 1874 to supply wines and spirits to the professional middle classes. As it was a cooperative, the members owned the company and any profits were re-invested for their benefit. They published fully annotated wine lists four times a year and regularly sent out special offers; I learnt almost as much from these publications as I did from books. The Wine Society remains unchanged – now just bigger and better – and I have never had a bad bottle from them. If anyone asks me how to go about buying wine, my reply is always the same: 'Find a wine merchant you can trust.' Today is a golden age for every kind of wine drinker, but this rule remains valid. The Wine Society remains a beacon.

To supplement my training I read many books on wine, starting with Tommy Layton's *Wine Primers*, moving on to such exotica as Ian Maxwell Campbell's *Wayward Tendrils of the Vine* (1948) and Maurice Healy's splendid *Stay Me With Flagons* (1940), and I devoured the marvellous books by Alexis Lichine, learning much of them by heart. Alexis, Russian by birth but a naturalized American, had been on General Eisenhower's staff towards the end of the World War II and had spent time freeing Bordeaux from German occupation. By the mid-1960s he had purchased Château Prieuré-Lichine (fourth growth Margaux) and set up a consortium to take over the much larger Château Lascombes (second growth Margaux) as well as creating his own *négociant* business in Bordeaux and Burgundy, where he was the first to encourage growers to bottle unblended produce from their own vineyards.

In Burgundy, as in every wine region in Europe until perhaps the 1970s, the *négociants* or merchants controlled the market, having not only bottling facilities for quantities large and small, but also sales people at home, importers abroad, and clients, to whom the actual producers had no access. The vignerons were farmers, selling their grapes to the merchants or, if they had cellars to make the wine, selling it off in bulk after the harvest. The merchants decided the price, which the growers had to accept. In the mid-1930s, a small group of top estates such as Marquis d'Angerville in Volnay, Henri Gouges in Nuits-St-Georges, Comte Georges de Vogüé in Chambolle-Musigny and Armand Rousseau in Gevrey-Chambertin began 'domaine bottling', still selling some wine in bulk while they built up sales, but even in the 1960s this was still uncommon. Alexis encouraged growers to invest in their own cellars and practise domaine bottling; he would sell these unblended Meursaults or Volnays with both his and the growers' name on the bottle.

Alexis also opened Château Pieuré-Lichine to sell direct to the public, an approach new in Bordeaux, especially in the Médoc (there is a French expression *'snob comme le Médoc'*), though increasingly commonplace today. Not many of the classed growth châteaux were lived in, the owners preferring Bordeaux or Paris addresses, but even if the owners were in residence, their doors were firmly closed to commerce. Wines were sold to the *négociant*/merchants known collectively as La Place de Bordeaux. The owners knew each other and knew the brokers and merchants, whom they entertained for lunches and dinners. The occasional importer, wine writer – or even a lowly trainee – might be invited, but never the public. Alexis was derided by his neighbours, thought vulgar for openly encouraging visits and tastings to offer 'the château experience'. These usually ended in sales of his wine and of his books: he promoted himself and his brand in the most elegant way – and created a growing mailing list.

I first met Alexis in 1964. I had been invited through a friend to a lunch at Woburn Abbey in Bedfordshire where we were greeted by the vivacious and charming Nicole, Duchess of Bedford. After a glass or two of champagne, lunch was announced and the doors to the 'Canaletto Room' flung open. I walked in to see 16 paintings by the Venetian master, painted during the years he had worked in England. Had I failed to find a start in wine, I would have applied to join Christie's auction house as a trainee, so nothing could have impressed me more. Lunch began with an empty place either side of our hosts but soon the missing guests were announced, and in came Alexis with Arlene Dahl, one of the most beautiful Hollywood actresses ever; they had just flown into London from New York for the start of their honeymoon. It doesn't get much better than that when you are just 23 years old.

I got to know Alexis well from the early 1970s and our friendship lasted until his death in 1989. It continues with his son, Sacha. Sacha sold Prieuré-Lichine after his father's death and finally, after many ups and downs, bought a beautiful château in Provence and began to produce France's most expensive Rosé de Provence under the name of Château d'Esclans. He always sends me the new vintage to taste and, sending him my notes recently to congratulate him on its quality, I told him that Alexis would have been proud of him. His reply was brief: 'Papa always appreciated success.'

Life at Christopher's continued well, despite the strictness, for I was learning all the time. In spring 1964 two things happened that were to have a very deep effect on my life: meeting Bella Lawson, who was to become my wife, and receiving a cheque for my shares in Hilton Gravel Ltd, the company that Grandpa Spurrier had founded in 1922 to support his country pursuits, which had been sold to Blue Circle Cement.

First, meeting Bella. I was looking forward to a summer of parties in London and weekends in country houses. One of the places our group of friends met was the Queensway Ice Skating Rink in Bayswater, and on that particular evening I was with committed party-goer Ian Carr. The plan was always to get the skates on first, which suited me as it made me seem taller, and then go into the bar for a drink. Around girls I was still shy, so my deal with Ian was that he would look out for the girls and I would get the drinks. He pointed out a threesome near the bar and over we went, he opening smoothly with 'Hello, I'm Ian. This is my friend Steven who'd like to offer you a drink.' The girls accepted, two of them asking for something harmless like cider, the third for a gin and orange. Now, in the early part of the war my mother had been a cub reporter for the *Daily Mirror*, mostly on food and fashion. She had told me that gin and orange was the favourite tipple of Soho's *filles de joie*: orange for health, and gin to keep up their spirits, so I said Bella couldn't possibly order that because it was 'what tarts drink'. The 17-year old Bella replied: 'In that case, make it a double.' In fact Bella hadn't had a clue what to ask for; 'gin and orange' had just come into her head without her knowing what it was, but having just left a sheltered upbringing to come to London, she wasn't going to be told what not to do on her first evening out. We got on right from the start and still do, which is why this book is dedicated to Bella and to wine.

The other event actually created more problems than it might have solved, had there been problems to solve at the time. Hilton Gravel had become successful, with half a dozen large working pits, as they were known, and had expanded into ready-mixed cement and tennis courts. My father had told Nicky and me over the previous Christmas that a sale was on the cards. By Easter 1964 he said the deal was being concluded, adding that we would receive a cheque in the post. No other information was given and none asked for, and in April I did indeed receive a cheque – for £250,000, the equivalent today of over £5 million. I paid it into the Soho branch of Lloyds Bank along with my £10 weekly wage from Christopher's, and when the cashier looked astonished and asked if I wished to see the manager, I just said: 'No, thanks.' The Hilton Gravel cheque represented more than 200 times my annual income and I simply had no clue what it really meant.

At that time I was on a monthly allowance of £60 so, with my trainee's pay, I had £100 a month to spend. I was already having my suits and shirts made and thought of commissioning a pair of bespoke shoes from Henry Maxwell in Dover Street, since they were also makers of riding spurs on the Royal Warrant and had 'Spurriers to the Queen' on their window under their logo – but this was an unrealized extravagance. I had a busy social life: London parties, dinners in my new dining room with wines from The Wine Society (to which I had upgraded from the cheerful Peter Dominic's), restaurants and occasionally night clubs, but life was so cheap in those days. Five pounds would cover dinner for two at either the fashionable and very good Alvaro's or David Hicks' restaurant nearby, a couple of glasses of champagne and a dance at Annabel's club, and still leave enough for the taxi home.

My Saturday forays to the Portobello Road also usually resulted in some piece to add to the flat. I picked up some 19th-century Staffordshire pottery, including half a dozen 'cow creamers' (whose open mouths still grin at me from the kitchen shelves); lots of Jane Austen-like fashion plates which I arranged in an album and re-sold; similarly prints of eminent Victorians, all sold except one of the Duke of Wellington which I had framed for my father. Snobbish people used to say that the mark of the 'nouveau riche' was that they 'had to buy their own furniture'. I was certainly not nouveau riche, but I simply loved buying my own furniture, mostly from a clutch of antique shops in the New Kings Road.

Back at the Hollen Street cellars, Christopher's had a surprise for me: I was to be sent – at my own expense – to Burgundy for a week, and then on to Champagne for another, to work in the cellars at vintage time.

Bella and I were able to spend a few days together before I set off in early February to cross the Channel. That first evening I stayed in Normandy at a comfortable hotel with a good restaurant, and sent a postcard to Bella the following morning listing the menu and wines, signing off 'I miss you, but no doubt I will get over it'. I don't think she appreciated the joke.

My first job in Burgundy was with the *négociant* Thibault Liger-Belair in Nuits-St-Georges. The Liger-Belairs were local aristocrats. Two of Monsieur le Comte's grandsons have now revitalized the estate with parcels of inherited vineyards and great imagination, but in the mid-1960s the company was coasting along as so many were at that time. On my first day in the cellars I heard a succession of muffled booms, which turned out to be cannons firing buckshot into the black clouds. This, it was hoped, would break up the hail that was forming, turning it instead into rain which would cause less damage in the vineyards – and indeed Burgundy enjoyed a wonderful 1964 vintage. After work I would jump into my little red Triumph Herald, 'La Petite', and drive along the *route du vin*, passing through villages whose names I had only previously seen in books.

Then it was off north to Champagne, where I was lucky enough to be staying at Moët & Chandon's Château de Saran on the hillside vineyards outside its Epernay headquarters. At vintage time the château had a constant flow of visitors, both trade and social, and the social side was managed by Lady Moyra Campbell, a consummate hostess. I was lodged in one of the maid's rooms under the rafters and – of course – seated 'below the salt' at dinner, but nothing could beat this first experience of the true *vie du château*.

There was so much to learn: about the vineyards, the champagne method, the value that the main houses – the *grandes marques* – put on their individual style, and the huge stocks they needed to have in their seemingly endless cellars to keep it that way. I went to Reims to visit Ruinart, a small champagne company that pre-dated Moët & Chandon (and which the latter has now bought). It was run by a charming man named Bunny d'Ayala who, after a tour and a tasting, suggested we lunch at a place he liked outside the city. Seeing my open-top car, he suggested I drive him there as it was a sunny day. La Petite had been behaving oddly and it was clear as soon as we set off that something was not right. '*Mon cher, vous avez un gicleur bouché*', he said: a blocked carburettor nozzle. This was news to me as I didn't know what a carburettor was, much less that it had nozzles, but M d'Ayala jumped out, removed the offending outlet, blew into it, buffed it with his handkerchief, and off we went again as smooth as silk. Apparently he liked tinkering with cars. He told me that his sister was married to Nubar Gulbenkian, owner of many very splendid vehicles, and when he stayed with them in England he spent as much time as he could get away with chatting to the mechanics. I was beginning to learn that wine people are just as interesting as the drink they produced.

CHAPTER TWO
LIVING THE
TRADE

After completing a year as a *stagière* or trainee at Christopher's, I was sent abroad for eight months to work for the company's 'principals' (major suppliers) in France, Germany, Spain and Portugal. This was 1965. I let each firm know that since I would be with them to learn as much as possible and that I considered this a privilege, I would not expect to be paid. This proved an astute move. In my first posting to Bordeaux, for example, although I worked normal hours in the cellars and on the bottling line, I was also often called upon to set up the room for clients' tastings – and allowed to taste the wines afterwards. Sometimes I was asked to lunch at the Bordeaux headquarters or at one of their châteaux, a benefit my fellow interns did not enjoy, since they were busy earning their keep.

In the 1950s and early '60s, British adults could take abroad an allowance of only £50 each, so to support myself on this trip I took out a Letter of Credit – a splendid document, several pages long – with Lloyds Bank. By taking this letter, along with my passport, to any foreign bank I could draw down as much cash as I needed up to the limit of £2,000. Heaven knows how the tiny banks in Yugoslavia or Greece were ever paid back, but they all went along with it. Certainly £2,000 was a very tidy sum, but eight marvellous months on the road saw it all used up.

I had secured a billet for my three months in Bordeaux in a classic double-fronted town house managed by the charming yet formidable Madeleine Duret. Her husband Paul was half-English and a substantial size, taking up every inch of his fireside armchair in the evening. The house was bang in the centre of the city, just behind the elegant Allées de Tourny in the Rue Jean-Jacques Rousseau. Fifty metres further on was Place des Grandes Hommes, where the daily market offered a cornucopia of produce from the Gironde and beyond. Madeleine knew every stallholder by name and the Durets' table was recognized across the city for its quality – which probably accounted for Monsieur's splendid physique. I often helped Madame with the shopping, learning as I went along. Unlike the famous cuisines of Normandy, Burgundy and the Loire Valley, which are based on butter, or those of Provence based on oil, Bordeaux cuisine was relatively plain with few richly sauced dishes.

Bordeaux is France's finest 18th-century city. The Garonne and Dordogne rivers join there to form the Gironde estuary on their way to the sea, 100 kilometres further north, and give the city a fine trade catchment – it was already an established port, known as Burdiglia, under Roman occupation. By the middle of the 16th century, it had begun exporting to Bristol, London and Edinburgh as well as to Holland and northern Europe; by the 17th, its commercial and residential life on the Left Bank was thriving. Gold-coloured limestone from beneath the town and St-Emilion's vineyards was used along the quays and in the construction of the magnificent Place de la Bourse, one of the grandest and most harmonious squares in Europe. Behind the Quai des Chartrons' classical facades were the wine merchants' offices and vast *chais* (barrel cellars), the high water-table having prevented the building of underground cellars or *caves*.

During my time in Bordeaux I often visited Château Langoa Barton in St-Julien, a beautiful 1750s Chartreuse-style house that Anglo-Irish merchant Hugh Barton had bought in 1821, five years before he bought one third of the historic Léoville estate and re-named it Léoville Barton. During the 1971 vintage, the owner Ronald Barton said 'thanks to the 1970 vintage we were able to repair the château roof. Perhaps the 1971 will enable us to repair the roof of the *chai*?' Three decades later, when many of the surrounding châteaux were in full expansion mode, I asked his nephew Anthony, who had taken over in 1982, why so many new cellars were being built if the wines were so easy to sell. He replied 'Perhaps to store the money.' Times had certainly changed.

In the mid-1960s, when merchants ruled the roost, wines from the previous year were tasted and assessed in March or April, and the merchants set the price they were prepared to pay for them. Châteaux meekly accepted, grateful for the cash that would pay the winter bills and get them through to the next harvest. This system was known as selling En Primeur, since the wines would not be bottled for 12 months or more. Under this system, the importers added a small margin when selling on to their customers. Thus began the huge and ultimately greedily speculative En Primeur Bordeaux market, which reached its peak in price and volume during the 2011 summer with the good – but over-priced – 2010s. China was one of the largest buyers of that year but when, six months later, they saw prices beginning to go down, not up as they had been told they would, they simply cancelled their orders, causing the whole merry-go-round to grind to a halt. This and the unexciting 2011, '12 and '13 vintages saw prices decline further, to begin a slow but sure rise from the attractive 2014 and really excellent 2015 and 2016. Everyone hopes that the Bordeaux bubble will not burst again, but knowing the region's commercial history, that cannot be guaranteed.

Cash was so tight in the mid-1960s that there was even a pre-Primeur method of sale before the harvest had begun, known as *sur souches*. Wines were offered from mid-June at a time when the quantity of the coming vintage could, failing disaster, be gauged – but not, of course, the quality. Back in London after my eight-month tour, with money at my disposal, I looked into this with the merchant Borie-Manoux. Wines from good middle-of-the-road châteaux were being offered in lots of a single *tonneau* – four barrels or 1,200 bottles – at derisory prices. I ended up buying from 10 individual châteaux, paying for what would be 12,000 bottles the following month, and received a post-vintage telephone call from Borie-Manoux's Emile Castéja to say 'Steven, you are a lucky gambler'. The system was banned the following year, but not before it forced the sale of Château La Lagune, a well-regarded third growth Médoc. The vineyard had been ravaged by a pre-harvest hailstorm, which meant that less wine was produced than had already been sold three months earlier.

I was a new boy to everything in Bordeaux. The commercial side of things slowly revealed itself, while the well-structured social side was evident from the start. My first two jobs – with de Luze and Cruse – were on the Quai des Chartrons. The third was with Calvet just around the corner on the Cours du Médoc, and the fourth with another firm, a relative newcomer from the 1900s, located nearer the train station. All four merchants owned wine-producing châteaux. The *chais* were simply huge: almost 100 metres long, with the standard 225-litre oak barrels stacked three or four high. Only the first growth châteaux Haut-Brion, Margaux, Latour, Lafite Rothschild, and (then) top second growth Mouton Rothschild bottled their entire production at the château, so immense volumes came into the merchants' *chais* and the cellar-work never stopped.

The Cruse business was the largest of the *Chartronnais*. It owned two prestigious châteaux in the Médoc: Château d'Issan, a 15th-century moated castle with a fine history, a third growth Margaux, and the fifth growth Pontet-Canet in Pauillac. A decade later in 1972, disaster befell the firm as a result of what should have been a normal tax inspection.

Wine and tax have always been closely linked in France, and since the wine industry was Bordeaux's biggest employer and biggest earner, tax officials used to pay regular visits to châteaux and merchants to make sure all was in order. In those days, since very little wine was bottled at the châteaux and was thus of guaranteed origin, a little blending often went on to 'improve' what eventually went into the bottle. The inspectors usually contented themselves with an overview: only if something was found to be very wrong would the wine be destroyed and a fine be levied. Their visits were never announced in advance. One day they called at the Cruse headquarters to be told that everyone was too busy to see them and that they should return after lunch – and then, by the way, that they should use the tradesmen's entrance a few doors along. Return after lunch they did, but this time with the police, who impounded their books before starting a thorough investigation. What they found was a massive, though in terms of what went into the bottle quite acceptable, fraud.

At the base of the Bordeaux quality pyramid was the simple appellation 'Bordeaux'. 'Bordeaux Supérieur' had to be red, but Bordeaux could be either white or red wine. After the war there was considerable replanting of the vast stretch of vineyards that lay between the Garonne and Dordogne rivers (known as Entre-Deux-Mers), mostly with the same white grapes that had been there in the past. By the early 1960s there was a huge over-supply of these nice but light wines, and they were sold off in bulk, below cost, carrying the appellation Bordeaux.

At the same time there was vast over-production of sturdy red wine from the Languedoc-Roussillon departments, known as le Midi, and during the next decade over 100,000 hectares of vineyard would be grubbed up. What Cruse had been doing was selling the AC Bordeaux Blanc to Germany to be turned into cheap Sekt or sparkling wine, then buying similar quantities of honest-quality red wine from the Midi, making a pleasant blend with the Bordeaux reds they held in stock, and using official paperwork to sell it as AC (red) Bordeaux. This was sensible and beneficial all round – but it was also illegal.

Tax departments in France were under pressure from the finance ministry to make a profit by uncovering such abuses and the Bordeaux authorities, perhaps piqued by their haughty reception from the powerful Cruse family, threw the book at them, creating one of the biggest scandals Bordeaux has ever known. In 1974 classed growths Châteaux Pontet-Canet and Château Lafon-Rochet had to be sold to the owners' Tesseron cousins from Cognac; one family member took his life by throwing himself into the Garonne, and the company was broken up and sold.

While the Cruses had managed their own fraud, the fourth firm I worked for might be said to have had fraud thrust upon them. Christopher's had a small market for Graves Supérieur, a semi-sweet white wine made in the south of the region using an appellation that most producers by the mid-1960s had abandoned in favour of drier styles. The firm was Christopher's supplier, but when the annual order came in, there was no stock available. I was at the time spending a few days working in the firm's laboratory, where every element in the wine is tested. The sales team passed the problem to the technicians, who quickly came up with a solution. They had a stock of red Graves, so a bottle was ordered, the wine put through a charcoal filter to remove the colour, filtered again to remove the tannins, white-wine flavours were added, as was sweetening and a little more alcohol to make it richer, and finally colour, to match the pale-gold of the previous year's sample. After this experiment I was offered a glass of each wine for comparison – one from before and one after modification – and concluded that there wasn't much between them, so off the doctored bottles went.

On the plus side this company (which is still trading – such experimental adventures being definitely a thing of the past) owned a fine range of châteaux: Gruaud-Larose and Talbot in St-Julien, Meyney in St-Estèphe, Clos des Jacobins in St-Emilion and Lafaurie-Peyraguey in Sauternes, as well as many others in minor appellations. With these wines, the firm introduced me to vertical tastings – that is tasting a selection of vintages of from one property, starting with the youngest and working back to the oldest (a horizontal tasting is of many different wines from the same vintage) – from which I learned a great deal.

My third firm was Calvet, second only to Cruse in the Bordeaux rankings. The Calvets came from the Auvergne in the centre of France, which is known for its farming community's hard-headed approach to business. An early Calvet would have introduced the red wine to Bordeaux from nearby Hermitage in the northern Rhône. There it was used during the 19th century to 'improve' the wines of even the finest châteaux in weaker years, Bordeaux merchants outbidding others to obtain the best barrels. In the 1880s it was not uncommon to see Margaux Hermitagé selling at prices higher than those of Margaux itself.

The Calvets had exclusive rights to many châteaux, especially those around St-Emilion on the Right Bank, the feather in their cap being Château Cheval Blanc. Between the châteaux and the merchants were 'courtiers' or brokers. They visited all the estates, assessing the vintage, collecting samples and receiving a small commission from both sides for their advice if the deal went through. Brokers had been an integral part of Bordeaux business for centuries and were respected as the essential middlemen. Calvet sent me off for several trips with one of their brokers, who took me behind the scenes to very varied estates on the Right Bank (or the Libournais as it was known, after the city port of Libourne). He and I often had lunch there at the Hotel Robin in front of the train station. The Robin sisters still owned Lafleur in Pomerol and had also part-owned its nearest rival Petrus until it was bought by Jean-Pierre Moueix (another Auvergnat family) in the 1950s, but in those days the restaurant made more money.

Station hotels, Hôtels de la Gare, were mostly a sure bet. Few commercial travellers could afford cars, and since French train links were excellent, this was where they tended to eat and sleep. High standards in the kitchen kept them coming back. I used to seek them out and some were famous for their wine lists as well as their food, the most memorable being the Hôtel de la Gare at Montbard in northern Burgundy. The chef had two Michelin stars and had cooked for many years on the great liner SS *Normandie*. About four years after my stint at Calvet,

Bella and I stopped at the Hôtel de la Gare en route from Provence to England for Christmas. The red wine I chose was Chambolle-Musigny Les Amoureuses 1934 from Domaine Comte Georges de Vogüé which was, as expected, magnificent. Towards the end of dinner Bella briefly left the table and, my own glass being long empty, I finished the sip left in hers. This has never been forgotten and Bella has not allowed it to happen again.

Jacques Calvet, the elderly (it seemed to me) head of the family, invited me to his home in the centre of Bordeaux, which was full of the most wonderful furniture and paintings. Seeing my interest, he told me of a street near the Musée des Beaux Arts where all the good antique shops were. These were fascinating to visit and, while I was not antique-shopping on the first few months of my tour, I did buy a pair of Louis XV silver candlesticks. I showed them to Jacques later; he nodded his approval and asked me what I had paid for them. When I told him, he wrote a short note and put it in an envelope for me to give to the dealer on my next visit. Thinking it was just a word of greeting from a busy man, I presented the note some time later. The dealer smiled and gave me a few banknotes. It appeared that M Calvet had told him I had been overcharged; his connoisseur's eye and Auvergnat spirit coming to the fore.

My next stage was at the Cognac house of Delamain in the tiny town of Jarnac in the Charente. Delamain was a small company specializing in buying, ageing and blending cognacs from the two best sub-regions, Grande and Petite Champagne. Their famous brand Pale & Dry averages 25 years of age. It is still one of Cognac's finest houses, now with a majority investment by Champagne Bollinger, thanks in part to my suggesting the firm to François Sauzey, one of the family shareholders. He told me in the 1980s that the company was looking for outside investment from like-minded people. I had first met François at Delamain while I was working there: he was a gangly teenager and his father was the firm's general manager.

My short time in Jarnac, a total contrast to the *haut commerce* of Bordeaux, was spent carefully labelling the precious bottles, all filled by hand and slowly polished dry. I learnt to 'nose' the different barrels and blends and then visited the small estates that supplied the young spirit from their copper stills. The other, larger, Cognac house in Jarnac was Hine, well known in England in part because the founder originated from Beaminster in Dorset. I went to Cognac itself to visit Hennessy, founded in 1765 by James Hennessy, which was one of the big three along with Martell and Rémy Martin. Hennessy was one of the many 'Wild Geese' – as were the Bartons and the Lynchs of Bordeaux – who decamped from their native Ireland during English rule. There were two other trainees there to show me around and it was a young Hennessy who introduced me to cognac and tonic, the drink they were launching to attract younger drinkers. This was interesting and different from the ubiquitous gin and tonic, and for the next two years back in London it was what I ordered in nightclubs. Today, if I drink spirits as a long drink, apart from one G&T a year to remind me how good it is, I drink brandy and soda, which is refreshing and can be heavily diluted without completely losing the flavour.

Just before I left Jarnac after an inspiring week, M Delamain asked me to join him for lunch. When his formidable cook-housekeeper served the coffee, he asked her to bring us the bottle of 1870. She expressed surprise: surely his guest was 'far too young for such a treasure?' He insisted, and as he poured a little cognac into a small tulip-shaped glass ('balloon' brandy glasses are deemed vulgar by the classic producers), he told me that the last person he had shared this particular bottle with was Winston Churchill. Thirty years later I saw a bottle of the 1870 in a Christie's auction and bought it to give to François Sauzey in memory of that moment.

My next brief trip was to Anjou in the Loire Valley, where I visited Domaine Baumard in the Côteaux-du-Layon region. Baumard was and still is one of the main producers of sweet Côteaux-du-Layon white wines, made from Chenin Blanc, whose natural acidity brings freshness to the finish. Baumard also produced the richer and much rarer Quarts de Chaume, which in the 18th century had been reserved solely for the royal court. My hosts were charming, but it was clear that business was poor. Wines were bottled with high levels of sulphur to stave off oxidation while they waited for a sale. Things are better now; the wines of Anjou and neighbouring Touraine are some of the purest 'country wines' of France and very good value, but many of the historic estates did not survive.

With the weather getting warmer and La Petite's top down whenever possible, I set off north to Alsace for a week with Hugel et Fils in Riquewihr, east of the Rhine. Hugel, still owned and managed by the direct descendants of the 1639 founder, is perhaps the best-known wine name in Alsace, although the

Trimbach estate in the next village, Ribeauvillé, is older, founded in 1626 and still going strong. Riquewihr, with its steep cobbled streets and timber-framed houses, rivals St-Emilion as France's most popular wine town.

Alsace is a varietal wine in the sense that Vin d'Alsace is the only appellation; the wines are labelled with their grape variety and further information according to their quality. While houses such as Hugel and Trimbach own many vineyards, as *négociants* they also buy in grapes and unfinished wine from other growers. They use labels such as *réserve* and *réserve personnelle*, except where the wine might come from a single vineyard, as is the case with Trimbach's Clos Ste Hune. In the mid-1960s, it was the *négociants* whose names ruled the market here, as in Burgundy. Now they share it with the individual estates, and quality has never been better.

Quality was always at the heart of Hugel, and the great Jean 'Johnny' Hugel, the family's roving ambassador, was well known and loved in every export market. He oversaw the wines from grape to bottle – but refused the title of winemaker, saying that such a word did not exist in the French language (logically it would be *fabricant du vin* or 'wine fabricator'); he also eschewed *œnologue*, or oenologist, as it hinted at the laboratory. He simply had all the right feelings in his DNA, and respect for the wine all through its life. Johnny was almost single-handedly responsible for the *Sélection des Grains Nobles* from grapes picked at a concentration far beyond late-harvest, and by setting the bar higher and higher for such wines, he ensured that the small quantities of them that reached the market were truly great.

The Hugel cellar was lined with tall, narrow vats or *foudres* of Slavonian oak in which the wines fermented and remained until bottling. This process threw off tartaric acid, which solidified on the sides of the vats like blocks of sugar, though it was perfectly tasteless. The vats themselves could not be moved, but this coating had to be dislodged every few years. The job could be done only by someone slim enough to squeeze through the small detachable 'door', who would then have to bang on the vat's sides with a wooden mallet to bring the tartaric crystals showering down around him. Since the cellar workers were exclusively male in those days and the Alsatians mostly of impressive size, this job usually fell to the trainees. It was sticky work.

In practical terms, Germany and its wines were pretty much unknown to me, so a week with the Villa Huesgen in the Mosel's Traben Trarbach was a revelation.

I had studied German at 'A' level but had had almost no chance to speak it, so I was surprised how easy it was. (In my 'O' level French oral exam I was asked *Que fait votre père?* / What does your father do? Unable to find the words for 'he is the director of transport for a sand and gravel company', I replied '*Hélas, il est mort/* Alas he is dead.' Luckily my French had improved by this time.)

Once again I spent a little time in the laboratory, did some tasting, worked on the bottling line and stacked bottles in huge bins 72 across and 48 deep. If the cellar master could then extract a bottle from the centre without the whole bin shifting, that was a job well done.

The Huesgen wines were mostly Rieslings, a few Sylvaners and a little sparkling. Dry or trocken wines were not made in the mid-1960s; entry-level wines were off-dry with no more than 10% alcohol and 10–15 grams of residual sugar. The alcohol reduced and the residual sugar increased as the quality rose to Spätlese/late harvest; Auslese/very late harvest; Beerenauslese/very late harvest of individual berries, and finally a supremely sweet wine, almost treacly textured Trockenbeerenauslese made from single, raisin-like berries. The cellar tastings did not cover the last two, but on the second evening I was taken across to a fine turreted castle to meet Frau Huesgen, who welcomed me into a panelled dining room where there was a small table with a half-bottle of wine, a bowl of wild strawberries and a glass. A white-gloved butler poured me a glass of something wonderful, and Fr Huesgen said I should come every evening to taste a different wine with some different berries, and make some notes. So three more times I appeared, suitably spruced up, to be received by the butler, who waited while I tasted and wrote up my impressions of the very classy wines.

When Traben Trarbach's early-summer wine fair came around, I was packed off with a glass – a small tumbler, not the usual green-stemmed Mosel glass – to attend my first-ever wine fair. It was full of boisterous jollity and friendly cheer, and although the road back to my host's house was straight, by late that evening it didn't seem so to me.

My second German stage was in the city of Worms am Rhein at Langenbach. Wines of the Rheingau are broader and richer than those of the Mosel; it is even warm enough there to make a little red wine. The best are the Pinot Noirs grown around Assmannshausen. Thanks to global warming and careful work in the vineyards and cellar, some German Pinot Noirs are now rivalling the finest from Burgundy, both in quality and price, but such wines were rare in the mid-1960s.

Returning from a brief visit home I stopped off in Chablis. Chablis, a name often 'borrowed' by other countries to promote their own wines, was slow to get back on its feet after the devastating 1956 frosts. They were so severe that (as in St-Emilion) the ground froze to a depth of many feet, killing the vines stone dead. The following year, less than 750 hectares from a possible 6,834 were in production, effectively stopping the post-war recovery in its tracks. By the mid-1960s things were better, but financially for the vignerons, not by much.

My two employers in Beaune were the merchants Joseph Drouhin and Louis Latour, both long-term members of Beaune's elite. Whereas wine ruled only a part of Bordeaux, it ruled the whole of Beaune. The cellars below the cobbled streets were all working cellars and the magnificent 14th-century Hospices de Beaune, alms-houses in the historic centre, owe their survival in part to inherited vineyards. Grand and premier cru wines are sold by auction each year over the third weekend in November, a festival known as *les Trois Glorieuses*.

Négociants controlled the market as the *Chartronnais* did in Bordeaux, being the only clients for the growers' wines in tank or barrel. A handful of top domaines bottled their own wine, but the merchants bought, blended, bottled and sold, and for the most part did a good job. As in Bordeaux, the *négociant's* name, more than that of the appellation, was the selling point.

Joseph Drouhin's 13th-century cellars were (and are) in the oddly named Rue d'Enfer / Hell Street. Inside were row after row of 215-litre barrels (smaller than Bordeaux's 225 litres) with the Burgundy appellations stencilled on their front or head, and bin after bin of unlabelled bottles identified only by a bin number. Over time the barrels acquired a coating of black, mushroomy fungus caused by the humidity: it was soft and velvety to the touch and generally reckoned to be a good thing.

Managed by the tall, elegant Robert Drouhin, whose father Maurice had been one of the great names in Beaune's history, Drouhin was much admired and remains a beacon for quality. I spent much time in the Côte d'Or vineyards meeting the vignerons who, in mid-June, were looking forward to a good harvest, only to see their hopes dashed by almost constant rain later in the summer. Very few 1965s were good enough for export; 1963 had been just as poor, but 1968 was so bad that the annual Hospices de Beaune sales did not even take place.

Louis Latour's working cellars were a little to the south in the village of Pommard, and their offices and other cellars were at the family-owned Château Corton Grancey. They, too, had ancient vaulted cellars in the centre of Beaune. Their US importer was Frederick Wildman and Sons, and the high-spot of my time at Latour was when I helped set up a vast stone tasting table for Colonel Wildman's annual visit. I stood in the background listening to the comments and was allowed to taste the wines after he and the directors had left for lunch. I also remember Louis Latour Sr (the eldest son is always named Louis) having me to a family lunch and asking me to help his granddaughter with her English homework.

I spent some free time touring the rich countryside, and found that by far the best food was to be had a 15-minute drive south to Chagny. The Lameloise family ran a restaurant that they had held for two generations; it had a Michelin star, to which a second and then a third were soon added. My weekly treat was a visit there, where my meal started with a Kir (a dash of crème de cassis topped up with Bourgogne Aligoté), then half a bottle of white, half a bottle of red and sometimes a marc de Bourgogne with coffee. There was usually change from a Fr50 note.

My last stage was with Jaboulet Aîné in Tain l'Hermitage, then the greatest name in the northern Rhône. Northern Rhône vineyards run 65 kilometres from Vienne to Valance and cover a handful of appellations on both sides of the river, Hermitage and Côte-Rôtie being the most famous. Their red wines are made entirely from Syrah. Louis Jaboulet welcomed me at his offices and cellars. I have always known the patriarchal head of the firm as *Oncle* Louis; he was a bachelor and had many nephews, one of whom, Gérard, was my age and became a great friend. Louis was always kind to me. On my very first day he gave me a beautifully illustrated set of art-deco maps of the French wine-growing regions from Louis Larmat's *Atlas de la France Vinicole*. Gérard then took me up to the steep terraces of the Hermitage Hill before Louis introduced me, vintage by vintage, to his revelatory wines.

Although Hermitage was used during most of the 19th century to bolster the wines of Bordeaux, it fell completely out of fashion following the devastation by phylloxera in the early 1900s, and had not yet recovered. Knowing that I had just been in Burgundy, Louis told me that his single-vineyard Crozes-Hermitage Domaine de Thalabert was selling for the price of a Beaujolais cru, his Hermitage for that of a Côtes de Beaune-Villages and his iconic Hermitage La Chapelle for that of a Volnay or a Pommard; prices far too low for wines of such quality. Perhaps there had been too much to absorb in Bordeaux and perhaps many of the burgundies I tasted did not have quite the precision or sense of place that they do today, but I certainly connected with the northern Rhônes (also with Jaboulet's Parallele 45 and Châteauneuf-du-Pape's Les Cèdres from the south), and have continued to connect ever since.

I told Louis that my parents had visited the Hôtel du Midi, 30 minutes up the hill at Lamastre, and he suggested we go there for lunch. When I told him that two *stagière* friends from Bordeaux would be joining me, as well as three charming girls from London, he told Mme Barratéro to reserve us the private room and have the chef prepare his classic menu: *Pâté d'écrevisses sauce cardinale* (crayfish pâté with sauce made from their pounded shells); *poularde de Bresse en demi-deuil sauce albufera* (truffled Bresse chicken poached in a pig's bladder); local cheeses and *Vacherin aux fruits rouges* (a meringue-and-ice-cream cake with raspberries and strawberries). This was one of the most marvellous meals I had ever had and – because one of the London guests was Bella – so memorable that I asked Michel Roux of London's Le Gavroche to re-create it for our 40th wedding anniversary in January 2008. With the cheese, *Oncle* Louis had offered us a bottle of La Chapelle 1961, a wine that I saw on the list at Hôtel Pic in Valence a few years ago at €15,000 a bottle. Four decades later I couldn't match this at Le Gavroche, but we did have fine burgundies from my children's birth years: 1971 and 1973.

In those days, although Bella's parents knew that she and I were seeing a lot of each other, the idea of their daughter travelling across Europe with me (which we'd planned as a link to my next work with Christopher's' suppliers in Spain) would have been unacceptable, so the two 'travelling companions' she arrived with were a front. I had told my father this, saying that I hoped we would get away with it, but we nearly did not. When we eventually arrived in Jerez, I collected mail at the hotel where we were staying to find a letter from him saying 'The game is up, you were spotted by Bella's cousins in Venice and Madrid. Prepare for the worst.'

There was nothing to be done and Bella was understandably nervous when she returned later that month, to see her father coming to meet her with a distinctly determined look on his face. Happily he was brushed aside by her beautiful mother who welcomed her saying 'Darling, how sensible to have travelled round Europe with Steven – so much more comfortable than with the two girls.'

After our fabulous dinner at the Hôtel du Midi, we waved goodbye to Tain l'Hermitage and headed south to Avignon, where we found a top-floor room at the Hôtel l'Univers with just the minimum facilities but a view – if one stood on a chair – over to the Palais des Papes. One evening we dined at Hiély-Lucullus, where white and red Châteauneuf-du-Pape *de l'année* was served *en carafe*. With no one around we swam in the Gard River, diving in from a ledge below the Roman Pont du Gard aqueduct. Next stop was Aix-en-Provence, passing the beautiful Château Simone, then the sole producer (and still the best) in the tiny appellation Palette, and afterwards on to Nice, where we stayed in the old town near the flower market, spending mornings on the pebble beach and discovering the city by night.

We then headed to Italy to spend a few days in Venice. On our last night we were invited up to the lovely hill town of Asolo, where the family of one of the Bordeaux *stagières* had a villa. The next day, having passed through Trieste, a truly international port which boasts churches of practically every denomination, we arrived in Yugoslavia, which was then under the firm rule of President Tito. We drove down the Adriatic to spend a couple of nights in Dubrovnik; passed through Pécs, famous for its inexpensive Riesling; and on down through Skopje, crossing on a car ferry to Greece. From here it was a lovely drive to Athens.

Stopping to fill up with petrol, we were accosted by a matronly woman laden with baskets of vegetables and two live chickens, who asked to be taken to the city to see her daughter. She and her menagerie piled in, and as we drove along she treated us to a lively rendition of songs in her local dialect. When she made it plain that we should reciprocate, my mind went blank. It was the early days of the Beatles but I couldn't remember a tune, let alone any words, so we ended up singing the Cumberland hunting song 'D'ye ken John Peel (with his coat so gay)?', which seemed to satisfy. We dropped the lady off in the rather down-at-heel centre of town. Since the tour was unplanned, we relied in Athens, as we had in Yugoslavia, on being approached with propositions along the lines of 'My friend has good room!', which worked well. Hosts were charming, rooms were clean; on one occasion we even ended up in a bunk bed in a room off somebody's kitchen. Happily Mamá was a good and generous cook. We visited Delphi, then Corinth, and took the ferry from Patras to Bari. Bella was furious with me for taking second-class tickets, which obliged us to sit up all night with nothing to eat.

Our pattern for the trip was to alternate, where possible, between smart and cheap-and-cheerful hotels, but occasionally in the countryside we slept in the car, which I am not sure Triumph Heralds were designed for. At that time, we had no way of keeping our picnic wines cool. I overcame this problem later with my next car, a convertible Triumph Vitesse, by installing a fridge in the boot. In August 1966, I stowed a bottle of champagne in it before driving to Bella's family home to see her on her birthday. When I arrived late in the afternoon, her father suggested we open a celebratory bottle. 'I had the same idea!' I told him, heading for the car.

'But it won't be cold,' he protested.

'It will, Sir: my car's got a fridge.'

'Fella's got a fridge in his car!' he exclaimed in disbelief. I always was a touch too modern for Bella's charmingly conservative father.

Back in fridge-free La Petite, Bella and I were heading to Jerez de la Frontera in the very south of Spain, where I hoped to learn something about sherry. We planned to stop off for a few days in St-Tropez, where a great friend was based during the summer season. Even in August, St-Tropez then still felt like a village. Locals dominated the Place des Lices, the large open square set back from the port, which was almost entirely given over to the game of *boules* or *pétanque*. I had never seen this game before. Crossing the square one evening, I noticed a ball rolling towards me and several men shouting and waving their hands in my direction. Naturally I thought they wanted their ball back, so I picked it up and rolled it towards them. I was not allowed to walk across the square after that. The fashionable Leï Mouscardins at the end of the port was the best place for fish which, if accompanied by Domaines Ott Blanc de Blancs served in its signature amphora-shaped bottle, made for a very good meal.

From St-Tropez we drove overnight along the coast to Spain – we often did this to save time, as there were so many places and things we wanted to see. Having crossed the border for a Spanish breakfast of coffee and *churros* (deep-fried strips of dough dredged in sugar – much lighter than they sound), we pushed on to Madrid for the Prado Museum and a bullfight, before continuing south.

After a marvellous few days in Seville, we arrived in Jerez to spend the first two nights in the Hotel Los Cisnes, the classic and best hotel in town, moving to cheaper premises when the Feria week started on the first Sunday in September. All at once a quiet, sleepy little town transformed into a glorious pageant celebrating the history of Andalucía, alive with horses and bulls, handsome boys and pretty girls, colourful food and delicious sherry. I had already met Beltrán Domecq of the illustrious local family in Bordeaux – we were about the same age – and seeing him leading the procession on a fine horse impressed me enormously.

The MacKenzie house, where my sherry induction began, was not in the same league on the international market as those of the Domecq or González Byass families, but it was a fine company with big stocks of old wine in a superb bodega (above-ground cellar). Diego Ferguson, of Scottish descent, was the director in charge of blending, the art that lies at the heart of sherry's reputation. In the bodega and in the tasting room he introduced me to the fabulous range of styles, all made from the Palomino grape, from the pale fino; the darker, aged fino known as amontillado; the classy palo cortado; the richer oloroso and finally the extra-rich Pedro Ximénez, known as PX, from the grape of the same name. He also showed me the Jerezano hangover cure. Dipping his *veneʒia* (a pipette or 'wine thief') deep into a cask of PX in the darkest part of the bodega, he filled a copita and handed it to me, telling me to hold on to the cask and down it in one. The explosive impact brought stars to my eyes – but it worked wonders.

After two days' learning in the bodega, a visit to the vineyards was planned, and I asked if Bella could come along too. The vintage was in full swing, the women picking, the men collecting the grapes in large boxes and humping them onto an ox-drawn cart to be taken up to the pressing room. It was too much to resist: I asked the man in charge if he needed a hand, and within five minutes I was on the back of the cart. My hosts were so surprised that they telephoned Christopher's to say that trainees were not expected to join the workers; the reply was simply that I was unreliable. I joined the vintage for three days. The MacKenzie family got over its shock of my penchant for vineyard work and on the last evening invited Bella and me to join in a magnificent party they were giving for their daughter's

Working in the vineyards at Vargellas was a useful apprenticeship. Eight years later, it was all hands to the pump when there was a mechanical failure at a vineyard I part-owned in the southern Rhône.

21st birthday. It was a wonderful way to end a magical week. The next day, after one last lunch with Bella on a terrace overlooking the city, I drove her to the airport and headed up to Oporto.

I had been advised to stay at the British Club in Vila Nova de Gaia, where all the great and small port houses or 'lodges' were. Many of the famous producers' names were (and still are) of British origin, including Cockburn, Croft, Dow, Graham and Taylor. The splendid 18th-century Factory House in Oporto with its 'double-cube' dining room – one half for eating, the other for drinking port – is open to members of the British family firms only. The British Club had a cricket pitch and a wine list that included Château Cheval Blanc 1947 – but the streets of Oporto were much more fun. I took the train up to Pinhão, the little town central to the Douro vineyards, where I was welcomed by Bruce Guimaraens of Fonseca, then went up to Quinta do Vargellas, owned by Taylor. At that time Dick Yeatman (the company's full name was Taylor, Fladgate and Yeatman) was the managing director, and his wife Beryl managed the Quinta.

While Europe was modernizing in the mid-1960s, Vargellas was not. What electric light there was came from a generator, I was given a candle to take to bed to read by and brought hot water in a pitcher in the mornings. It was as if I had stepped back in time, but the pace fitted perfectly with the slowness of the whole process of port, from treading the grapes in large granite *lagares*, to the wines' maturing in oak pipes. A selected vintage would be bottled in its second year, and mature for another 50. Dick stressed that a great vintage port should always have 'a touch of green' at the start, the equivalent of tannin in claret. When guests came, vintages were opened, but the after-dinner port was usually a 15-year-old Tawny OPW (Old Partners' Wine), which was and still is reserved for the Quinta. I was introduced to white port, Taylor's Chip Dry, which they liked to serve iced with a splash of tonic water, and took part in the grape-treading, a piano accordion-player providing the rhythmic beat to stomp to. One of the great strengths of the wine world is the families that make up a large part of it. The Douro is blessed with a wealth of such families.

By now it was late September and vintage time in France, though the 1965 vintage is not one to be remembered. Driving north from Oporto I crossed over into Spain and called in at López de Heredia in Haro, the historical centre of Rioja. The company was started, along with Marqués de Riscal, by members of the family who had worked in Bordeaux. Cabernet Sauvignon was planted in the late-19th century, making way for Tempranillo only after the devastations of phylloxera.

López de Heredia is unique in Rioja in maturing wines for a time in large upright casks, then a longer time in small barrels, and finally allowing the wine to settle in bottles before sale. The cobwebs in the reserve cellar get thicker every year. The current management, while modernizing, quite rightly maintains this family tradition.

A week in Bordeaux allowed me to see the vintage first hand and to revisit my former employers, but by this time I was keen to get back home. A final few days at Moët & Chandon was on the programme, again staying at the Château de Saran, and then it was back across the channel to London. La Petite (number plate 201 R), made it home without complaint, but when I took her to the dealership for a service after so many thousands of miles, she gave up the ghost. I remember her with great affection.

Shortly after my return, I presented myself at Christopher's to ask if they had a place for me, but they did not. I applied to Dolamore, an established merchant in Baker Street from whom my parents bought wine when they were 'going smart', but was turned down there as well. When I heard about a new company called Murray and Banbury, which had premises under a car showroom in Knightsbridge, I went along and, as the Christmas period was warming up, they took me on.

Murray and Banbury were David Murray-Threipland, a charming but serious gentleman from Wales, and Bill Banbury, an expansive and expanded bon viveur who had a passion for wine and a brilliant palate. They were an oddly matched but surprisingly complementary couple, only a few years older than I was. I stayed with them a year and a half, and had tremendous fun, becoming a director and – of course – investing some money, accompanying Bill to tastings and lunches in London and on buying trips to France. At this time the established London wine trade was in the last stages of a post-War boom before declining in the face of competition from supermarkets and start-ups such as Oddbins and Bottoms Up.

Murray and Banbury's premises combined both cellar and shop, being a rather more sophisticated version of the more mainstream Peter Dominic. Bill Banbury's upbringing had given him a taste for the best – we even imported wines from Domaine de la Romanée-Conti – while David Murray was more down to earth but liked to discover new things. Both approaches were very appealing to me. We imported a luxury champagne from the House of Lenoble in the Vallée de la

Marne, whose flagship brand was Prince André de Bourbon-Parme, and pitched it as a rival to Roederer Cristal. We also imported a range of wines from the Loire – Ménétou-Salon, Châteaumeillant, Cheverny and Quincy – quite unknown at that time, but which I came across again in the wine bars of Paris some years later.

Murray and Banbury were not the only merchants of 'country wines'; the best at the time was Gerald Asher, whose company Asher Storey went as far afield as the Jura, and whose wines took another half-century to become popular in London and New York. Asher's business did not survive the harsh economic climate that followed and he retired to France, later splitting his time between Paris and San Francisco as in-house wine writer for *Esquire*. His articles were erudite, poetic and not pretentious; long enough but certainly not lengthy. Full of admiration, I asked him one day how he did it. 'I sit down and pretend I'm writing a letter to my mother,' was his reply. Another favourite wine writer who wrote in quite a different style, short and to the point, was Frank J Prial, wine correspondent for 25 years for *The New York Times*, a great friend of Alexis Lichine and a reporter at heart. I said to him once: 'You must like writing since you write so well.'

'No', he replied: 'I like having written.' I'm more a Prial than an Asher.

Working at Murray and Banbury introduced me to a part of the London wine trade that I had heard of, but not seen, when I was at Christopher's: the shippers, importers who were established in the City of London and had warehouses down by the docks. Some were of foreign origin, such as Deinhard and Sichel from Germany, and some were very British, with names such as International Distillers and Vintners (IDV) that reflected mergers with other companies.

The shippers, keen to supply our up-and-coming retail outfit, would invite Bill to their offices for tastings, and after a time they asked me, too. A memorable one was at Sichel, where John Salvi (an Englishman – a count, indeed – who had learnt the business from the very bottom before becoming one of only 20 Masters of Wine in the world) had called us in to taste some German wines as well as some Bordeaux. The latter included Château d'Angludet owned by Peter Sichel, and Château Palmer, co-owned by the Bordeaux branch of the Sichels, both in Margaux. During lunch – it was unthinkable that a morning's tasting would not be followed by lunch, and this is when older vintages would be shown – John received a telephone call from Bordeaux to tell him that his wife had just been delivered of a son, the future Count Salvi. This, he said, calls for a celebration. Knowing what was in the company cellar, he immediately asked for a bottle of Château Margaux 1900 to be decanted, dismissing our weak protestations by saying that his bosses probably didn't know it was there, and if they did, they wouldn't miss it anyway. He was wrong on both counts.

Back in London, I caught up with contemporaries, many of them working in the City, who introduced me to Coates's Wine Bar in Old Broad Street. This was a long, dimly-lit establishment that served good plain English food and had a wonderful wine list, being part of the Corney & Barrow stable. Most of the clarets were London-bottled and the 1953s and '55s were offered by the glass or carafe at ridiculously low prices in the restaurant, and by the bottle to take away. I have pleasant recollections of Château Macarthy St-Estèphe and Langoa-Barton 1953 both at 13/6- (65p) a bottle, Pichon-Comtesse just two shillings (10p) more, and a whole raft of 1955 classed growths at the same sort of price. What with these, and the wine lists from the Army and Navy Stores, Patens of Peterborough and The Wine Society, really good claret was easy to come by.

The re-opening of Christie's Wine Auctions in 1966 was a significant event in terms of my wine education. This was where I first met Michael Broadbent. (Fifty years later, at the anniversary dinner in 2016, wines from the 1966 vintage were served in Christie's Great Rooms in St James's. Michael, then 89 years old, was on splendid form.)

Regular auctions were held in the King Street premises just off St James's, and these were preceded by tastings of many of the wines that were offered in several-case lots. One day a range of post-War vintage ports might be offered, another might show sherries and Madeiras, and of course claret was a staple. I remember watching Michael go down the line with a little red notebook assessing colour, nose, palate and aftertaste in a precise manner that I had not come across before. It showed me that wine tasting could, and actually should, be structured. Michael was the first person to put this structure into words in his book *Wine Tasting* (1968), and the importance of his having done so is impossible to exaggerate.

As Michael led Christie's to great heights in the 1970s and '80s, some of these auctions came to be of historic size and quality, but even in the early days there was a cornucopia of wines on offer. Of the many successful bids I placed at that time, perhaps the best was for 24 half-bottles of Château Gazin Pomerol 1945, bottled by Sichel. The wine was simply marvellous: robust, from Pomerol's '*crasse de fer*' iron-rich soil, with mature concentration. One of these bottles formed part of a lunch that I made up to brighten the day of a good friend who was spending a short spell in London's Brixton Prison. I had gone to Harrods for the food – pâté de foie gras, half a cold grouse (it was the autumn) and some fruit and cheese – and at reception the goodies had to be unwrapped for inspection and listing. The officer in charge spelled out the contents as he recorded them: 'Slice of meat paste, one half bird, cheese and fruit' and coming to the wine, which I had uncorked as I didn't imagine Brixton would supply corkscrews, 'shatto gazin one nine four five… what's the number for?' 'It's just its number,' I replied: 'Your guest has a number and so does the wine.' Some time later, when my friend was 'out', we shared another half-bottle, but he said he had appreciated the Brixton one more.

As I was a regular at the Christie's pre-auction tastings, Michael and I got to know each other, and every now and then he took me through some of the wines. Had it not been for his teaching, his book and his friendship in those days, my Paris wine school the Académie du Vin would never have existed.

Spring 1966 rolled around and Bill Banbury and I went on a buying trip to Champagne and Alsace. In Champagne we visited Lenoble, whose style I admired so much that the wine was served at my wedding a couple of years later. In Alsace I went back to say hello to the Hugels, we visited Trimbach and discovered a grower named Louis Sipp, one of the very few vignerons at that time to farm organically, and we took his wines on for the UK. Alsace is the most beautiful wine region, prompting Louis XIV to remark on his first visit *quel beau jardin! /* what a beautiful garden!, and its wines are varied and delicious, but at that time they were difficult to sell. As a result, they became known as 'wine merchants' wines', for the merchants bought them, couldn't sell them, so drank them themselves.

In the 1960s, one of the most sought-after invitations of the year was to the Lebègue Wine Tastings in mid-June. These, along with Centre Court tickets at Wimbledon and a box at Ascot, were recognized high-points of the Season. Lebègue, with merchant houses in both Bordeaux and Burgundy and offices in London, showed their full range of wines starting with a morning tasting, followed by a splendid lunch for the several hundred guests at which the finest

British products were served: Orkney lobsters, barons of Angus beef, Stilton cheese and of course strawberries (washed down with Château d'Yquem). The Bordeaux range went from the minor wines right up to the first growths and the burgundies from 'village' wines, through premiers to grands crus, ending with the wines of the Domaine de la Romanée-Conti. Held in the vast Lebègue cellars underneath the arches near the London Docks, the tastings were wildly impressive, especially to someone as young and new to the trade as I was. Bill, David and I took the tasting part very seriously, while for others it was a social event. Quentin Crewe, author and journalist with *Queen* magazine, was also there and wrote his review describing how he had navigated the many dozens of wines on offer: 'I followed the young man in the pink shirt.'

As 1966 drew on, my large inheritance began to slip through my fingers. The decisions were all mine, but I always expected the results to be better than they were. I was an easy target for adventurers who needed backing for a nightclub or for making a movie, and since they all seemed like good ideas at the time and were proposed by friends, it was both tempting and flattering to go along with them. A 30-minute documentary movie, *Dolly Story*, which I was involved in *almost* sold to a US distributor… and then didn't. Branches of Sybilla's, an ultra-fashionable nightclub, which we envisaged opening in the Bahamas and New York, never quite came off; a Chelsea restaurant did see the light of day briefly before it closed, taking some of my wine collection and artworks with it. Also, fitting in with this disappointing trend, I broke up with Bella.

Bill Banbury and I went to Burgundy for the Hospices de Beaune weekend, and before joining the festivities, we had a long tasting with Henri Leroy. Henri had been co-owner since 1945 of the Domaine de la Romanée-Conti alongside the de Villaine family, and his daughter was the formidable Lalou Bize-Leroy, one of Burgundy's figureheads for many years. I tasted some of the Leroy range and some from the DRC, concentrating hard, picking out the various aromas in Broadbent-trained fashion, and was pleased to hear M Leroy remark: 'This young man knows how to taste.' Two decades later I was at the Hospices tasting alongside Lalou, and afterwards she asked me which cuvées had particularly impressed me. I selected two or three which I thought were knockouts, to be told 'My poor Steven, you seem to taste for the present, while I taste for the future.'

Bill's and my sortie was one of the very few occasions I have attended all three manifestations of *les Trois Glorieuses*. The Saturday evening was the grand dinner at the Château du Clos de Vougeot hosted by the Chevaliers de Tastevin. This six-course banquet for at least 500 people included wines that had been *tasteviné*, that is selected on a blind tasting from many samples and awarded the prestigious Chevaliers de Tastevin label. A percentage of the price of every bottle goes towards the upkeep of the 12th-century château, which was for centuries a Cistercian monastery. The building dominates the 50-hectare walled Clos de Vougeot appellation. The formal dinner was punctuated by the singing of popular songs – *bans bourguignons* – and culminated with everyone waving their large linen napkins above their heads. The dinner on Sunday evening, *le Dîner aux Chandelles*, used to be a candlelit banquet for a much smaller number in the nave of Beaune's senior church, but has now transferred to the Hospices itself. Here only wines from the Hospices vineyards are served – and very good they are, too.

The final celebration is a lunch known as *la Paulée de Meursault*, an occasion rustically robust compared to the previous evenings, at which once again scores of guests – this is a highly prized invitation – gather for a full afternoon's lunch. Here, to match the local white wine, the main course is a local river fish known as *pocheuse*, but the main attraction is that *la Paulée* is a glorified bottle party. Bottles are provided, of course, open on the trestle tables, but everyone also brings his or her own – good bottles, and not just one of them – which are shared with increasing appreciation. Lunch never ends until well after dark, and then it is time for a 'cellar crawl' from grower to grower.

When Bill and I were there, *la Paulée* was held in the vast cellars of the Château du Meursault, then owned by the Comte de Moucheron. This ancient Burgundy family had been substantial vineyard owners not just in the Côte de Beaune, but also in Musigny and Chambertin in the Côte de Nuits. By the mid-1960s the holdings had been reduced to the best plots of Meursault and Volnay and the beautiful 18th-century château, but a decade later these, too, were sold.

Back in London I continued my Saturday forays to the Portobello Road for antiques and odds and ends, building up a collection of 19th-century English glasses known as rummers and an increasing range of Staffordshire pottery figures. I had also discovered an art gallery at the King's Road, World's End, run by a charming old boy named John Denny who filled a whole house, floor to ceiling, with pictures. His office (and his whisky bottle) were to be found at the top. He seemed to have only three prices: £500, £1,500 and £5,000 – and I was in the middle range. His 'attributions' were not wholly convincing. The George Stubbs painting I bought of a horse being frightened by a lion was unlikely to have come from the hand of England's greatest animal painter – the lion resembled a wind-up toy – but it was 'School of Stubbs'. However, the paintings were good to look at and, apart from the Stubbs and an Italian landscape by (School of) Gaspard Dughet, I still enjoy them.

My enthusiastic acquisition of art and antiques meant that I was soon looking for somewhere with more room, and in late 1966 I bought a four-storey house in Fernshaw Road, SW10. It was habitable but needed total renovation, which I went about with gusto. The tired stretch of lawn in the west-facing garden was replaced by slabs of York stone, in the middle of which I had a fountain built, whose large basin could accommodate many bottles of wine for summer chilling. The basement became a dining room and large kitchen, while in the hallway I installed face-to-face wine racks that held 360 bottles each. There was a 'coal hole' under the pavement which I had cleaned out to make space for wine in wooden cases.

Life was marvellous. The dining room seated eight comfortably and the whole house buzzed with activity. My friend (and later best man) Giles Townsend had one of the upstairs rooms, so on evenings when I wasn't going out we enjoyed cheerful dinners together. I had cooked quite a bit before, but now took it up in earnest. Elizabeth David's books were invaluable, making it all the more exciting when I discovered that Mrs David was one of Murray and Banbury's clients. Although we had a van driver, I often delivered her wines myself in the hope of meeting her. There were still very good food shops of all kinds in the area: a superb fishmonger from whom I would buy wild sea trout, and Curnicks, an excellent butcher. My brother Nicky then lived around the corner with his wife and two children, and was a regular there. Nicky's wife would have shopped every day for the family; I shopped only now and again for indulgent dinner parties. One day I called in to collect a rib of beef and my name was shouted to the back of the shop. 'Is that the rich Mr Spurrier or the poor Mr Spurrier?' came the reply.

A young Swiss au pair from Zurich, Susi Spörri, had the other room on the top floor. She was trying to get into the music business and one evening, returning from dinner, I found the sitting-room filled with her friends. A young black guy clutching a guitar got up and said: 'Hi, I'm Jimi, who are you?'

'I'm Steven,' I replied, and wishing them a good evening went up to bed. The following morning Susi asked me if I had enjoyed meeting Jimi Hendrix.

In early 1967 I was elected the second-youngest-ever member of Boodle's. Boodle's is one of three gentleman's clubs a stone's throw from each other in St James's Street. They were founded in the 1760s as places for gentlemen to meet, first as coffee houses with gaming rooms – everything was bet on in those days, from horses, to which drop of rain would reach the bottom of the window-pane first – then as substantial private houses with saloons, dining rooms and bedrooms. A mild rivalry exists between them and there is a saying that 'the members of Brooks's think they run the country, the members of Boodle's run the country and the members of White's own the country.'

Despite the poor investments I was making, I still had substantial capital at my disposal and I began to think of a place in the sun – France of course. I was fascinated by a 30-hectare plot of land outside Bagnols-en-Forêt in the Var department, midway between St-Tropez and Nice, both of which I knew quite well. The property had a ruined farmhouse on it and I was told that the owner was an Australian architect who was now living in England and had to sell up. This seemed like an interesting adventure, so I got in touch with David Langlands, an old friend who had spent some time in St-Tropez, and suggested he join me to check it out. The day we chose to leave, the Governor of the Bank of England, Lord Cromer, had announced that Sterling would undergo devaluation and that times were tough economically, so the country should 'tighten its belt for the future'.

The property, known as Bayonne, had views south to the sea and north to the Alps and I fell for it immediately. I subsequently met the vendor, Paul Calder, in London and we shook hands on a deal. Paul would sell me the land and the ruined farmhouse, and design a house for me which (this being around April) I said I would hope to build the following year.

In summer 1967 I left Murray and Banbury and, always on the lookout for a distraction, began to think of going into the antiques business. Meanwhile, Bella and I bumped into each other occasionally and she told me she was going to spend the summer in America, visiting cousins. Her 21st birthday was in the middle of August and I phoned her parents to ask for an address so that I could send a birthday telegram. Her father was unhelpful, but her mother said it was a nice idea and off the telegram went. On her return in early September, Bella called to thank me for it and I asked her to the (second) opening night of Rupert's, a restaurant I was briefly involved in. She accepted and we talked the evening away… I walked the few blocks back home in a very good state of mind. Slowly but surely, Bella and I got back together. I kept a notebook of the dinners at home and who was there and what was drunk, and Bella re-appears for a dinner for six (Puligny-Montrachet La Garenne 1961, Gevrey-Chambertin 1955) on 11th October, again on the 13th (Hermitage le Chevalier de Sterimberg 1964, Chambertin-Clos de Bèze 1955) and once again, just the two of us (half bottles of Corton-Charlemagne 1957 and Château Figeac 1952) on the 20th… and then almost without a break. A few weeks later Nicky took me aside and said that I should ask Bella to marry me: 'You lost her last time and you can't afford to lose her again', he said. I recounted this to Bella when we next met. Her response was that this constituted a suggestion, not a proposal, so I went down on one knee to propose, and – very happily – was accepted.

Both sets of parents had to be informed and while my parents were thrilled, hers were a little less so. We were apprehensive about their meeting but when they were introduced they found they knew many people in common; my father charmed Bella's mother, and her father fell for my mother, so all was well. The date of 31st January was set for the wedding in London, which didn't leave us much time to plan for the future.

The UK was in a poor financial state in the late 1960s and the government was determined to 'squeeze the rich until the pips squeak'. I had discovered a loophole whereby capital could be whisked out of the country to the Cayman Islands, and then to Switzerland. This was especially interesting in relation to the Provence project, since at the time the Bank of England permitted no more than £5,000 to leave the country, and that would be nowhere near enough to realise my plans. The big risk was that if it didn't work out, the Cayman banks would hold on to the money. But I took the risk and luckily it worked, so about half of the inheritance I had paid across the Lloyds Bank counter in early 1964 found its way to Geneva.

Bella and I flew down to look at the property, and I asked her if we should go and live in the south of France. 'Why not?' she replied. Bella didn't have capital to export, but we needed to get the Bank of England's permission to export ourselves to become non-residents for tax purposes. The fact that we had a place to export ourselves *to* clinched the deal, although it allowed us no more than 90 days a year back in the UK. This decision, taken almost on a whim, turned out to be the best – perhaps the only good – financial decision I have ever made.

Since we had designated the unbuilt house at Bagnols-en-Forêt as our primary residence, we were allowed to keep the house in London, so nothing had to be moved. My plan now was to become an antiques dealer, and for this I needed a

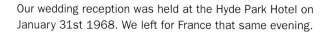

Our wedding reception was held at the Hyde Park Hotel on January 31st 1968. We left for France that same evening.

large station wagon. I ordered, via Citroën's London agent, a DS Safari, and we arranged to collect it on our arrival in Paris the day after our wedding.

The wedding itself had our friends all looking dashingly glamorous and/or eccentrically exotic. A wayward artist known as 'Boots' Bantock arrived with his shaggy black spaniel under his arm to be announced as 'Mr Boots and Lady Hermione Bantock'. Michael Fish, owner with Barry Sainsbury of London's most fashionable haberdasher, refused my suggestion that he shouldn't desert his clients just to come to a wedding, saying 'the shop will be shut: all the interesting clients will be at the wedding'. I got up at five o'clock that morning to go to Covent Garden to shop for lunch for my best man, Giles Townsend, and the four ushers, having commandeered (in January!) punnets of *fraises des bois* from Morocco that had been destined for Annabel's. Getting up that early and making lunch for six on my own wedding day does seem a bit odd now, but it didn't at the time. Afterwards we trooped off and they all watched while I had my hair cut (Bella said she hardly recognized me from the back as she walked down the aisle at the Brompton Oratory).

That evening I carried Bella over the threshold at Fernshaw Road. We changed out of our wedding gear and collected the marvellous packed supper my mother had prepared, as well as a bottle of Château Pape Clement 1953 to sustain us on our voyage. We left Victoria Station on the luxury boat-train, the *Golden Arrow*, in two first-class sleeping compartments – 'one to be sick in and one to be in afterwards' as my father had advised – heading to Paris, where we would begin a new life together in France.

CHAPTER FOUR
VAR FROM THE
MADDING CROWD

After arriving at the Gare du Nord, we sped to our hotel on Paris's superb Place Vendôme, only to be told that the rooms we had booked were being renovated and we were to divert to the sister Hôtel du Calais nearby. Here our room boasted a fine *lit matrimonial* which, if a few francs were inserted in the slot, would vibrate for 30 minutes. We saved our money.

The following morning we went to the Citroën showroom to collect our new car, then the most advanced of the range. In repose, it sat on its haunches, the body almost touching the ground; but once started it rose hydraulically about a foot. The brake was not a pedal but a large button, which had to be treated with respect. Heading off around the Arc de Triomphe, hazardous at the best of times, I stamped on it to avoid a taxi and the car almost stood on its head. The headlights could swivel, either manually or automatically, to lead you around hair-pin bends, which were always announced by a sign reading *attention aux lacets*. To describe tight corners as shoelaces seemed rather elegant.

We pushed on south to the ski station of Méribel, where a friend had lent us a chalet as a wedding present. I hadn't skied since my prep-school days, but Bella had. I made the best of it until we decided to take the lift right to the top and ski down to Courchevel on the other side. This was a black run, two grades more difficult than the blue I was comfortable with. I kept to the easier runs after that.

Motoring down to Provence, we found the vendor of the Bagnols-en-Forêt property had designed a substantial villa along classical lines and had moved himself, his wife and young daughter down to Fayence, a nearby village, to oversee the works. Once the house was finished, I planned to furnish it with antiques, pictures and objects, all of which would be for sale. The idea was based on Mallett Antiques, one of England's oldest dealers in fine art and antiques, whose showrooms were arranged to re-create the atmosphere of a private house.

We had rented a house in the lovely Provençale countryside, and in order to become bona fide French residents went to the Prefecture at Draguignan to apply for our *cartes de séjour*. My papers needed a few justifications: 'Profession?' My passport said I was a wine merchant but that was no longer the case, so I replied: 'Writer.'

What was I writing? 'A book.'

'What is its title?' Momentarily stunned by this, I had a flash of inspiration (with apologies to Thomas Hardy) and replied: '*Var from the Madding Crowd*.' My papers were signed and we left as legal residents of France, where we were to spend most of the next 14 years.

Apart from the occasional trip to St-Tropez, Cannes, Nice or Grasse, most of the time we were in Bagnols-en-Forêt was spent getting the building going. For the first 18 months or so I have to admit that this was very much teamwork alongside Calder and his Tunisian work force. This manual work, lots of heavy lifting, was a welcome change from the previous two years of partying in London.

The property was spread over 30 hectares, mostly terraces of cork oaks, leading down from where we planned to build the house to where the ruin was, tucked into the side of the hill. The hill rose steeply to a red volcanic-rock peak where we owned another portion of land, on which was what appeared to be a small sunken chapel. All that was visible above ground were the remains of a semi-circular vaulted roof. The builders cut a path up through the long-abandoned tree- and scrub-covered terraces and dragged a wheelbarrow, picks and shovels up to what we called the pagan chapel. Over the next year they dug it out, tipping the stones and earth onto the terraces below. A few years later when we were installed in Paris, I received an agonized communication from a geological expert who had known of and researched the 'chapel', discovering that it had been a Roman cistern. He had returned to the region to find the chapel/cistern totally demolished; 2,000 years of history unceremoniously pitched over the edge.

We were entirely alone on the side of the hill running down to the sea; nobody lived there because there was no running water. Our vendor – a good draughtsman but not, it later transpired, a qualified architect – solved the lack-of-water problem by discovering a natural spring almost a kilometre from the house, which we tapped into a holding tank. This pool came in useful the following March, after some picnickers accidentally started a small fire.

I could see flames leaping from tree to tree and told Bella to pack some valuables, a change of clothes and be prepared to evacuate. Within an hour, it was a full-scale fire. Canadair firefighting planes flew over, dumping water from a nearby lake, and the Fayence fire brigade turned up with two engines and a full team to ask us where the pool was! The following day in the local *Var-Matin* newspaper there we were, photographed standing by the house surrounded by charred and smoking trees with the caption 'Monsieur and Madame Spurrier were saved thanks to the water in their swimming pool....' Fortunately the vegetation grew back surprisingly well and surprisingly quickly.

Wine still played a part in my life at that time. At a Christie's auction of stocks lying in Bordeaux I had bid for five cases each of châteaux Pichelèbre and Canon de Brem 1964 from Fronsac (Fronsacs were underrated then and still are, but in the late-19th century they outsold all but the best St-Emilions). At Bagnols-en-Forêt there was La Bagnolaise Coopérative Vinicole which provided a range of wines from the surrounding vineyards, none of which could support a commercial business on their own. I remember with great affection a 20-litre glass demijohn we used to have filled with the 11% red, which we would then bottle to keep us in everyday wine. A few of the local wines styled themselves *crus classés*, notably Château Minuty for whites and rosés, and Châteaux de Rouët and Ste-Rosaline for reds. All three are still leaders in the Var.

In February 1969 I turned up uninvited at the first French professional tasting of my life: la Foire d'Orange, which concentrated on the wines of the southern Rhône. My passport still classed me as 'wine merchant' so I was admitted to the cellars under Orange's magnificent Roman amphitheatre and joined a panel of three, tasting on an upturned barrel in murky light. My French was just good enough to express my views, but I was surprised to find that, though many of the wines were poor, they were not criticized.

That autumn we were asked to spend a week of the vintage at Château Langoa-Barton, where we had stopped for a couple of days on our way to Spain the year before. En route we stayed in Cahors, famous for its 'black wine' which was used to bolster some lesser Bordeaux reds, but also for a two-Michelin-starred restaurant with a marvellous wine list. I chose the Haut-Brion 1952 to accompany *confit de canard*; Bella tasted it and declared it 'a bit flat'. I disagreed.

We had arranged to have lunch with Peter Sichel in Bordeaux the following day before driving up the Médoc to Langoa. Peter had kindly secured for me a copy of Edmund Penning-Rowsell's just-released book, *The Wines of Bordeaux*. This seminal work, I confidently predicted, would prove Bella wrong. When we met Peter I grabbed the book (hardly thanking him for it, to my shame) and turned to the chapter on the Graves to find 'the Rowsing Pencil's' comment on the 1952: 'a good wine, but a bit flat on the finish'. I have long since admitted the superiority of the female palate.

Two dinners during this visit stick firmly in my mind, for very different reasons. The first was at Langoa midway through our stay. Since it was vintage time, the château was full and there were frequent visitors, and Ronald Barton suggested that for one special evening I help him choose the wine. Bordeaux châteaux have a tradition of exchanging wines with each other, so the cellar was filled with many names from many vintages, and it was customary that if a fellow château owner was present, his or her wine would be served. Ronald himself had recently retired from the merchant house Barton & Guestier, but had retained close contacts with the Hugel family in Alsace and the Lupé-Cholet sisters in Burgundy, so had exchanged wines with them as well. At such dinners, champagne – always from Paul Bara, a fine *récoltant-manipulant* in Bouzy – would be the apéritif, a dry white would be served with the first course, three reds would follow, and Sauternes with dessert. Since it was autumn – Bordeaux vintages began in early October in those days – Ronald decided to skip the white and go for four reds, each a decade apart. He selected Cantemerle 1953 as the owner Henri Binaud would be present, then Langoa 1947, and hesitated on a wine from the 1930s, which had been an appalling decade for Bordeaux. (Only 1934 had been respectable, the other passable year being the lean 1937, which Ronald Barton's nephew Anthony told me 'came round 30 years later for about 15 minutes'.) Looking around, his eyes fell on a bin of

Pommard 1934 from Lupé-Cholet, which he thought would go well with the meal as well as being a surprise. The final wine was to be Léoville-Barton 1928.

At these dinners the wines are traditionally served blind, and a guessing game goes around the table for a few minutes before the identity is revealed. Henri Binaud recognized his Cantemerle 1953, Edmund Penning-Rowsell was spot on with the Langoa 1947, while the third wine was much admired and prompted much discussion: certainly Right Bank, but was it Pomerol or St-Emilion? The young Peter Sichel said it was so rich it could almost be burgundy, and was told to stop being silly. When Ronald told them what it was, most of the guests pushed away their glasses: they hadn't come to Langoa to drink Pommard. Bordeaux and Burgundy were different countries in those days; their wines seldom deigned to occupy the same cellar.

Martin Bamford MW, who managed Château Loudenne in the Médoc, was one of the six people who joined us for the second memorable dinner that week, at Restaurant Darroze in Villeneuve-de-Marsan. The Darroze wine list was famous, and we were there as guests of our American friend David Fromkin to drink the 1806 Lafite. David had spotted this wine on the list the year before but was then on his own, and felt it needed to be enjoyed in company. The 1806 had been re-corked at the château in 1953 and, on the advice of Raymond Baudoin, founder of *La Revue du vin de France* and adviser to the country's top restaurants, six bottles each were sent to Le Chapon Fin in Bordeaux, Taillevent in Paris, Le Coq Hardi near Paris at Bougival, and Darroze. The Lafite was the reason David had convened us, in addition to the superb burgundies he so much enjoyed. We were to have Dom Pérignon as an apéritif, probably the 1955, then Chassagne-Montrachet Marquis de Laguiche 1962 bottled by Drouhin, and compare Domaine Rousseau's Gevrey-Chambertin and Chambertin Clos de Bèze from 1952. The order was left to me and I suggested that the Lafite should be the first of the reds and that it should not be decanted, but poured directly into the glasses after opening. A seventh glass was poured for Monsieur Darroze, who took it around the room to share with other guests. We approached the wine with reverence: the colour was still a fine, if light, red; the nose showed fragrance and purity of fruit; the palate was delicate yet also firm, and for 20 minutes or so it was beautifully, captivatingly alive, before fading into dryness as our glasses emptied. A moving experience, and certainly the most memorable wine – along with the Cockburn 1908, 102 years its junior – I have ever tasted. The price on the Darroze list was Fr1,500, about £120. In an auction at Christie's in London in late 2017, one of the bottles from Le Coq Hardi cellar was sold for £38,000.

The plans that Calder had drawn up for the Bagnols-en-Forêt property were elegant and impressively simple: five bedrooms, with our suite and three others having views down the valley to the sea 15 kilometres away; an open-tread spiral staircase led to the ground floor and out onto a wide terrace that ran the whole length of the façade and had seven French windows. To the left there would be a reading room, a triple-bay salon and then my study; to the right would be summer and winter dining rooms. There were kitchens and store rooms behind and of course a cellar, dug deep into the rock.

We built the basic structure at a cost of physical labour only, rolling the volcanic rocks and stones that littered the hillside opposite down the slope and pitching them onto our flatbed truck. But the interior was never remotely finished. After two years, when it became plain that the sum Calder had accepted to complete both the servants' quarters and the main villa had already been spent, our relationship soured, coming to an acrimonious end via a long drawn-out court case.

With the collapse of the house project and facing a seemingly interminable legal battle, we decided to leave our life in Provence. Bella thought we should return to London. My response was that we hadn't gone to all the trouble of moving to France to return so soon. In any case, the London wine world seemed too 'old boy' for me, so I suggested instead that we move to Paris. There I would find a job in the wine trade, which was basically all I knew.

We finally closed up the unfinished property in the autumn of 1970, packed the car and headed north. In due course we sold the place to a developer from Cannes, who turned what was planned as a self-indulgent dream into a kind of hotel, splitting up the spacious rooms to provide additional accommodation. Out of curiosity, we made a detour on our way home from Italy to visit the site in August 2015. We found access barred and the entire property abandoned, which made me very sad. The views and the potential of the space were still amazing, and they really should have been enjoyed.

CHAPTER FIVE
BONJOUR PARIS

Although our base had been in Provence, we also had friends in Paris so we knew we would not be alone there. Having had so much space both in London and in the Var, I wasn't keen on moving into a flat, but it seemed that was all Paris had to offer until one sunny, late-September day when Bella and I were crossing Pont Alexandre III. We were admiring the barges, big and small, moored along the Right Bank. On the largest and smartest, a drinks party was in full swing. We went down to ask who the owner was and when he appeared, I asked him where one could buy a barge like his. He pointed to the wheelhouse and said: 'Ask in there.' M Van Den Bosch, who was busy adjusting the electrics, said he dealt in canal barges and would soon have one – 'better than this one' – for sale. A few days later he showed us a 39 x 5-metre 1950s barge that had been built for transporting petrol. It had one more trip to make before it was to be retired; M Van Den Bosch was then going to strip it out ready for living quarters to be installed in the hold. We put down a deposit there and then, and he said he would be in touch when the boat, *Orion*, was returned to his yard.

With our accommodation fixed for the future, we needed something for the present and the *Paris Herald Tribune* classified ads provided the answer. I found a large flat on the second floor of a 1900 block of buildings in Rue des Martyrs, ninth *arrondissement*. The rooms were spacious and light, the rent was reasonable and the street was buzzing with shops of all kinds. Later that month, when I told one of my smart Paris friends where it was, there was a momentary pause before he said 'How chic, my dear Steven. No one has lived there since Proust.' Viewed from his smart St-Germain apartment, this may have been a fair comment, but I was delighted some 40-odd years later to see *The Only Street in Paris: Life on the Rue des Martyrs* (2015), written by Elaine Sciolino, former Paris bureau chief for the *New York Times*. Her book celebrated the rich history and vibrant life of a street in which she had once lived.

Ours was an ideal introduction to Paris. Rue des Martyrs makes a long slice through the city, starting at the Eglise Notre-Dame-de-Lorette on the northern edge of the sedate old financial district, where it bursts into life right away. It rises steeply as it heads north towards the Boulevard de Clichy (once the haunt of such painters as Picasso, Van Gogh and Degas), and ends in the 18th *arrondissement* near Pigalle, where there were nightclubs and racy shows. The food shops were amazing and the weekend market one of the best in Paris; shopping was a joy.

It soon became clear that the wine trade I had imagined might resemble London's, with structured importer/wholesalers and retailers, did not exist in Paris. The wholesalers were there all right, albeit in the process of being evicted from Les Halles au Vin in the fifth arrondissement to be housed in big warehouses at Bercy in the 12th near the Gare de Lyon; but the wines they dealt in were mostly branded *vins de table*. The retail sector was dominated by the Nicolas family, whose massive cellars further out of Paris at Charenton stored millions of bottles, from *vins ordinaires* to burgundy grands crus and Bordeaux first growths. These cellars supplied the many Nicolas shops dotted throughout the city, four or five in every *quartier*. Then there were independent shops ranging from those announcing *vins-charbon-bois* (wine, coal, wood) to well-stocked *cavistes*, right up to luxury establishments for the carriage trade. But there was no place in any of these for a young Englishman with only passable French, however much he knew about wine, so setting up on my own was the only answer.

One bright autumn day as we were threading our way through a lively market on the way to lunch, my friend Christopher Mitchell-Heggs and I passed a small wine shop called Cave de la Madeleine which looked as though it had seen better days. I told Christopher that this was exactly the kind of shop I would like to buy. 'Let's go inside', he said. Behind the huge chest that acted as a counter stood an elegant lady of a certain age who asked if there was anything we wanted. 'Yes,' said Christopher in his very good French: 'My friend would like to buy your shop.' Mme Fougères asked us to return later, and when we did she told us that the shop had been unofficially for sale since her husband – *un grand caviste* – had died, two years earlier. She was keeping the business going with her sturdy little helper Mauricette (who was also her housemaid and cook) and Bernard Hopquin, who did the heavy lifting and made deliveries.

As discussions continued – me never doubting the outcome, Bella with her supportive 'Why not?' attitude – Madame began to question whether I would be able to manage the business to the high standard she expected. Remembering the useful strategy of my *stagière* days, I suggested I work for her unpaid for six months, and that at the end of that time if I had gained her confidence, we would finalize the deal. Madame agreed, and on April 1st she handed me the keys to both the shop and the cash desk (although she continued to do the accounts for several months). The following day I placed a classified ad in the *Herald Tribune* headed: 'Your wine merchant speaks English.'

In the interim there had been an important family event: our son was born on 21st February in London. Within a week or so, Bella and the baby were back in Paris. For a first name we wanted something that would be as easy in French as it was in English, so we chose Christian. Bella's father thought this was a girl's name, but we softened the blow by adding 'John' in front of it. Nicky generously suggested he could take the family name of Marston, but though we kept the M initial, we used it instead for Mark. John Christian Mark Spurrier was christened at the Marston church, an event afterwards referred to by my grandfather as the 'Gipsy Christening' because of the flamboyant early-1970s finery that the parents and godparents were all wearing.

Much of Cave de la Madeleine's turnover came from *vins ordinaires* which were bottled from tanks at the back of the shop and a big barrel in the cellar. These came from a reliable producer called Prefontaines and we sold them in the classic six-star litre bottles with plastic stoppers. All over the country such wines were the daily drink, out of tumblers in workers' kitchens and out of crystal glasses on the dining tables of the bourgeoisie. Brands were dominant, one of the biggest being Gévéor, which billed itself as *le velours de l'estomac* / velvet for the stomach – though it

An Englishman in Paris. In those days *cavistes* were more likely to sport a dark wool beret than a pale silk tie.

was anything but. To buy such wines, clients brought in empty bottles that were filled directly from the tanks. (At the time the social status of a *caviste* was on a par with that of a *pompiste* or petrol-pump attendant.) This might have made sense at La Bagnolaise Coopérative Vinicole, I thought, but not in a charming little street whose neighbours were embassies and luxury shops on the Faubourg St-Honoré.

I was in a hurry to put into practice the ideas that had evolved during my six months as the shop's delivery boy and general dogsbody. Madame had informed her suppliers of the change of ownership and the suppliers – she had never set foot in a vineyard herself – came to be introduced. When I told the Prefontaines salesman that within the week the tanks and barrel at the back of the shop would be gone and the bottling a thing of the past, he was horrified, telling me that I would lose 'half my clientele'. That half was precisely the one I intended to lose.

I had to buy all the stock from Madame, and while there were some nice wines from the major French appellations and the usual champagnes, M Fougères's influence had been succeeded by safe purchases of popular brands. During the trial period Bella and I had discovered several cafés that specialized in wine, and we talked to the owners about their suppliers. I also checked out the three major Paris *cavistes*, whose shops were a revelation: Jean-Baptiste Chaudet and Jean-Baptiste Besse on the Left Bank, and Lucien Legrand on the Right. I bought bottles from all three and got in touch with the producers, always citing whose shop they came from, if I wanted them for my own selection. Bit by bit we lost the brands, especially those of spirits and apéritifs, even though we were offered incentives to keep some of them.

The Cave was in the 'golden triangle' between the Place de la Concorde, the Gare St-Lazare and the Arc de Triomphe, in an area known also as Cité Berryer. Only the best salesmen came by. My aim was to sell wines from producers I knew to people I knew would like them, so it had to be personal. It didn't take long for the Press to come looking to see what was going on.

The ever-cheerful Mauricette continued to work with us, while Bernard moved a couple of floors up in the building to start delivering hand-washed shirts instead of wine. To replace him I employed a succession of 'junior year abroad' students, some of whose parents worked at the British Embassy nearby. Wines came and went, the range always expanding. My major suppliers were Pierre Coste for Bordeaux and Pierre Ferraud for Beaujolais and all the crus; my burgundies came from small domaines as did the wines from Alsace, the Loire and the Rhône which later became household names but in those days were hardly known.

One afternoon, strolling past a bookshop, I spied a copy of *Connaissance du Vin* (1970) by Constant Bourquin remaindered at five francs (40p). This book influenced my life in wine more than almost any other. The Swiss author had founded the Académie Internationale du Vin (AIV) in Geneva in 1971 with the intention of waging war on poor quality in wine. These days, when 90 percent of wine is not only good to drink but also true to its origin, it is hard to remember the situation as it used to be.

The *Appellation d'Origine Contrôlée* (AC) rules were laid down in 1933 thanks to Baron Leroy de Boiseaumarié, co-founder of the AIV and owner of Château Fortia in Châteauneuf-du-Pape. The first AC went to Châteauneuf itself, the second to Quincy in the Loire. Not until after the 1953 vintage was AC ranking given to the commune of Margaux, which had previously been under Haut-Médoc. The rules were based on *usages francs, loyaux et constants* / above-board, true and enduring practices learnt from the past. They could not prevent poor wines from being made, but they laid down what was, and what was not, allowed, and began the process of protecting France's distinctive vineyard terroirs.

The concept of origin that is now accepted all over the world – basically a 'sense of place' due to soils, climate, exposure, grape varieties, winemaking and ageing – did not bother the UK market when I started in the trade. At about that time *The Sunday Times* exposed a massive fraud in Suffolk: two vast vats of wine, one white and one red, had been discovered waiting to be bottled under dozens of different labels. Over in Bristol, the great Ronald Avery, doyen of one of the country's oldest wine merchants, did not hide the fact that many of his red burgundies were 50 percent from the village of origin and 50 percent from 'the south' to give them more body.

Bourquin's preface (simply entitled 'Argument') asserts: 'What I write won't please everybody, not because of my opinions, which no one will lose any sleep over, but because of my stance, which some will find shocking. I have brought unworthy practices to light, and will continue to highlight them until they are remedied.' His overriding theme was that naturalness was everything, and that 'improving additions' represented the thin end of the fraudulent wedge. This book was a revelation to me and an inspiration, and was responsible not only for many additions to the Cave de la Madeleine range, but also for two ground-breaking ideas.

The first concerned champagne. Bourquin did not approve of dosage, the *liqueur d'expedition* added after *dégorgement*. This liqueur was a blend of still champagne, sugar and brandy, which enriched the final blend to as much as 12 percent residual sugar for a champagne calling itself 'brut', thus masking the wine's high acidity. I had come across *Vin Nature de la Champagne*: still, unsweetened wine now known as AC Côteaux Champenois, at the Restaurant Drouant in the Place Gaillon, where it had been served to judges of the literary *Prix Goncourt* since 1914.

Bourquin's stance made so much sense to me that I decided to create a *non-dosé* champagne to sell at the Cave. I called on Lucien Legrand, whose nearby shop was a wine-lovers' mecca, having noticed that he sold a non-dosed Vouvray Nature, a sparkling wine from the Loire Valley. Legrand, also very much a purist, agreed to help me. In January 1972 we set off to see François Legras in the premier (now grand) cru Chouilly in the Côte de Blancs. Legras strongly advised against the idea and said he would go along with it only if we guaranteed to buy the whole cuvée. This didn't deter us. After tasting, we settled on a 1966 'dosed' only with a 1959 that Legrand had kept intact for further blending. I suggested we call it Brut Intégral (the Pigalle Club advertised its nightly shows as *Nues Intégrales*) and presented it to my mostly English clientele as 'naked in its purity'.

Brut Intégral caught on fast and we followed it with a Brut Zéro from Bonnaire-Bouquemont in the grand cru Cramant. Competitors came up with Brut de Brut and Brut Sauvage, and then, as fashions changed in the later 1970s, the market went back to more classic blends. These days *non-dosé* is back, principally from single growers, and superb examples have been made such as Pol Roger Pure and Louis Roederer Brut Nature, but thanks to Constant Bourquin, Lucien Legrand and I got there first.

The second, more important, inspiration from Bourquin's book arose from his detestation of chaptalization: adding sugar to the fermenting must to bolster the alcohol content. This practice was named after Professor Chaptal and declared legal by the Institut National des Appellations d'Origine Contrôlée (INAO) for most French regions except the south. It was particularly evident in Beaujolais where, in Bourquin's opinion, it countered the freshness of the Gamay grape. Again, Lucien and I travelled down during vintage time in 1973 to find a source for what we were going to call Beaujolais à l'Ancienne. My supplier Pierre Ferraud introduced us to one of his growers in Brouilly who agreed, like François Legras, to make it, provided we purchase the whole cuvée – this time a much larger volume. Barrels were shipped to Legrand for bottling, the wines labelled Beaujolais Nouveau being embargoed for sale until the third Thursday in November. The following day I filled my shop window with our bottles, two lumps of sugar tied around each of their necks, under a banner saying: 'If you want sugar in your Beaujolais, add it yourself.' But the display was short-lived, as our adventure was written up in the Press and soon came to the government's attention. Since sugar for chaptalization came from sugar-beet farmers in northern France (who had a lot of votes), I was advised to withdraw the presentation or face a substantial fine.

At around that time I bumped into the commercial director of the region's *négociant* Georges Duboeuf, and asked him how his En Primeur sales were going. 'In spite of your efforts, Monsieur Spurrier,' he replied, 'very well, thank you'. Today, chaptalization is almost a dirty word. Constant Bourquin was a prophet.

Following the launch of Brut Intégral, I wrote to Constant to thank him for his informed reflection, and in his reply he put me in touch with his nephew, Bernard Furth-Bourquin, who also lived in Paris. Bernard's day job kept him travelling, but in his spare time he ran a little wine company called DIVO-France, an offshoot of his uncle's *Défense et Illustration des Vins d'Origine* (DIVO-Suisse), based in Geneva. Bernard's small selection, all from 'wine purists' admired in Bourquin Sr's book, was impeccable. Among them were Champagne Leclerc-Briant, Huet in Vouvray, Gouges in Nuits-St-Georges, Marquis d'Angerville in Volnay, Chave in Hermitage, Rougier of Aix-en-Provence's Château Simone, Peyraud from Domaine Tempier in Bandol and Dr Parcé from Banyuls, all of which I added to the ever-expanding list at Cave de la Madeleine.

That December Constant invited me to the meeting of his Académie Internationale du Vin organization. I brought my copy of *Connaissance du Vin* for him to sign, which he did, adding 'a reader, and already an accomplice'. Before

Orion moored in the Seine in 1972 opposite the Gare d'Orsay, the station and hotel that was inaugurated for the World Fair in 1900.

the 1973 meeting I was informed that I had been elected as a member, the youngest by a long shot and the first from the UK. Since then I have attended almost every December meeting and many of the summer excursions, even hosting a tour of English vineyards in Kent and Sussex in May 2013, and have become truly committed to Constant's quest for *le vin vrai, le vin nature, le vin noble* / true, natural and noble wine, which has grown immensely in stature and influence.

Early in 1971 Monsieur Van den Bosch contacted me to say that our barge, *Orion*, had been retired from active life and was ready for conversion into a floating apartment. The hold alone gave us the largest space we would ever own in Paris. I roughed out a floor-plan: entrance via steep steps, lavatory underneath, a passageway off which were two bedrooms, a bathroom and a kitchen-dining room (with a 120-bottle wine rack), leading to a 5 x 5-metre salon with a retractable roof.

The Van den Bosch team rose to the challenge and the result was splendid. I did not know, though, and they forgot to tell me, that boats, even stationary canal barges, are lower in the water at the stern than they are at the prow, so our lavatory had to be raised by a metre, rather reducing headroom. That summer we left the Rue de Martyrs and Bella and I, baby Christian and Digby, a fine Briard sheepdog we had acquired in Provence, moved in. We were happily moored upstream from the Pont de la Concorde, with the Gare d'Orsay (later to become the Musée d'Orsay) on the opposite bank.

The two years we spent on *Orion* were simply wonderful. We had no phone connection and there were no mobile phones in those days, so friends just drove or walked by and if we were on board they joined us for a glass of wine or a meal. When we came to sell up after Easter 1973 – Bella was by then expecting our daughter Catherine (Kate) – our ad in the trusty *Herald Tribune* was headed 'A Penthouse on the Seine'. Quite often, while we dined on deck, the large *bateaux mouches* (excursion boats) that passed up and down the river would turn their spotlights on us to show how good life on the water could be. My father didn't think much of my running a small wine shop and living on a barge – 'You behave like hippies!' – until at the car-rental desk at Bordeaux airport he was asked: 'Are you Monsieur Spurrier the Paris wine merchant, by any chance?' This prompted our first parental visit, which went off very well.

CHAPTER SIX
STEVEN SPURRIER,
MARCHAND DU VIN

Early in 1972 an imposing gentleman strode into the shop and introduced himself as Sir Guy Salisbury-Jones, owner of Hambledon Vineyards in Hampshire. He told me that HM The Queen and Prince Philip would be paying their first official visit to Paris around Easter, that he and his wife would be there, and that he would like me to import his wine so that it too would be present for the occasion. Major-General Sir Arthur Guy Salisbury-Jones GCVO CMG CBE MC was a retired British army officer and marshal of the diplomatic corps. There had been a vineyard in Hambledon in Roman times, and Sir Guy had replanted it with hybrid varieties such as Madeleine Angevine to make a pleasant, just off-dry white wine. I agreed to take 60 bottles, which were duly flown into Orly Airport.

When I turned up at the customs office I was told it was '*Pas possible*' to collect them, for the simple reason that English wine did not exist in the customs books, so how could he clear delivery of something that did not exist? (I was to hear '*Pas possible, Monsieur*' quite often during my life in France.) The following day I returned, pointing out to the officer that the five cases did indeed exist: there they were on the floor just behind his desk. Still '*Pas possible*'. I ventured to ask: 'Does your job exist?'

'*Bien sûr, Monsieur*, I am a custom's officer.'

'Well, soon your job may not exist, since these wines are due to be served to President Pompidou by HM The Queen this very evening at the British Embassy.' At the mention of *son Président* he snapped into action, the papers were hastily stamped and I took the wine away with me. (It was of course never supposed to be served at the Embassy.) I filled the Cave window with Sir Guy's bottles, added a fine photograph of the Queen with the proclamation *Il y a deux bonnes choses qui viennent d'Angleterre: la Reine et le Vin* / There are two good things that come from England: The Queen and wine.

It was thanks to Hambledon's wine that I met Jon Winroth, wine correspondent for the *Tribune*. Since taking charge of the Cave I had sent the odd bottle to him at their offices, but had received no reaction. An English wine, I thought, would surely do the trick, and I took it along personally. When I introduced myself he said 'Oh, *you're* the guy sending me all these wines! I'm off to lunch, why don't you leave the bottle here and join me?' We went to one of the noisy brasseries that have now sadly disappeared from the eighth *arrondissement*, shared several glasses of Beaujolais with the plat du jour and separated as firm friends.

Jon was of Swedish descent (his surname appropriately meaning 'wine root'), only a few years older than me, and had moved from Illinois to Paris with his wife Doreen. Doreen's employer was involved in helping students from the US to learn as much as they could from the few weeks they spent in France on their 'junior year abroad' programme. One of the things they had to learn about was wine, and Jon gave them afternoon lessons.

By now I had built up a clientele of mostly North-American expats from the finance and legal professions, both of which were strongly represented in the centre of Paris at the time. Many of their offices were within walking distance of the Cave, and IBM was in the next street. On Friday evenings many of them crammed into the shop to taste and to hear me talk them through my new discoveries. One of the regulars said that if ever I could do this on a more structured basis, he would love to take a wine course. Jon and Doreen were frequent visitors to the barge, and Jon introduced me to wine bars in every part of the city. We felt something could be done along these lines, but where? Then, as luck would have it (the 1970s was a very lucky decade), the locksmith next door, whose premises were separated from the Cave's by only a stairway, closed down. The space went up for auction and since nobody seemed keen to continue in the locksmith business I was able to acquire it at a modest price to convert it from locksmith into an organization that communicated the history and qualities of French wines. The original

I unpack the Cave's latest consignment while the
window displays a unique novelty in France: English wine.

name I had in mind was the *Ambassade du Vin*, but I found that that had already
been taken, so I tried for the Académie du Vin and this simple, generic name had
not. Another piece of good fortune.

The ground floor was to be the tasting room, the upstairs much-needed office
space and later a lending library. The authorities warned me that I would not be
allowed to sell wine that was to be consumed on the premises, since that was the
prerogative of cafés and restaurants. Everything around alcohol was licensed in
France. For the shop, selling to take away (the equivalent of the UK 'off-trade'),
I had a License No 1. License No 4 was the ultimate, allowing premises to offer
alcohol of any kind with or without food, while License No 3 was for the sale, with
food, of wines and grape-based products of 20% alcohol or less. I could apply for
neither of these. License No 2 appeared to be for special occasions when normally-
unlicensed premises – such as a church or school – wished to present wines on a
commercial basis. I thought this would suit, but '*Pas possible, Monsieur*': I was told
that I couldn't apply as I would be selling wine on a regular basis. My answer to

this was that I was selling education, not wine; the wine was merely part of the teaching process, but that I would indeed need a License No 2 for events such as the launch of Beaujolais Nouveau, where education was not part of the package. We reached agreement at last.

Thanks to Jon's contacts, I was invited to be a judge alongside him at the *Foire Agricole de Paris* and the *Foire de Mâcon*. At the former, out at the Porte de Versailles in early April, one of the halls was reserved for food produce of every shape and size, raw or cooked, and the wine stands were part of that. In the vast adjoining halls were the animals, fish, fowl and of course the four-legged beasts of the field, whose bellowing, moo-ing, bleating and baa-ing could be heard as we settled at tables to taste the just-bottled or about-to-be bottled wines. The rules for the tasting tables were that there should be two judges from the region concerned, one a producer, the other a merchant; and two from Paris, one a merchant and one from the Press. Jon and I fitted the Paris bill well and the first year we found ourselves tasting Alsace, flanked by two burly Alsatians. Ranking was on the 20-point scale, the whole 20 being used in those days, and the difference between their marks in the high teens and ours, which barely reached double figures, caused heated exchanges. In future years we opted for the calmer waters of the Loire Valley.

The fair was crammed with Parisians hoping to absorb a sense of their countryside. It was a great place for producers to make contacts so that they could sell direct to the public, and the same producers came back year after year. In the early days, even established growers such as Gaston Huet, Mayor of Vouvray (who 20 years later forced the Paris–Bordeaux TGV line to be diverted around the Vouvray vineyards rather than through them), was behind a table to make the sales. With few export markets in those days, these sales accounted for an important part of his annual production. I was already a Huet client, but my annual visits to the Paris Fair always delivered something new.

The Mâcon Fair in the middle of May was smaller and more focused on central France. Both awarded Gold, Silver and Bronze medals and the international wine competitions today still use the same system, the ranking for most now being on the 100-point scale. While the Porte de Versailles was just a metro ride away, Mâcon (before the TGV arrived) entailed a two-day drive south through

Chablis and Burgundy, tasting at a few domaines on the way. Jon had been a judge for some years and Pierre Ferraud, my Beaujolais supplier, made sure we got onto some good tasting tables. It wouldn't have mattered had he not, since the atmosphere was both more professional and more convivial than in Paris, and the hard morning's work produced good results. I continued to attend right into the mid-1980s and always enjoyed it.

After the 1974 tasting I saw a photographic session being set up on the tree-lined terrace of the hotel-restaurant that overlooked the Chénas vineyards. It was an advertising shoot for Piat Beaujolais, a leading brand that had recently been taken over by International Distillers and Vintners (IDV) who owned Château Loudenne in the Médoc. The brand was managed by my old friend Martin Bamford. I jokingly told the gentleman from the London advertising agency that if he needed some real Beaujolais drinkers, we would be in the restaurant. Half-way through out first course the man rushed in to say that one of the male participants hadn't turned up, so could I please come and take his place right away before they lost the light. My Briard dog Digby had travelled down with me, and since he had been stuck in the car on a hot day, I said I would certainly stand in as long as I could bring my dog along. The man had no choice but to agree. When the moment came to take the final images, I made sure I was not photographed drinking a wine that I wouldn't have wanted in my shop.

The full-page advertisement duly appeared in the UK in *Punch* and other magazines with text in French to show how very *Français* Piat Beaujolais was. It went something along these lines: 'Recreate La Belle France in summertime by drinking Piat de Beaujolais nice and cool. We love to get together with friends every weekend and have lunch outside under shady trees, and we like our drinks to be fresh, too. You may be surprised to learn that Piat de Beaujolais' seductive aroma is best enjoyed well chilled – you should try it this way, and perhaps it will help you to forget the miseries of your terrible English summers.'

When the photograph appeared, I received a furious phone call from Martin: 'What the hell are you doing in my ad with that damned dog of yours?' Digby had unfortunately already fallen foul of Martin the year before at Loudenne. The château had a wonderful butler-and-cook couple, Sylvain and Josette, who had previously worked at Moët & Chandon's Château de Saran outside Epernay.

Sylvain was always perfectly turned out in a striped waistcoat during the day and a dinner jacket in the evening. Martin and the house guests (including me) were comfortably lounging in the salon late one Sunday morning when the telephone rang. Sylvain burst in, dashing to get to the telephone, waking Digby with a start. The dog's protective, intruder-alert instincts kicked in, he rose to his feet and with a single bound caught Sylvain on the shoulders with his front paws, bringing him to the ground. The telephone rang off. After a short silence Martin turned to me and said: 'Steven, will you please get your dog off my butler.' The Piat advertising campaign was a great success and Martin never mentioned his displeasure again.

Back in Paris my burgundy-loving friend David Fromkin, who had made a small investment in the Cave, treated me and a few others to some marvellous wines in restaurants with great cellars. We made a series of successful forays to the seafood restaurant Prunier, only a few streets away on the Rue Duphot, where we had the bright idea of ordering meat – generally a superbly prepared steak tartare – which meant that we could plough through their red burgundies from the late 1940s and early 1950s. Other customers didn't consider these wines suitable for their oysters and *sole meunière*.

Just next door in the Place de la Madeleine was Caviare Kaspia, which had a shop downstairs and a restaurant upstairs serving caviar (of course) as well as other fine dishes with a Russian twist. The main attraction was its collection of 1928 champagnes (the vintage earned a full five stars in Michael Broadbent's *Great Vintage Wine Book* (1991)), which it was selling at the same price as current vintages. Over one week, we treated ourselves to a horizontal of Bollinger, Mumm, Perrier-Jouët, Pol Roger, Louis Roederer and Veuve Clicquot: three more than even the great Broadbent managed to record.

David loved the wines of Burgundy and decided to buy a house there, stipulating that it had to have a vaulted cellar to store his wine collection. He told me his price range and I set off on a house-hunt for him with Jean-Pierre Pavillard. Jean-Pierre, an accomplished still-life photographer, was Bella's tutor and then part-time employer. He subsequently became godfather to our daughter Kate and took a series of quite superb photographs of wine colours for my Académie du Vin *Wine Course* publication. He and I looked around for a suitable property, starting south of Chablis, ending up on the first day in Semur-en-Auxois, just on the edge of the Côte d'Or. At a small estate agent just off the main square, I presented our requirements: an old house with a vaulted cellar priced at around Fr300,000. 'You don't get a heap of stones any more at that kind of price,' the agent told us, but added that he had something interesting at Fr1,500,000. The agent had assumed that we were talking in old francs (100:1) and had replied in kind, so the house he wanted to show us was actually priced at around £1,250.

We went to a tiny village a few miles south to look at it. A fine 18th-century *maison de maître* on three floors, it had a heavy stone roof, two vaulted cellars, a bread oven and 2,000 square metres of tatty grass in the front. The roofless *pigeonnier* had been turned into an outhouse lavatory, it had no running water, and the well at the back had a dead sheep in it. It had been abandoned for years. My knowledge of antiques told me that the 18th-century carved doors alone, with their original handles, were worth more than the asking price, and I immediately put down a 10 percent deposit to take it off the market. I said I would be back next week with my wife.

Back in Paris I told David that I had found him a house with cellars and that he didn't even have to pay for it, just send down his wine and come and stay whenever he wanted. This suited him fine. We drew up the deeds with the elderly owner, Mme Degouve des Nuncques, in her grand house in Dijon; she seemed glad to be rid of it. I put the renovation in the hands of an Australian, Peter Ryan, who with his wife Brooke had become close friends in London. Peter, Brooke and their twin girls shared our lives for about nine months, renting a small place in the village next door. Peter put together a team of workmen, helped by the estate agent (whom I thanked with some nice wines), and our house took shape. We used it only from April to October, Burgundy winters being very cold indeed, but it was a marvellous place to spend weekends and summer holidays.

The Académie premises were finished by the end of 1972. The tasting room had terracotta floor tiles, oak beams on the high ceiling and an exposed 16th-century stone wall at the end, offering a very congenial space. I hadn't thought how the wine school was to be set out until the architect/builder called me to say that a marble-topped bar in a café that was being demolished near where he lived was about to be dumped. If I was interested in salvaging it, he said, I needed to come and take it away immediately before it went onto the tip. This was an astounding piece of luck: it turned out to be a horseshoe-shaped Napoleon III (1870) bar, complete with all its ormolu fittings. Somehow, using my delivery van and a few taxis, this century-old work of art arrived in Cité Berryer to set the Académie off on its road to success.

Another happy arrival in the Cité in late 1972 was Patricia Gallagher, a young American writer. Patricia hailed from Wilmington, Delaware, where her ancestors had landed in the early 1600s. She was an occasional client in the shop, wrote for newspapers back home and sometimes for the *Herald Tribune*. We got on well, and although we didn't see each other too often, Patricia always seemed to appear at the right moment. One such was during the November launch of 1972's Beaujolais Nouveau. She knew Jon Winroth a little from the *Trib*, so (once we had dismissed the rained-off 1972s) we starting to talk about the wine school. Patricia said simply 'what you two need is someone to run this', and she was right. What he and I had started on a 'let's do this and hope it works' basis, Patricia turned into a completely structured business which provided something new and ultimately hugely valuable in Paris. I am far prouder of the Académie and its achievements than I am of any of many other wine ventures I started during my time in the city.

Another venture that grew tremendously in size and influence long after I had ceased to be part of it was Le Chemin des Vignes with Lucien Legrand and Bernard Bourquin. After the success of the *non-dosé* champagnes and Beaujolais à l'Ancienne, Legrand and I were in regular contact and I suggested that both our businesses needed somewhere to expand to. I mentioned that many wholesalers in London had warehouses under the city's railway arches, which had perfect conditions for wine storage, and that we should look out for something similar.

Legrand found some abandoned arches – about two square kilometres of them – under the Paris–Tours railway lines on the outskirts of the city. The bus stop outside the entrance was called Le Chemin des Vignes, so it seemed pre-ordained and we went ahead. Bernard sold me his shares after a couple of years, but Legrand was the major partner, the bulk of the business being bottling. My interest was in storage for my ever-increasing wine purchases. The Paris wine trade was impressed by our ambition and the Press compared our venture with the low-quality wholesalers at the Porte de Bercy, calling ours *un Bercy intelligent* / a Bercy with brains.

In the early days in London, while I worked at Murray and Banbury, I had met Nicholas Barrow. He had left for Bordeaux in the early 1960s to buy a tiny vineyard and house, called Château Courant, in the Médoc. One of Nicholas's bright ideas was to create a mobile bottling company that could turn up on demand, thus obviating the need for châteaux to install their own bottling line. This was not a new idea: there was already such a company based in St-Emilion where the average size of the estates was much smaller, making the purchase and upkeep of an automated bottling line uneconomic. In the Médoc the estates were larger, but in the early 1970s they had very little money to invest, so the Barrow Bottling Line served a real purpose. Nicholas needed funds for his business and I could see the potential – even Léoville and Langoa-Barton hired him to bottle their 1972s – so I became his sleeping partner.

The company didn't prosper, however, and Château Courant had to be sold. Nicholas admitted that the collapse of the company was his fault and, being a gent, since he was unable to return even a part of my investment, he made over to me instead his shares in a nine-hectare vineyard in the southern Rhône. It had an attractive stone farmhouse (*mas*) and was called Le Clos du Caveau. His former partner in the business, Richard, lived there with his wife and two small children.

Richard looked after the vineyard and made the wine, but he wasn't over-industrious and when I first arrived I found the place a mess. For a week in August I helped him bottle the very good 1973s, using a borrowed hand-pump because the mechanical one was broken. Patricia Gallagher, who had by now taken on the running of the Académie, said that the house would make a wonderful summer school (which of course it would have), but we were both too busy in Paris to take this idea much further.

Crédit Agricole approached me and said that they were about to foreclose on the property for its debt of around £7,000 and added that if I gave them guarantees to settle this and refinance the company, they would indeed foreclose, evict the family from the farmhouse and return the company to me. I wasn't keen on that scenario, so I set about raising funds from my well-off clients in Paris instead. Once again the *Tribune* carried my classified ad, this time headed 'Invest in the Booming Wine Trade', and I prepared a sales document. This quickly raised around £15,000, which would have paid off the bank and put the *mas* back into shape for the new investors to stay in. I planned to rent out the vines to neighbours and shut down the wine operation. So I repaid the bank and told Richard that I had saved the company from going under and would now run the house on a profitable basis, so he and his wife would have to find somewhere else to live. But there was a problem: I had only 49 percent of the business, and Richard's wife did not wish to move. In a few months the place was sold instead to one of the Testut brothers from Chablis. My investors were repaid, and to make up for their disappointment I gave them bottles of the 1973, which I had labelled the Cuvée des Actionnaires / 'Shareholders' Blend. The property was lovely, tucked into the spiky ridge of hills known as the Dentelles de Montmirail that ran past Gigondas to Beaumes de Venise… but I had a lot on my plate. That was the one that got away.

By Easter 1973, Bella and I had sold the flat in London and with the proceeds bought a second-floor flat in the Rue des Hospitalières-St-Gervais, bang in the middle of the Marais. The area was just recovering from a century of neglect to become one of the city's most sought-after places to live. Furniture from the London flat looked good in Paris and Burgundy, and there was just enough wall space for my pictures. Bernard Hopquin's wife, Thérèse, had by this time become our child-minder, looking after Christian and Kate, and life seemed to settle down into a more structured existence.

The shop was doing well, as was the Académie. We held a six-session Tour de France course, followed by a four-session in-depth course on specific regions. Jon continued to teach his 'junior year abroad' students about wines, which he matched with cheeses from Barthélémy, his favourite *fromagier*. I overheard him showing the group a Condrieu, the seductively aromatic yet dry wine made from the Viognier grape in the northern Rhône, and saying that there wasn't really a match to drink it with. A young woman put up her hand and volunteered: 'What about a good-looking guy?'

The Press soon got wind of the Académie and we began to give courses in French, Bernard Bourquin introducing his friend, Parisian wine writer Michel Dovaz to the team. We held comparative tastings, both vertical and horizontal, often with the proprietors present to talk about their wines. It seems embarrassing to say it, but in terms of wine appreciation, promotion and communication, the Académie du Vin was the only game in town.

CHAPTER SEVEN
THE JUDGEMENT
OF PARIS

By the mid-1970s I was firmly part of the *Gault & Millau* tasting team, having barged my way into their Côtes de Provence tasting at the Hotel George V (Paris) with a bottle from Bernard Laudon's Domaine des Férauds a couple of years earlier.

Restaurant critics Henri Gault and Christian Millau had founded their restaurant guide, *Gault & Millau*, in 1965, bringing chefs out of kitchens onto their pages, to be followed by vignerons, sommeliers – and eventually *cavistes*. All their tastings were informative; some were truly ground-breaking. One, in autumn 1975, covered non-vintage champagne from the *grandes marques*. The wines were mostly formed from the rained-off and unripe 1972 vintage as a base wine and the quality was very poor, hardly any wines across the board achieving double figures. When the results were reported to the Champenois, they refused to believe them and threatened to withdraw their advertising from the *Gault & Millau* Christmas issue unless the tasting was held again with their own representatives present.

One month later, Christian convened the same judges plus *a huissier de justice* / court officer to add weight to the proceedings, and the wines were re-judged in front of a group from Epernay and Reims. Christian asked us, the judges, to make sure we got there before the others arrived, and then instructed us to 'rank the wines as you feel, but start your marks at 5/20'. Honour was saved and the magazine got its Christmas advertisements.

At around that time Alexis Bespaloff, wine columnist for *New York* magazine, had come to Cité Berryer bringing with him a few bottles of wine from California wineries that had been admired in New York. Discussing who else in Paris might be interested in trying them, I suggested ex-New Yorker now Paris resident Michael Goldman. Michael's attitude to buying wine was that of a true collector. He attended auctions up and down the country, and every December studied the special offers from Nicolas's vast cellars. Each year, all the better-placed shops were allocated a few bottles from reserves of historical vintages, wines such as Château Brane-Cantenac 1928, Château Climens 1947, Musigny Comte Georges de Vogüé 1945 and so on. Realising that just a few bottles would not be enough for his cellar, but that visiting every shop personally to secure the limited supplies would not be possible, Michael hired four taxis, taking one himself and dispatching three friends in the others armed with lists of wines to buy and the cash to buy them. As the various shops' managers called head office at the end of day to report significant sales of the old vintages, it became plain that a raid had taken place – but by then it was too late for Nicolas to do anything about it.

Michael was also into music and had bought a rambling basement across the street from his apartment with the intention of opening a jazz club, but planning permission never came through, so instead he turned it into one of the largest private cellars I have ever seen. This became the venue for many parties with his, and his wife Jackie's, friends. I took Alexis not to the cellar, but to Michael's apartment, for my introduction to California Cabernets. I remember finding them a bit 'cooked'. I put this down to their being from a warm country, the only other Cabernets I knew being from Bordeaux with its cool Atlantic climate – but they were undoubtedly impressive.

The inspiration for an event at which the Académie showed a range of California Chardonnays and Cabernet Sauvignons to nine of the finest palates in France came from Patricia Gallagher. Because the shop and the school were in the centre of Paris – and more importantly because we spoke English – we had begun to receive visits from California winemakers and US wine writers, but for a couple of years running Patricia had tried without success to find some California wines in Paris to show our students on July 4th, American Independence Day.

Patricia takes up the story, explaining why she was so committed to show-ing these wines to their advantage on the occasion of the American bicentennial: 'I had a personal reason and a professional one. Personally, the Declaration of

Patricia Gallagher and I wait for students to take up their
tasting stations around the Académie's marble-topped bar.

Independence was signed 20 minutes by car (an overnight ride on horseback
in 1776) from Wilmington, Delaware, where I was born. Ours is a colonial
family, having emigrated from England in 1634, so I was definitely caught up in
the excitement of celebrating our 200th anniversary. Professionally, I had organized two 4th July events at the Académie du Vin in 1974 and 1975, which had been
disappointing because of the poor quality of California wines available in Paris
at that time, even from the luxury shops Fauchon and Hédiard. From a passing
acquaintance with some of Robert Mondavi's books and Robert Finigan's *Private
Guide to Wines*, I knew there were better California wines. The challenge would
be selecting them and somehow getting them to Paris.'

Patricia goes on to recount that just before her 1975 summer vacation in the
USA, Glenda Cudaback, a friend from her *Herald Tribune days*, and her husband
David, both natives of the Napa Valley, suggested she extend her trip and drive
north to Napa. David's parents offered hospitality there and a car to tour the vineyards. As their guest, and with Robert Finigan's introductions to Ridge, Heitz,
Montelena, Mayacamus and Stag's Leap – as well as his company part of the way
– she visited them all. She didn't bring back samples, but the people she met and
the quality of their wines made a hugely positive impression.

When she returned, raving about the quality of the wines she had tasted, I remembered what I'd thought of Alexis's Cabernet Sauvignons, and the following day I put a glass of white wine in front of her and asked her opinion. 'Far too high in acid,' she said. 'I hope you're not buying it.' This was a Bourgogne-Aligoté with its characteristic 'green' acidity. The fact that Patricia's palate was rejecting such a style of wine after two weeks of California's food and wine made me think that if we were to impress our potential panel of tasters with wines from the West Coast, we should take the French palate into account.

As the autumn progressed, Patricia began the groundwork for the tasting. In California she had met and visited wineries with Joanne Dickenson, whose husband had started a company called Wine Tours International. Joanne was planning a wine tour in France to be headed up by the great André Tchelistcheff (1901–1994), who had worked as a farmer in France before turning to wine. His professor of œnology in Bordeaux had recommended him to Comte Georges de La Tour, owner of Beaulieu Vineyards in Napa, as the new winemaker, his brief being to resurrect the winery following Prohibition. After 30 years at BV, as it was known (his 1946 Pinot Noir is one of the greatest wines I have ever tasted), he retired in the mid-1960s and became a consultant to up-and-coming winemakers including both Mike Grgich of Chateau Montelena and Warren Winiarski of Stag's Leap Wine Cellars.

The plan for the tour was for André and his Napa colleagues and friends to return to the regions and people he had known during his time in France. Joanne and her wine tourists were to play a pivotal role in *our* tasting by importing the selected California wines for the event.

After the busy Christmas period, Patricia and I began to think about who we would invite to taste these New World wines. (I think of them now as 'judges' but then they were just 'tasters', as the notion of a comparative France-California tasting had not yet occurred to me.) The idea was simple: it would be another enjoyable, informative event put on by the Académie, but this one would be in honour of the 1776–1976 Bicentennial. We wished to present wines from California for the first time ever in France, hoping to obtain recognition for their quality. Since we were known, respected and liked, we threw our net wide and high to construct the panel, which needed to be balanced between producers, writers and restaurateurs. Those who accepted our invitation were: Pierre Bréjoux, Inspector Générale of the Appellation d'Origine Controlée (INAO) Board; Michel Dovaz, one of the early *profs* to teach the Académie courses in French; Claude Dubois-Millot, from *Gault & Millau*; Odette Khan, editor of *La Revue du Vin de France* and its sister publication *Cuisine et Vins de France* (and the ruler of the roost among Parisian wine writers); Raymond Oliver, Bordeaux-born chef and owner of the three-Michelin-star Le Grand Véfour; Pierre Tari, owner of Château Giscours, the Margaux third growth, and later Secretary General of the Association des Grands Crus Classés de St-Emilion; Christian Vannequé, head sommelier at the three-Michelin-star La Tour d'Argent, in charge of the city's most famous cellar; Aubert de Villaine, co-owner and co-director of the Domaine de la Romanée-Conti; Jean-Claude Vrinat, owner of the three-Michelin-star Le Taillevent, having trained under his father as a sommelier before taking over the reins in 1973.

The next step was to find a suitable place to hold the event, the tasting room at the Académie being too small. We had already chosen a date – May 24th – and our first approach was to Ernst Van Dam, a friend and client of the shop who was Food and Beverage Manager of the Intercontinental Hotel a few blocks away. I was just after a reception room with good natural light, but Ernst came up trumps, offering a ground-floor room with picture windows leading to an interior courtyard, which he said we could have from 3pm until just before 6pm, when it was to be prepared for a wedding reception.

Almost the last piece in the jigsaw was for me to go – with Bella – to California to make the final selection of wines. We went at the end of March and Robert Finigan helped us with our itinerary, as he had helped Patricia. Through his restaurant review guide he knew everyone and everything that was happening in the Bay area, and one night he booked us into Chez Panisse, a restaurant in Berkeley that had been created by Alice Waters. Chez Panisse served only a set menu in the evening and the chef at the time was Jeremiah Tower, soon to become San Francisco's leading culinary light. He was a tall, strikingly good-looking man with a combative temperament. We arrived late enough to cause some concern for the front of house, but we immediately ordered the wine, and the four-course meal began. The main course was roast lamb, and Robert's dish arrived with some fatty bits on it. He complained; the three of us offered to swap plates, but no: he was a restaurant critic and this should not happen to him, so he told a waiter to take the plate back to the kitchen. A few minutes later the waiter returned with the same plate, to Bob's intense annoyance. 'What did the chef say?' he asked.

'The chef said "tough shit", Mr Finigan,' came the straight-faced reply. We had to laugh.

Patricia had given me a list of wines and wineries to check out, our aim being to choose six Chardonnays and six Cabernets to illustrate what was going on in California. After the tasting, we were often asked why there was no Mondavi, no Beaulieu Vineyards or Buena Vista, and the answer was that we were only looking for small, family-run wineries, described in France at the time as 'boutique'.

Nine of the 12 wines came from Napa and three from the Santa Cruz Mountains south of San Francisco; wineries representative of the new age of California wine. They were generally small operations run by the founders who were, for the most part, on a second career. While I was there I began to realize that many of the winemakers used France as their model – Paul Draper of Ridge Vineyards had previously worked with Cabernet Sauvignon in Bordeaux and Chile – while the others intended simply to get the best out of their soil and their grapes.

Thanks to Patricia's groundwork and Robert's assistance, the visits went well – although the visits to Heitz in Napa and Ridge in Santa Cruz almost didn't happen. My call to Joe Heitz, well-known in the Valley as a 'charming curmudgeon', began with a brush-off: 'If you are a journalist, I don't receive them; if you are a merchant, I don't export; and anyway I don't have time.' I told him that he was so famous that a visit to Napa would be incomplete without him, and was grudgingly given a time slot to call in at the winery on the Silverado Trail, east of St Helena. During a tour of the cellars, I admired the large, upright redwood storage tanks and wondered what on earth a redwood-stored wine would taste like. He said he had just time to show me two wines, the first being his Chardonnay, and he asked me to comment on what was probably only the third California Chardonnay I'd ever tasted. I said it reminded me of a Meursault. Heitz beamed and said that Meursault was his wife's favourite wine, and this was what he tried to make. This broke the ice well and he offered me the full range to taste. I left with two bottles of Heitz Martha's Vineyard 1970.

Ridge Vineyards I knew was a must, although it was a two-hour drive away. I called and was told that they didn't have a tasting room, didn't expect or receive visitors and anyway, once again, they didn't have the time. Bella and I simply turned up one morning to be met by one of the partners, David Bennion. Seeing an Englishman getting out of the car, he shouted over: 'Aren't you the fella I told not to come? Well, since you're here you'd better taste some wine!' We ended up staying for a scratch lunch and leaving with two bottles of Ridge Monte Bello Cabernet Sauvignon 1971.

By the end of the week the selection had been made and the wines delivered to Joanne Dickenson's home in San Francisco. Joanne had already prepared the ground by asking the TWA (Trans World Airlines) representative who was working with her on the Tchelistcheff-led tour whether it would be acceptable for wine to travel with the group. TWA was at the time trying to establish a 'Wine Bridge' linking the wine-producing areas of the world, and the representative replied that they would be delighted to handle it. Had the group not agreed to carry the 24 bottles over to Paris, the tasting would not have taken place, since even if had they arrived by other means, they would have been blocked in customs.

The California wines on their way to Paris, were:

CHARDONNAY

Chalone Vineyard 1974

Located 160 km (100 miles) south of San Francisco, Chalone was deemed to have soils similar to Burgundy and in 1923 was planted with Chardonnay, Chenin Blanc, Pinot Blanc and Pinot Noir. Dick Graff, a young banker, bought into the winery in 1965 and in a few years his wines were receiving high praise from both Julia Child (the American teacher, author and TV personality who brought French cuisine to the US) and André Tchelistcheff. This was my bet for the best Chardonnay.

Chateau Montelena 1973

Dating back to the glory days of early California wine, the vineyard and winery were created in the late 1880s by Alfred L Tubbs (and are still on Tubbs' Lane). Then more famous for its red wines, Montelena did not survive Prohibition, but was acquired by Los Angeles lawyer James (Jim) Barrett and partners in 1972. Mike Grgich, a disciple of André Tchelistcheff and then at Robert Mondavi, was hired as winemaker.

David Bruce Winery 1973

David Bruce, a student at Stanford University, bought a 16-hectare plot above the town of Los Gatos in 1961. At 670 metres (2,200 feet) of elevation and with well-drained sandy soil, it seemed perfect for Chardonnay and Pinot Noir. Both a technician and an experimenter, Bruce used very little sulphur in his wines, the lack of which unfortunately led to his 1973 being out of condition when it arrived in Paris. This wine had been recommended by Robert, who described the bottle we tasted at the winery as having 'the essence of Chardonnay'.

Freemark Abbey 1972

I had met Jerry Luper, the winemaker at Freemark Abbey, in Aix-en-Provence and was impressed by his French-influenced approach in the cellar. The 1969 Chardonnay had already bested some top white burgundies in New York. The 1972 struck me as being very elegant, and was my second bet after Chalone.

Spring Mountain 1973

The ebullient Mike Robbins (who had once dated Grace Kelly) was a real-estate developer with a passion for wine. In 1962 he bought a fine Victorian home north of St Helena, which became known as Chateau St Clement, with a small vineyard and winery. From the early 1970s his Chardonnays were regular Gold-medal winners. This was Robert's bet for the tasting.

Veedercrest Vineyards 1972

AW (Al) Baxter, a home winemaker with serious ambitions, bought 120 hectares of land on Mount Veeder on the western side of the Napa Valley. While the planting was progressing, grapes were bought in. The 1972 came from Winery Lake Vineyard in the cool Carneros district, soon to become famous for its Chardonnays and Pinot Noirs.

CABERNET SAUVIGNON

Clos du Val Winery 1972

John Goelet and Bernard Porter, the two men behind Clos du Val, were both born into the French wine business: Goelet a partner of merchant Barton & Guestier;

Portet the son of Château Lafite's technical director. Goelet had employed Portet to travel the world to study wine regions for potential investment and he had recommended two: California's Napa Valley and Victoria in Australia. Being French-owned and made, this wine was an obvious choice.

Freemark Abbey Winery 1969

This was the only winery to have two wines in the tasting. A blend of 88 percent Cabernet and 12 percent Merlot, the wine was chosen for its maturity and elegance although in the tasting, its maturity did it no favours against the younger reds.

Heitz Cellar Martha's Vineyard 1970

Joe Heitz had been stationed in California during World War II and decided to stay, joining the wine programme at UC Davis. He then worked at Gallo, from 1951 to 1958 at Beaulieu Vineyards under Tchelistcheff, then left to buy a small vineyard and winery south of St Helena. In 1965 he bought Cabernet Sauvignon grapes from Tom May, from a vineyard in Oakville that May had named after his wife, Martha. As these grapes turned out to make the best wines, Heitz decided to bottle them separately using Martha's Vineyard on the label, and another Napa icon was born. The 1970 cost more than twice the price of all the other Cabernets.

Mayacamas Vineyards 1971

Bob Travers joined Joe Heitz as a cellar-worker in 1967, and the following year bought Mayacamas when its owners retired. (Mayacama means 'cry of the mountain lion' in the language of the Wappo, the indigenous people of northern California.) He quickly reduced the production to just Chardonnay and Cabernet Sauvignon, holding the latter back from selling for longer than his neighbours did. I had been really impressed by the 1970 I tasted with Robert, but the winery was out of stock. Travers agreed to sell me the not-yet-released 1971. Not until the 30th anniversary of the tasting did this one show its real quality.

Ridge Vineyards Monte Bello 1971

Vines were first planted on the 700-metre (2,300-feet) elevation Monte Bello Ridge in the 1890s. There were just 10 hectares of vines left by the time David Bennion and three friends from the Stanford Research Institute bought the 32-hectare farm in 1959. The partners expanded the vineyards, but needed professional help. Paul Draper joined them in 1969. He made the 1971, noting that 'our Cabernet grapes reached their balance in 1971 at slightly lower sugar than usual and produced a wine with more elegance and finesse than we have yet seen.' How right he was.

Stag's Leap Wine Cellars 1973

Warren Winiarski was on the way to becoming a professor at the University of Chicago before a visit to Italy introduced him to wine in 1953. He started making wine in his college apartment before spending a week during the vintage at the Martin Ray Winery, after which he set out in 1964 to start work with Lee Stewart at Souverain Cellars in Napa. From there he moved to become assistant winemaker at Mondavi, buying his first vineyard in the Stag's Leap district and planting his first Cabernet Sauvignon in 1970. The 1973 was these vines' first vintage.

When Joanne's tour group arrived at Roissy Airport and I saw the two cases of wine on the carousel, I was overjoyed. Joanne was horrified, as one carton was stained red. The breaker was one of the Freemark Abbey 1969 bottles, but I needed only one bottle for the tasting. The following day I gave the group a 'Tour de France' tasting from the major French regions at Chemin des Vignes, after which they headed off to Champagne for the start of their own tour. It was to culminate 15 days later at Alexis Lichine's Château Lascombes in Margaux.

Now that everything was lined up for May 24th, a thought began to nag at me. The tasting was designed to gain recognition for California wines via the selection that Patricia and I had made. Looking through the list of tasters, I realized that only two of them would ever have tasted these wines before: Aubert de Villaine, whose wife Pamela came from San Francisco, and Christian Vannequé, who had been introduced to California wines by the film director John Frankenheimer (in Paris to make *The French Connection*, 1971). I became concerned that the other judges, all wine experts and leaders in their fields, might view California, being just north of Mexico on America's West Coast, as a 'southern' country like Portugal or Spain. Good though the wines were, then, the tasters' innate Frenchness might result in their judging the wines from a biased perspective. With just a week to go, I decided to turn the event into a blind tasting, showing the Californias along-side four of the best white burgundies and four of the best Cabernet Sauvignon-dominated red Bordeaux from my shop. The wines I selected to match the vintages from California were:

WHITE BURGUNDY

Bâtard-Montrachet Grand Cru Domaine Ramonet-Prudhon 1973

From one of the five grands crus across the Chassagne- and Puligny-Montrachet vineyards, Bâtard-Montrachet is considered, along with Chevalier-Montrachet from a slightly higher elevation, second only to Le Montrachet itself. I had both the 1972 (a fine but lean vintage) and 1973 (more ripe and open) in the shop and phoned Monsieur Ramonet to ask which vintage he would recommend.

A few years earlier, M Ramonet had been on the cover of *Gault & Millau*, and had pronounced that he 'had been put on earth by God to make great wine'. My question was met with some surprise and the reply that both were excellent, so I went with the 1973 to match four of the California Chardonnays. The wine turned out to be low in acidity and was not well received by the judges. (The following autumn, on a buying tour of Burgundy, I was physically thrown out of the Ramonet cellars by M Ramonet's son André for having caused such an insult to the family name.)

Beaune Premier Cru Classé Clos des Mouches Domaine Joseph Drouhin 1973

Joseph Drouhin is one of the oldest and most respected of the *négociant-éleveurs* in Beaune and the walled Clos des Mouches is its flagship vineyard.

Meursault Premier Cru Les Charmes Domaine Roulot 1973

The village of Meursault is to white burgundy what the little town of Nuits-St-Georges is to red, being well known by wine drinkers as the benchmark of its type. Guy Roulot pioneered the elegant style of this sometimes slightly robust Chardonnay, and the domaine reached spectacular heights under his son Jean-Marc. Incidentally, American Ted Lemon was in the Roulot cellar for the 1973 vintage; he went on to become the producer of top Chardonnays and Pinot Noirs from his Littorai Winery in California's Sonoma County.

Puligny-Montrachet Premier Cru Classé Les Pucelles Domaine Leflaive 1972

The village of Puligny produces some of the world's greatest white wines and the most revered producer is Domaine Leflaive. The gentlemanly Vincent Leflaive said he was looking for 'elegance and harmony' in his wines, and some believe that Les Pucelles in his hands might have been ranked as a grand cru.

RED BORDEAUX

Château Haut-Brion Premier Cru Classé Graves 1970

Founded in the 15th century, Haut-Brion has a Bordeaux history second to none. The vineyards are now surrounded by the city, but they have remained intact since that time. In 1935 Clarence Dillon, a Francophile American financier, bought the estate (apparently the weather was too foggy for him to visit Château Cheval-Blanc in St-Emilion, his alternative choice for purchase) and his descendants continue his good work. The year was excellent: highly regarded at the start, it became even more so as it matured.

Château Mouton-Rothschild Premier Cru Classé (1973) *Médoc* 1970

Bought by the Rothschilds in 1853 in a comparatively run-down state, Mouton did not attain the ranking of first growth in the 1855 Classification, but was placed top of the second growths. This was the first Bordeaux estate to bottle at the château all the production sold under the château label. In 1973 under a determined Baron Philippe, the classification was amended and Mouton raised to a first growth to match the reputation it had enjoyed for five decades.

Château Léoville-Las Cases Deuxième Cru Classé St-Julien 1971

According to Bordeaux historian Edmund Penning-Rowsell, the commune of St-Julien produces 'quintessential claret'. Las Cases is considered (and considers itself) superior to its two second growth Léoville neighbours Barton and Poyferré. Lighter and less tannic than 1970, 1971 was a good year, very suitable for the tasting.

Château Montrose Deuxième Cru Classé St-Estèphe 1970

St-Estèphe is the most northern of the four major communes, and produces some of the most robust wines from a high percentage of Cabernet Sauvignon grapes.

Under the careful ownership and consolidating influence of the Charmolüe family, the wines were consistently classic, and the 1970 was a great vintage.

I certainly did not stint on the origins and quality of the French wines to give the California wines a head start! Patricia and I set off for the venue, the Intercontinental, hoping only that the tasting would achieve our objective and would not be a waste of time for the judges. Of course we wanted recognition for the Académie as well as for the California wines, but we had not invited wine writers from *Le Monde*, *Le Figaro* and *Libération* and the weekly magazines *L'Expres* and *Le Point*, since our panel of tasters were of sufficient importance in their own right.

Patricia had remembered that a George Taber of *Time* magazine had recently taken one of our wine courses, and suggested I call him to see if he could attend. Since American wines were there, she thought, he should be too. He accepted, with the caveat that if something else cropped up, he wouldn't be able to make it. On the day, nothing did and he was there, as was Bella to take some photos. Had George not been present to witness the tasting and to report the story in *Time* on June 7th under the title 'Judgment of Paris', our little adventure would probably have sunk without trace.

Before the tasting could start, we had to establish the order in which the wines would be poured. Alphabetical order would have put two heavy-hitters first for the whites and grouped the Bordeaux in the middle for the reds, so I plumped instead for random order. I wrote the names of all the wines on scraps of paper and, once we had arrived at the hotel, asked our Académie intern to draw them out of a hat. The bottles were marked Chardonnay 1–10 and Cabernet 1–10.

We were seated at a long table with one judge at each end, me in the middle with Patricia on my right and the elegant Odette Khan on my left. I said a few words of welcome and announced that, instead of just tasting Chardonnays and Cabernets from California, I thought it would be interesting to match them against some benchmarks of similar vintages from Burgundy and Bordeaux in a friendly 'glasses across the ocean' blind tasting. It would, I said, be part of a celebration of the War of Independence, which the French General Lafayette had himself supported, fighting on the American side. Fortunately they accepted,

Odette Khan, seated beside Patricia and me, focuses
her attention on the second of the 10 Chardonnays.

with murmurs of '*bonne idée*' and '*pas de problème*' all round. Tasting sheets were handed out, the wines to be marked out of 20 as was then the norm, with the whole range being used. (In later years the 20-point scale began at 10 and the 100-point scale began at 50.)

Patricia gave George Taber the identity of the wines and the tasting order. In Chapter 19 of his book (*Judgment of Paris*, Scribner, 2005) under the title 'A Stunning Upset', he describes what he saw and heard:

'The nine judges seemed nervous at the beginning. There was lots of laughing and quick side comments. No one, though, was acting rashly. The judges pondered their wines carefully and made their judgements slowly. As I stood only a few feet from them, I could listen to their commentary and I copied into the brown reporter's notebook that I always carry with me such phrases as: "This soars out of the ordinary", "A good nose, but not too much on the mouth" and "This is nervous and agreeable". From their comments, though, I soon realized that the judges were becoming totally confused as they tasted the white wines. The panel couldn't tell the difference between the French ones and those from California and they began talking to each other, which is very rare in a tasting. They speculated about a wine's nationality, often disagreeing.

'At one point Raymond Oliver was certain he had sipped a French wine, when it was a California one from Freemark Abbey. Shortly after, Claude Dubois-Millot said he thought a wine was obviously from California because it had no nose, when it was France's famed Bâtard-Montrachet. The judges were brutal when they found a wine wanting. They completely dismissed the David Bruce Chardonnay, Pierre Bréjoux giving it 0 and Odette Khan just 1 point out of 20. The David Bruce was rated last by all of the judges. Robert Finigan had warned Spurrier that he'd found David Bruce wines at that time could be erratic, and this bottle appeared to be erratically bad.

'After the white wines had been tasted, Spurrier called a break and collected the scorecards. Using normal procedure for wine tastings, he added up the individual scores, divided this by the number of tasters (his and Patricia Gallagher's marks not being noted) and ranked them from highest to lowest. The judges spoke quietly to each other and I talked briefly with Dubois-Millot. Even though he did not yet know the results, he told me a bit sheepishly that: "We thought we were recognizing French wines when they were Californian and vice versa. Our confusion showed how good California wines have become."

'Spurrier's original plan had been to announce all the results at the end of the day, but the waiters were slow clearing the tables and getting the red wines together and the programme was getting badly behind schedule, so he decided to announce the results of the white wine tasting. He had been personally stunned and began reading them slowly to the group:

Ch Montelena 1973 (14.67)
Meursault-Charmes 1973 (14.05)
Chalone Vineyard 1974 (13.44)
Spring Mountain 1973 (11.55)
Beaune Clos des Mouches 1973 (11.22)
Freemark Abbey 1972 (11.11)
Bâtard-Montrachet 1973 (10.44)
Puligny-Montrachet les Pucelles 1972 (9.89)
Veedercrest 1972 (9.78)
David Bruce 1973 (4.67)

'When he finished, Spurrier looked at the judges, whose reaction ranged from shock to horror. No one had expected this, and soon the whole room was abuzz. The scores of the individual judges made the results even more astounding. California Chardonnays had overwhelmed their French counterparts. Every single judge had rated a California wine first, Chateau Montelena was given top rating by six judges, Chalone being rated first by the other three. Three of the top four wines were Californian. Claude Dubois-Millot gave Chateau Montelena 18.5 points out of 20, while Aubert de Villaine gave it 18. Chateau Montelena scored a total of 132 points, comfortably ahead of second-place Meursault-Charmes which got 126.5.

'As I watched the reaction of the others to the results, I felt a sense of both awe and pride. Who would have thought it? Chauvinism is a word invented by the French, but I felt some chauvinism that a California white wine had won. But how could this be happening? I was tempted to ask for a taste of the winning California Chardonnay, but decided against it. I still had a reporting job to finish and I needed to have a clear head.

'As the waiters poured the reds, Spurrier was certain that the judges would be more careful and would not allow a California wine to come out on top again. One California wine winning was bad enough; two would be treason. The judges, he felt, would be very careful to identify the French wines and score them high, while rating those that seemed American low. The French reds, with their classic, distinctive and familiar tastes would certainly stand out against the California reds.

'There was less chatter during the second wave of wines. The judges seemed both more intense and more circumspect. Their comments about the nationality of the wine in the glass were now usually correct. "That's a California, or I don't know what I am doing here," said Christian Vannequé of La Tour d'Argent. I looked at my card and he was right, it was the Ridge Monte Bello. Raymond Oliver took one sip of a red and proclaimed: "That's a Mouton, without a doubt." He too was right. Because of delays in the earlier part of the tasting, the hour was getting late and the group had to be out by 6pm, so Spurrier pushed on quickly after the ballots were collected. He followed the same procedure as he had for the Chardonnay tasting, adding up the individual scores of the judges and dividing the total by nine. The room was hushed as he read out the results.

Stag's Leap Wine Cellars 1973 (14.17)

Ch Mouton Rothschild 1970 (14.00)

Ch Haut-Brion 1970 (13.89)

Ch Montrose 1970 (13.55)

Ridge Monte Bello 1971 (11.50)

Ch Léoville-Las Cases 1971 (10.78)

Mayacamas 1971 (9.94)

Clos du Val 1972 (9.72)

Heitz Martha's Vineyard 1970 (9.39)

Freemark Abbey 1969 (8.67)

'This time the stir in the room was even more pronounced than before. A California wine had won again! Who would have believed it? The judges sat in disbelief. The results for the Cabernet wines were much closer than they had been for the Chardonnays. Château Haut-Brion got the most first-place votes of all: three. French wines were rated first, in some cases tied for first, by seven of the nine judges. Stag's Leap was rated highly by most judges, but only Odette Khan put it first and Raymond Oliver had it in a tie for first. The French red wines rated much better overall, taking three of the top four positions, while California wines were relegated to the last four slots.

Based on overall scores, the results were very close. with only a five-and-a-half-point difference between the top four finishers. Stag's Leap won by just a point-and-a-half over second-place Mouton Rothschild. But, as the old saying goes, "close only counts in horseshoes". Stag's Leap was the winner that day. It was the Judgement of Paris.

'Spurrier's suspicion that the judges would attempt to identify the French wines and score them higher while rating the California ones low appears to have taken place. In the Cabernet tasting the judges had a significantly wider scoring range than with the Chardonnays. The judges may have honestly felt the quality differences were that great, but they also may have been out to make sure a French wine won. Odette Khan, for example, gave two wines (Clos du Val and Heitz Martha's Vineyard) only two points out of 20, one (Freemark Abbey) five points and one (Ridge) seven points. All her other Cabernet scores were in double digits, but if she was trying to score California wines low overall, she didn't succeed, for her two highest scores went to Stag's Leap and Mayacamas. Four other judges also had the same pattern of rating several California wines in single digits, which is unusual in a fine-wine tasting.

'The California reds did very well on Spurrier's and Gallagher's scoring cards. Spurrier in a moment of indecision had a four-way tie for first: Château Montrose, Château Mouton Rothschild, Ridge and Stag's Leap. Gallagher gave first place to Martha's Vineyard.

'After the final results were announced, Odette Khan marched up to Spurrier, gathering together all the force of her strong personality, elegant presence and aristocratic demeanour. As editor of *La Revue du Vin de France* she realized better than probably anyone else in the room what had just happened and the impact this wine tasting might have. "Monsieur Spurrier, I demand to have my scorecards."

"I'm sorry, Madame Khan, but you're not going to get them back."

"But they are my scores."

"No, you agreed to take part in this tasting and your scores, like those of the others, belong to the Académie du Vin."

'The judges lingered for a little while longer, sharing a glass of champagne and talking freely about the results of the tasting. I spoke with five of the nine. Their immediate reactions were candid. They were generally complimentary about the California wines they had just tasted. Most said they had heard that winemakers in California were doing interesting things, but they had little first-hand experience of the wines.

'Said Aubert de Villaine: "I tasted my first California wines in 1964 and since then there have been more and more good wine houses there." Pierre Bréjoux told me: "I went to California in July 1974 and I learned a lot – to my surprise. They are now certainly among the top wines in the world, but this Stag's Leap has been a secret, I've never heard of it." Pierre Tari said: "I was really surprised by the California whites, they are certainly the best – after France. They have come a long way but they have a long way to go." Christian Vannequé told me: "The white wines approached the best of France, without a doubt. The reds, though, were not as good and didn't have the character of a Bordeaux. They are a bit minty, very strong in tannin and lack finesse."

'There were also a few sour grapes among the judges. Tari complained that "French wines develop slower than California wines because of the climate, so the test was not completely correct". Added Aubert de Villaine: "In general there is still quite a difference, the French wines are still superior." Sniped Odette Khan: "It was a false test because California wines are trying to become too much like French wines."'

After closing up at the Hôtel Intercontinental, Patricia and I walked back to the Académie, toasted each other with a glass of Brut Intégral and said how pleased we were for California that it had all been a bit of a surprise. When I got home, Bella, who had had to leave after the Chardonnays to collect Christian and Kate from school, asked how it had gone for the reds. I replied that I hadn't expected it, but California had come out top there as well. I read the children a bedtime story, Bella prepared supper, and we talked about something else.

The person who wasn't talking about something else was George Taber. He called Patricia the next day in order to track down the Dickenson-Tchelistcheff group and tell them the news. Patricia told him that they would be having lunch at Alexis Lichine's Château Lascombes in Margaux. When George called, the group were enjoying an apéritif on the terrace with château owners, who had been very keen to meet them. George Taber once again takes up the story.

'Dickenson spotted Barrett [of Chateau Montelena] across the room, walked over and told him he had a phone call. He was surprised and thought it must be bad news [...] Once Barrett identified himself I asked him: "Have you heard that your wine came first in the tasting that was held on Monday in Paris?"

"No, I haven't. That's great."

"Well, you won in the white part of it. And a California red wine also won, so it was a California sweep. What's your reaction to beating the French at their own game in Paris?" Barrett's mind started racing, but the careful Los Angeles lawyer came to the fore and after a second's hesitation he said: "Not bad for kids from the sticks." With this, I knew I had a quote.

'After our conversation ended, Barrett returned to the pre-luncheon reception which was just ending [...] He sidled up to Dickenson and said: "That was *Time* magazine, the reporter told me we had won Steven Spurrier's tasting." He then sat down for lunch. Bob Travers, the owner of Mayacamas who also had a wine in the Spurrier tasting, was sitting across the table and asked if everything was OK. Barrett looked at Travers with a smile as wide as a bottle of Chardonnay and said "Yes, everything's just fine". The results of the Paris Tasting began to spread quietly but quickly from Californian to Californian across the room.

'Some 90 people attended the formal lunch, which was done in the best French style. Dickenson was seated to the right of Alexis Lichine, while André Tchelistcheff was on his left. After lunch Lichine made a gracious, though condescending, speech saying how nice it was that Americans had come to learn from the French how to make great wine, and how, if they worked hard, some day they too might be successful. For Dickenson it was hard to take that speech, all the while knowing that California wines had just beaten some of the best of France's in Spurrier's tasting. After lunch the Californian delegation politely thanked their hosts and got back onto their bus. Everyone waved goodbye as the vehicle pulled away from Lascombes. As soon as it had passed the last pine tree and was safely out of sight, the group erupted like football fans whose team had just won the Super Bowl. Everyone was screaming with elation. Barrett hugged Tchelistcheff. There were two more tastings that afternoon to bring the number of wines the Californians had tried in three weeks in France to more than 250, but the group walked through those in a dream. They were more excited about what had happened in Paris.

'Once they had arrived at their hotel, Barrett sent a telegram to the staff at Chateau Montelena that read – STUNNING SUCCESS IN PARIS ON MAY TWENTY FOUR STOP TOOK FIRST PLACE OVER NINE OTHERS WITH PREMIER CRU WINE STOP TOP NAMES IN FRANCE WERE BLIND TASTERS STOP. The staff wasn't sure what Barrett was referring to, but they learned it was something important when Miljenko "Mike" Grgich, Montelena's winemaker, got a call from *The New York Times* asking to send a photographer to take his picture. After that call, Grgich didn't know what to do so he started dancing around the winery shouting in his native Croatian: "I'm born again! I'm born again!" No one could understand a word he said, but who cared? Barrett's son Bo watched Grgich from a second storey window and thought he had gone bonkers.

'The next day the group flew back to San Francisco. It was near dinner time when André Tchelistcheff and his wife Dorothy reached their home in Napa, and

Dorothy thought it might be a good moment to call Barbara Winiarski and tell her about the results of the Paris Tasting [...When] Barbara casually mentioned that their wine had won "that wine tasting in Paris", Warren also had a tough time remembering which tasting it was. Without realizing the profound impact the Paris Tasting would have on his life and on his winery, he said simply: "That's nice."'

It did not take long, however, for Warren to find a way of describing the importance of that day in Paris. 'I called it a Copernican moment [Nicolaus Copernicus (1473–1543) discovered that the sun, not the Earth, was at the centre of the universe]: nothing was the same after that. We looked at what we could do with different eyes.' From the following year he was involved in tasting after tasting to re-run his wine's triumph in Paris. I was often at these events, so much so that Warren said that he and I were 'joined at the hip'. I was the first person he called when the sale of Stag's Leap for $185,000,000 had been finalized with Château Ste Michelle in 2007, after 30 successful years as a leader in Napa Valley winemaking.

In his autobiography Robert Mondavi wrote that 'The Paris Tasting was an enormous event in the history of California winemaking. It put us squarely on the world map of great wine-producing regions. I saw the impact everywhere I went. Suddenly people had a new respect for what we were doing, for they saw we could make wines as good as France's best. I think it is no coincidence that the first vintage of Opus One, the joint venture in Napa between Robert Mondavi and Baron Philippe de Rothschild of Château Mouton Rothschild, was the 1979.'

After the initial shock, intelligent wine producers went to California to see what all the fuss was about. What they found was a vibrant wine region committed to investment in quality and determined to prove themselves. Outside investors were there to help it happen, in stark contrast to France where such third-party financing was rare. Within a year or two, this first chink in France's dominance of the wine world began to promote an outward- rather than an inward-looking mind set, particularly amongst the younger generation. Taber's headline 'The Historic Tasting that Revolutionized Wine' was prophetic.

France's first reaction was to blame the judges. I became a persona non grata in certain circles, but since both the shop and the Académie continued to do well, I paid no attention. Claude Terrail, owner of La Tour d'Argent, chastised Christian Vannequé for having taken part and forbade him to do so again, telling him it was 'very bad for the French wine business'. There were calls for Pierre Bréjoux to resign from the INAO, and Lalou Bize-Leroy, Aubert de Villaine's partner at the Domaine de la Romanée-Conti, accused him of treachery. Odette Khan got her side of the story into print in her magazine under the title 'On the Subject of a Small Scandal' insinuating that I had falsified the scores.

Tari's complaint that French wines develop more slowly than California wines because of the climate, and in general that the red Bordeaux were too young, was heard again and again, so in 1986 I held a tasting in New York organized by Dorothy Cann at the French Culinary Institute she ran in the city. We tasted the same red wines, again with nine tasters. Apart from Georges Lepré, head sommelier of the Paris Ritz, and Bartholomew Broadbent, they were all American: Michael Aaron of Manhattan wine store Sherry-Lehmann, Alexis Bespaloff of *New York* magazine, Barbara Ensrud of the New York *Daily News*, Peter Morrell of Manhattan wine store Morrell, Frank J Prial of *The New York Times* and Robert Finigan. There had been some criticism of my original (1976) scoring method, in which I added up the scores out of 20 and divided by the number of tasters, so this time I asked the judges to range their scores from nine for their first-choice down to one point for their least favourite. With eight tasters and nine wines, then, a perfect score would be 72, and the worst possible score eight. Here are the 1986 scores followed by their 1976 rankings:

> *Clos du Val* 1972 – 57 (8th)
> *Ridge Monte Bello* 1971 – 54 (5th)
> *Ch Montrose* 1970 – 45 (3rd)
> *Ch Léoville-Las Cases* 1971 – 43 (6th)
> *Ch Mouton Rothschild* 1970 – 41 (2nd)
> *Stag's Leap Wine Cellars* 1973 – 36 (1st)
> *Heitz Martha's Vineyard* 1970 – 35 (9th)
> *Mayacamas* 1971 – 34 (7th)
> *Ch Haut-Brion* 1970 – 23 (4th)

Three red Bordeaux had come directly from the châteaux at my request, but Haut-Brion refused to participate and the bottle was bought in New York from a top merchant. It had plainly been badly stored. Freemark Abbey admitted that their 1969 had faded, and as a result they declined to participate.

At the time of tasting, the Union des Grands Crus de Bordeaux was crossing the US promoting the region's very good 1985 vintage. When the results were announced, their president (and one of the original judges in 1976) Pierre Tari accused me of single-handedly wrecking their campaign. I decided it would be better not to repeat it in 1996.

When he was researching for his book in the early 2000s, George Taber told me that the judges still found the memory of May 24th 1976 extremely painful. When the 30th anniversary took place in 2006 I was in touch with all those still living and they confirmed that they had been given a really hard going over. It is to their immense credit that not a single one of them told me so at the time. They knew that the tasting that Patricia and I had created had been honestly handled and that we had had the best intentions.

Because the '86 tasting had ruffled so many feathers, I had not originally intended to hold a re-match 20 years on but I was eventually persuaded to take up the gauntlet again. With the encouragement of Jacob, Lord Rothschild (a substantial shareholder in both Château Lafite Rothschild and Château Mouton Rothschild) and Robert Mondavi, 30 years to the day after the original Paris Tasting we held two simultaneous tastings, again of the original red wines, in 2006: at Copia in Napa at 10am and at Berry Bros & Rudd in London at 6pm. The wines were sourced from the wineries, nine tasters were present on each side of the pond, including from the 1976 tastings Christian Vannequé in Napa as well as Patricia Gallagher, Michel Dovaz and me in London. With both panels' marks added together (this time the taster's top wine earned one point, their second wine two points and so on, so lower is better) the combined results were:

Ridge Monte Bello 1971 (61)
Stag's Leap Wine Cellars 1973 (79)
Heitz Martha's Vineyard 1970 (86)
Mayacamas 1971 (86)
Clos du Val 1972 (92)
Ch Mouton Rothschild 1970 (93)

Ch Montrose 1970 (106)

Ch Haut-Brion 1970 (116)

Ch Léoville-Las Cases 1971 (132)

Freemark Abbey 1969 (139)

The fact that the California Cabernets took the five top places rather dashed the argument that the red Bordeaux would age well and the Californias would not. The following morning I was interviewed on the BBC's *Today* news programme and asked how the Bordelais might feel about the result. I could only suggest they might be 'rather miffed'. But I should mention here that after this blind tasting in London, there was an open tasting for about 40 guests of the same or similar wines from the 2000 vintage, and here the Bordeaux wines simply wiped the floor with the Californias.

Aubert de Villaine had described the 1976 event as *un coup de pied dans la derrière pour les vins Français* / a kick up the bum for French wine, which indeed it was, and it turned out to be both necessary and beneficial. My conclusion from the 1976–2006 tastings across the 40 years is that in the early 1970s the benchmark Bordeaux were resting on their laurels, and by the late 1990s, the classic Californias were doing the same. The world of wine never stands still.

CHAPTER EIGHT
HERE, THERE AND EVERYWHERE

In Cité Berryer and in the Spurrier family, life was good. We were on the corner of the Rue des Francs-Bourgeois which led south to the Place des Vosges, one of the most beautiful squares in the city. Christian was in a school nearby in the Rue des Archives and I used to take him there on the handlebars of my bike before heading off to the Rue Royale. Kate was in a local crèche, which gave Bella a good half-day to continue working for Jean-Pierre Pavillard.

My ambitions as a Parisian wine merchant were moving ahead. The Cave (although my name had long since replaced that name on the shop front, I still answered the phone with 'Bonjour, Cave de la Madeleine…') was by the mid-'70s one of the best-stocked wine shops in Paris. Thanks to Constant Bourquin and my membership of the Académie Internationale du Vin, I was on good terms with the owners of some of France's finest vineyards, who were happy to sell to me. At least one weekend a month we went to a wine region to visit the established names and discover new ones, always bringing back two or more wines to cram into the shop. My approach was much more about 'communication' – 'Try this, you'll like it' – than commercialization. My aim was that my customers should have two reactions when opening a bottle for friends: 'Gosh, that's good!' and 'Where can I buy it?'

A quick tour of France via the suppliers, many little-known at the time, and many of whom became friends, would come up with the following names. From north to south: Alsace: Hugel and Trimbach of course, but also Leonard Humbrecht (whose son Olivier was France's first Master of Wine), Colette Faller,

A lively street market on the doorstep increased passing trade.

Marcel Deiss, Jean Meyer and André Ostertag. From Champagne: Etienne Gosset and Jean Vesselle; from Savoie, Jean-Pierre Quénard; and from the Jura, the Rolet family. From Chablis: René Dauvissat, whose wife made the best *gougères* (little cheese puffs – so good after tasting young wines being readied for bottling before going onto older vintages). From Burgundy, the long list would include Domaines Rousseau, Dujac, Rémy, Roumier, Grivot, Rion and Gouges from the Côte de Nuits; Tollot Beaut, Chandon de Briailles, de Mérode, Drouhin, de Suremain, Coche-Dury, Lafon, Roulot, Leflaive, Pousse d'Or, de Montille, Matrot, Blain-Gagnard, d'Angerville, Comte Armand and Thévenin from the Côte de Beaune; and Juillot and Michel from the Côte Chalonnaise. All my Beaujolais came from Pierre Ferraud and, apart from Beaujolais and Mâcon, I sold all nine of the crus, and the wonderful Pouilly-Fuissés from Château de Fuissé. In the Rhône I renewed my contact with Louis Jaboulet and his nephew Gérard, met Marcel Guigal in 1971, Gérard Chave and August Clape in the north and Pierre Perrin of Château de Beaucastel. In Provence it was Châteaux Simone and de Vignelaure either side of Aix-en-Provence, Clos Ste Magdeleine in Cassis and Tempier in Bandol, and in 1977 I was the first person to stock Domaine de Trévallon.

In 1972, the locksmith's next door became France's first private wine school.

Along the river Loire from east to west I visited Gérard Pétillat at St-Pourçain, Vincent Delaporte in Sancerre, Landrat-Guyollot in Pouilly-Fumé, Pierre Mardon in Quincy; Lucien Legrand and I bought a great deal of Sauvignon Blanc from Jean Gueritte in Cheverny and a little of the very rare white grape Romorantin; Henri Marionnet in Touraine, Gaston Huet and Prince Poniatowski in Vouvray, Pierre Couly and Charles Joguet in Chinon, Paul Maître in Bourgueil, Denis Duveau in Saumur-Champigny, Mme Joly at La Coulée de Serrant (before her son Nicholas created the biodynamic movement in France), and Château de la Roulerie in Anjou; M Boivin for his superb Château de Fesles Bonnezeaux, and from Muscadet Leon Boullault and his family at Domaine des Dorices, who made a marvellous *vin de grande garde* – it passed six years on its fine lees in cement tanks below ground before bottling, and Leon reserved it for me and for Jean-Pierre Coffe's restaurant La Ciboulette.

Going south towards Bordeaux, I bought Mme de St-Exupéry's Château de Tiregand, which led the Pécharmant appellation (and still does); there were some pleasant Bergeracs and my minor Bordeaux all came from Pierre Coste at Langon, who introduced me to Denis Dubourdieu's red and white Graves Château Reynon and his now-cult Clos Floridène. Much of my Bordeaux came from courtiers or brokers on La Place de Bordeaux, and the rest from personal visits to lesser-known appellations such as Fronsac, Côtes de Castillon, Côtes de Francs and Côtes de Bourg and Blaye. Moving east, I helped launch the Madirans of Alain Brumont, while in Cahors I bought grapes from the venerable Clôs du Gamot and the up-and-coming Château de Cèdre. There were many, many other wines from other regions, notably the emerging *vins de pays*, a category created by the INAO in 1973 to highlight and protect the local regional wines, sold previously as *vins de table*. My interest in these helped me to write my first wine book, *French Country Wines*, a few years later.

When I started in Paris I used to ask the salesmen who came to the Cave whether they had sold their wines to any of the city's three top *cavistes*: Besse, Chaudet or Legrand. If the answer was yes, this was already a reference for me to give them a try. By the mid-1970s my own name was being widely used as a reference, which was a flattering measure of recognition. The shop was always busy and the volumes we sold quite surprising considering the size of the premises and modest staff numbers. I remember Melvyn Master introducing me to a wealthy American wine collector who had heard of me.

'How many shops do you have?' he asked. 'One.'

'And how many employees?'

'Two.'

'Gee, I guess you must be kinda exclusive.' We weren't, but I wanted my customers to feel as though we were. Being bang in the centre of Paris was one of the keys: location, location, location – but the other was commitment: vocation, vocation, vocation. This was what I had been cut out for, and in the first few years of the Cave and the Académie I could not have been happier. The hours were long, but this wasn't work, it was a way of life.

I should have had enough to do with running the shop and teaching at the Académie, but I always found something to distract me from these two core activities, provided it centred on wine. One of my American clients, 'Stony' Stollenwerk was Paris bureau chief for the book department of Time Life, one of the US pioneers of mail-order sales. In France this was known as *la vente par correspondance*, and it was in its infancy. One of the earlier ventures, The Savour

Club, had started in Beaujolais in the early 1970s and specialized in the region's wines, which were supplied by Georges Duboeuf (later 'Monsieur Beaujolais'). He supplied all the local restaurants, including Paul Bocuse in Lyon and the Troisgros brothers at Roanne, who put their names and knowledge behind the Club's range.

Stony's experience of mail order was vast and, having seen the 'communication by education' effect on sales to students of the Académie, he suggested that these elements could be wrapped up in a mail-order package that would provide wines with a newsletter to match. What it needed, he said, was a name everybody would recognize. By chance, I had earlier registered the name Les Amis du Vin for use in France and the UK at some point in the future, and Stony and I adopted it for our venture.

We began work on our new enterprise and its newsletter. He introduced me to Anne Duval (whose husband-to-be, François Sauzey, I had first met in 1965 at Delamain in Cognac, where his father was managing director). Anne, an artist, provided illustrations and designed some of our 'own label' wines. We planned to offer six wines: three whites and three reds, and the mailing went out to about 50,000 addresses, drawn from Time Life and other lists. Stony would finance this, and it would be administered from offices above the Académie's tasting room. He was quite clear: if we did not get a positive response from two percent or more of the list, then he would not go ahead. Our initial mailing narrowly missed this target and, sadly, the idea died a death.

At around this time Neville Abraham, one of my clients who was at the INSEAD business school in Fontainebleau, was setting up a company to take advantage of the potential wine market in London, and needed a name for it. He had asked me to be one of his in-house wine suppliers. Since the Amis du Vin name was no longer any use to me, I gave it to him, complete with the logo. His business did well and in the early 1980s he opened what was to be a hugely successful wine bar in Covent Garden, naming it Café des Amis du Vin and modelling it on Michael Liekerman's and my Bistrot à Vin. Michael took 20 percent of this venture while I, again not paying attention to the value of a brand, had just 0.5 percent, but even with this I made a little money when Neville's restaurant empire, having by that time expanded into the Chez Gérard chain of brasseries and the fine Indian restaurant Chutney Mary, was eventually sold.

In 1977 we took on Isabelle Bachelard at the Académie. She had been studying in Portland, Oregon so spoke good English, which was useful, even though by this time the French clientele were almost outnumbering the Anglo-Saxons. Patricia welcomed another pair of hands and when, the following year, she married and started a family, Isabelle took over the daily running of the Académie.

Just a look at the Monday-night tastings we held in autumn 1977 shows our commitment to offering new and exciting wines. In addition to the regular courses – six evenings on the Tour de France and three on the Advanced – we created these tastings to allow our students to follow the evolution of *Appellation Contrôlée* wines in several vintages, and compare wines of the same vintage across the same appellation from different producers. They also provided an opportunity to taste rare and expensive wines that were no longer available on the market, and we did not limit ourselves to France. The Académie was fortunate to have the cooperation of embassies, *négociants* and the owners of various châteaux and domaines, without whom the tastings would not have been possible. Listed below is the autumn 1977 programme complete with charges (Fr10 equalled a little less than £1 at that time). The world of wine education was young and it was wonderful to be able to offer such experiences, but at those prices we never made much of a profit.

SEPTEMBER
- 1973 St-Emilion grands and premiers grands crus classés: Fr40
- Branded wines of Bordeaux: Fr30
- Pommard premier cru Les Epeneaux Comte Armand 1964–75: Fr50
OCTOBER
- Ch Talbot fourth growth St-Julien, eight 1960s and 1970s vintages: Fr50
- Volnay premier cru Clos des Santenots Domaine Jacques Prieur: Fr40
- 1971 Médoc grands crus classés: Fr40
- *Bordeaux premiers crus of 1957: Ausone, Haut-Brion, Latour, Margaux, Mouton Rothschild: Fr60
NOVEMBER
- The best wines of Austria from the Austrian Embassy: Fr40
- Musigny Comté de Vogüé, six vintages 1957–70: Fr60
- Beaujolais Nouveau with Pain Poilâne and Brie: Fr20

- Ch Giscours, third growth Margaux: Fr50
- *Romanée-St-Vivant grand cru 1962, '64, '66, '69 and '70: Fr75
DECEMBER
- The Best Wines of Chile from the Chilean Embassy: Fr40
- Château de Pez St-Estèphe, nine vintages 1945–71: Fr50
- *1928s of Brane-Cantenac, Carbonnieux, Margaux, Montrose, Palmer: Fr75
(*these wines had been supplied from Nicolas's vintage reserves.)

David Russell, a gentlemanly advertising executive whose large cellars were stocked mostly from the Cave (on his frequent visits he always ordered 'a dozen dozen'), introduced me to Julian and Sheila More. Julian, about 10 years older than me, was well known in the UK theatre world having written the book and the lyrics for three of the biggest musical successes of the 1950s: *Grab me a Gondola*, *Expresso Bongo* and *Irma La Douce*. He and Sheila were moving to Paris and David said we must meet, so I suggested a drink in the café Les Deux Magots on the Place St Germain. Julian asked how he would recognize me and I said I would be with Digby, my Briard. We got on superbly from the start, as did Bella with Sheila (who represented the works from the estate of Alphonse Mucha, the Czech Art Deco artist).

At one point during our many get-togethers, Julian said he was surprised that nobody had written a TV series or 'soap opera' on wine, as there were so many great stories. I agreed and suggested we sketch out a script. The title from the very start was *Corkscrew*, and our enterprise was planned as a 10-hour package. The idea almost sold to BBC 1 but didn't in the end, and although it garnered a good deal of interest during the time Bella and I spent in New York in 1981–82, it was pipped to the post by a soap named *Falcon's Crest*, based, of course, in California. The last script we wrote was in 1993, and it was on the verge of being accepted by Britain's Channel 4 – but even this never saw the light of day.

With both Christian and Kate at school, Bella was looking for something more to do during the day having by now learnt as much about photography as she could with Jean-Pierre Pavillard. Through the British Chamber of Commerce we learnt that Bernard and Laura Ashley were planning to open a branch of their shop on the Rue de Grenelle in the fashionable sixth *arrondissement*. Bella applied for a job and was taken on. Bella and Annie Bingham, whom we had met earlier and became a dear friend, were known as *les petites Anglaises* and they proved adept at selling the pretty fabrics and wallpaper that had made the brand's name.

Rules in French shops – even at the Cave – were strict: any payment by cheque had to be validated by a *pièce d'identité* or ID card. One busy Saturday afternoon, a very elegant Parisienne made substantial purchases, paying by cheque on the Banque de France. '*Pièce d'identité, s'il vous plaît, Mme,*' said Bella, to the woman's evident surprise. Bella repeated the request, pointing to the card in the shop that set out the rule, and adding that Mme should also write her address on the back of the cheque, please. From the depths of her very smart handbag the woman extracted and then presented the ID card, which showed that she was Mme Giscard d'Estaing, wife of the then President of France. On the back of the cheque she wrote 'Palais d'Elysée, Paris 8ème'.

Bella's time at Laura Ashley showed how much demand there was in Paris for *le style Anglais*, and in 1978 she, with friends, opened a shop in the Rue de Verneuil. I suggested a simple name, The English Trading Company, based on the successful store The General Trading Company (GTC) in London's Sloane Street. Their new shop, which soon became known as ETC, sold everything from oatcakes to kilts, made-to-measure in Scotland, and for a year or two it worked very well.

Meanwhile in London, my friend David Zambra had begun buying wine from me to sell on to friends and, becoming increasingly interested in the trade, decided in 1975 to leave his job with WH Smith and open a wine shop. He found ideal premises in the Chelsea part of the Fulham Road in an area known as 'The Beach' because the local clothes shops, cafés and restaurants were so appealing that casual strolling up and down was a pleasure. Naturally, he called the shop Cave de la Madeleine, and he bought from the same suppliers as I did for many years. We were friends so I didn't consider charging a royalty, and anyway it was nice to have an outpost of the Cave in fashionable London. In the mid-1980s the shop was taken over by Graham Chidgey of Laytons, and a few years later by Charles Lea and Patrick Sandeman, both ex-Laytons. Charles had spent a year with me in the early 1980s on his junior year abroad. Patrick was of the Sandeman port and sherry family. Lea & Sandeman are still in the Fulham Road and are one of the city's best retailers where I am always pleased to see remnants from the old days such as Vincent Delaporte's Sancerre and Marcel Deiss's Alsace on their shelves.

In June 1977 Lucien Legrand and I were invited as representatives of the Paris retail trade to Bordeaux's Cité du Vin, a complex devoted to wine on the Quai des Chartrons. We were to take part with a few dozen others in what was called *Les Premières Journées Mondiales*. This was a testing 'think tank' to discuss what in 1979 would emerge as Vinexpo, the international wine fair held in Bordeaux every other year, and later in Hong Kong and the US in alternate years. Jacques Chaban-Delmas, prime minister under president Pompidou, was the Bordeaux mayor planning to spend lots of the city's money to drag it into the modern world. In the early days, Vinexpo was small but well supported by the châteaux, who began to open their doors to visitors. This practice had been much frowned upon when it was pioneered by Alexis Lichine in the early 1960s.

After the Judgement of Paris I became a regular visitor to California. On the tasting's first anniversary, the Vintners' Club in San Francisco decided to hold a rematch with both the Chardonnays and the Cabernets, and invited me to co-host. Not surprisingly the results were again in favour of California, but I had already done my bit for the 'sunshine state' and was now more interested in meeting the people who made the wine. Robert Mondavi was at these tastings and invited me up to Napa. After showing me round his famous winery, he hosted a tasting of his Pinot Noir against a La Tâche from the Domaine de la Romanée-Conti, and his Cabernet Sauvignon Reserve against Mouton Rothschild. The first showed his ambition, but there was no thread that linked the two Pinots. There was, however, a sense of common identity between the two Cabernets.

Robert Mondavi was certainly the most forward-looking wine producer of his, perhaps any, generation, and when the first vintage of Opus One, his joint venture with Baron Philippe de Rothschild of Mouton Rothschild was unveiled in 1981, the wine world paid attention. His subsequent collaborations, always at his instigation, with Marchese Lodovico Antinori in Tuscany and Eduardo Chadwick in Chile's Aconcagua Valley, were perhaps even more innovative. Ornellaia's Masseto and Chadwick's Seña have now joined Opus One at the pinnacle of their respective regions' production.

The following year I went south for my first-ever visit to Los Angeles, where I was to give two tastings comparing California and French wines. I was put up in great state at the Beverley Wiltshire Hotel, where I saw my first mobile phone, brought to the table of a movie mogul, and that evening went to my first and last 'Roller Disco'. This was at Flipper's in a downtown converted warehouse, which had recently been opened by a friend from my London days. I had enjoyed roller skating as a boy and ice skating later at the Queensway Ice Rink, but was unprepared for the booming music and the speed and gyrations of the participants that evening.

Back in Paris, there were further temptations to expand the Spurrier brand. When I first noticed and thought about buying the Cave, I had been on my way to Le Moulin du Village, a restaurant in Cité Berryer. Le Moulin was just up the street, and on the sunny side. On two floors, with a large terrace that was always packed in summer, it was full at lunch and seemed to tick over in the evening. The owner, Monsieur Albert Bégot, was getting on in years and the menu was old-fashioned and repetitive compared to the nouvelle cuisine that had by then become fashionable. M Bégot's family was from Tain l'Hermitage in the northern Rhône, and much of the list was made up of wines from Chapoutier, which were not well thought of at the time. Nevertheless when the restaurant came up for sale at a fair price, it seemed too good an opportunity to miss. I put up a little over half the money to gain a majority share and was joined by my friend David Fromkin, who owned a little Russian-themed restaurant opposite. I raised the rest by offering clients of the Cave and Académie 30 percent off their forthcoming meals if they came up with Fr500 in cash. Le Moulin was to be managed by Chuck, the fiancé of one of our part-time Académie staff, and we had also engaged a young chef from Maxim's, so all seemed set fair.

Since Chuck was working for the Cave without residence- or work-papers, I turned to my original 'fixer' Félix Branger to get him the necessary permits, explaining that since the *quartier* was the centre for American banks and businesses and we would have a French chef and other French staff, it was logical that the manager should be American. This ruse succeeded – but within two or three years I was to regret having pushed it through.

The wines were all supplied by the Cave and I operated on a 300-percent mark-up, low in Paris at that time, certainly around the Place de la Madeleine. This made the wines' prices in Le Moulin around 60 percent higher than they were in the shop. For some people, la Cité Berryer was becoming la Cité Spurrier, and my taking over Le Moulin came to the attention of Robert Courtine, France's most feared and revered restaurant critic. He wrote in *Le Monde* under the name of La Reynière. He gave the restaurant a passable review, but described me as 'un monsieur touche-à-tout' or a jack of all trades; the implication, I thought, being that I was master of none. With the two pillars of Parisian gastronomy against me – Odette Khan and Robert Courtine – perhaps I should have been worried.

As if I didn't have enough on my plate, that same year I went into another restaurant venture with Michael Liekerman, the director of Terence Conran's Habitat store in Paris. Both being young(ish) Brits wanting to shake up the scene a little, and Michael having a more progressive vision of commerce than I did, we got on well. A business centre was being built on the Esplanade de La Défense on the outskirts of Paris across the Seine from Neuilly. Michael had the brilliant idea that it needed a modern bistro for the office workers. With the assistance of SICAREX, government-funded experimental wine producers at Listel near Marseille and our potential partners in this venture, we managed to obtain a site on the Esplanade in front of two already completed high-rise buildings. Michael hired the Habitat team to design and construct a single-storey metal-and-glass building with a large basement, we obtained a lease of 19 years and Le Bistrot à Vin opened its doors in time for Christmas 1978. The manager was Steve Steede, who had left the Cave the year before and was welcomed back into the fold; not an easy character but a very honest one, who knew all my wine producers and bought from them directly.

Most of the charcuterie came from the food hall Charcuterie Bobosse just north of Lyon, and we were the first wine bar to serve Beaujolais on tap from kegs. Half the basement was arranged as a wine shop, and we held occasional wine courses there. Michael planned Le Bistrot as a template which, if successful, we would reproduce in other major French cities, but sadly this didn't happen. Michael and I were both preoccupied with other interests and sold our shares in 1983, but Le Bistrot is still flourishing as one of the area's most popular venues.

I was in increasing demand as a wine judge, and the shop needed another pair of hands to help Mauricette and Mark Williamson. Mark had trained in the Savoy Hotel kitchens in London, and when we met was working his way through restaurants in Provence with a plan to return to the hotel business in London.

I suggested he stop off in Paris to learn about wine... and he never left. Step up Drew Harré, a New Zealand student violin-maker who lived in Neuilly. Drew was fiercely independent and now rivals Mark as the most successful former member of our '*Mafia Anglais*', having set up four restaurants, all cheek-by-jowl in the smart Rue de Seine in the sixth *arrondissement*.

I had recently been made Christie's representative in France, part of my responsibility being to pack up wine cellars for sale in London. One of the best was that of Restaurant Darroze in Villeneuve-de-Marsan. The elderly but very spry Monsieur Darroze had decided that his clients no longer deserved most of the marvellous bottles that he had so lovingly collected. Drew and I spent three full days cataloguing and packing, and each lunchtime we were offered a half-bottle of a Médoc first growth; there were burgundies for dinner and after that, the marvellous Darroze Armagnac, which is still a highly regarded brand.

At around this time, Christie's hosted a huge auction of Sandeman sherries. The company had recently been taken over by Seagram, who decided to close down the sherry arm. No doubt the thousands of butts of sherry maturing under the solera (year-to-year blending) system quickly found takers among the long-established Jerez bodegas, but the bottled stock was consigned to Christie's. Being their agent, I was well aware of the auctions. Once I saw the catalogue with over two thousand cases of all styles from the driest fino to the sweetest amaroso – and the estimated prices – I flew to London for the tasting.

Parisians didn't drink sherry, and if they drank port it was a light ruby as an apéritif. They bought Madeira only for cooking. My week with Mackenzie in September 1965 had shown how marvellous some of the older blends could be, and the quality of the Sandeman range was extraordinary. I ended up buying around 150 cases across the entire range. As they cleared customs through Bercy, the officer observed that this was more sherry than had been shipped to Paris in the past six months. Although I did (and do) not have a business bone in my body, I was good at promotion and communication, and this investment was a golden opportunity. My Anglo-Saxon clients had heard of sherry but had not tasted wines of this quality; my French clients were amazed by what was put before them. I made comparisons with the classics, aged fino being likened to the Jura's *vin jaune*, the extraordinary amaroso (sweetened oloroso) aligned with Château d'Yquem. *Gault & Millau* wrote them all up, my restaurant friends including Alain Dutournier of Le Trou Gascon put them on their list, and within a month or so there wasn't a bottle left.

In late May I had planned a short break in Florence with Bella and a couple of friends. As a surprise, I had booked a nice hotel on the left bank of the Arno away from the tourists. With the reservations in my pocket I set off alone, planning to stop at the Foire de Mâcon first. Bella meanwhile was to take the train from the Gare de Lyon that stopped at Chambéry at around 11.30pm, where I would join her in our sleeping compartment. After the tasting, my friend Tim Johnston gave me a lift to Chambéry, where we found ourselves with time on our hands before the train arrived.

The local cinema was showing *Saturday Night Fever* with John Travolta, so we persuaded the usherette to let us in, took our seats and (having already dined rather well) both promptly both fell asleep. We came to only about 10 minutes before the train was due to leave. After a quick dash back to the car to get my bag, we charged through the gates to see the train standing at the platform opposite, ready to leave. I sprinted across the tracks and opened the train door – mercifully unlocked – as it began to move. Tim, behind me, was just close enough to throw the bag into my outstretched arms. Gasping for breath but safely on board, I turned around to find myself face to face with the conductor, who surveyed me gravely and said *Mme vous attend* / Madam is waiting for you. Had we not made it, my planned surprise would have backfired as Bella would have arrived in Florence with not the first clue what to do or where to go. Once she had calmed down, we had a very good time.

After the Foire de Mâcon the following year, which coincided with Tim's 30th birthday, he and I spent a rather more relaxed evening together. I suggested we make up a small party to have dinner at the restaurant La Pyramide in Vienne, which was well known in the 1950s for the cuisine of the 'gastronomic godfather' Fernand Point, and was still renowned for its cellar. Tim and his wife Stephanie would be my guests and I'd host the wines for the table. The other guests were Bob Baker, Robert Finigan and Mark Williamson. I contacted Tim recently to check what we drank and he replied: 'We started with a Condrieu 1978 with their house label, but I reckon it would have been either from Vernay or Dumazet. We then moved on to 1976 Nuits-St-Georges Clos de la Perrière Blanc, the Pinot Blanc from Domaine Henri Gouges with very refined, crisp dry fruit. Then we had Château Haut-Brion 1961 on great form: magical. The centrepiece of the evening was a Marie-Jeanne [three bottles] of Château Lafite 1947 which was magnificent, a little dry with tannic structure, great elegance and a very long finish. What a wine! We finished with the Coulée de Serrant 1949 (Fr50 on the list!): quite extraordinary. I have always said that it was the only bottle of Coulée de Serrant that I have ever really enjoyed, and Nicolas Joly has certainly never made a wine that even gets close to it.

'I remember that your friend Geoffrey Roberts and his friend Christopher Selmes were at a table not far from us and were drinking Château Caillou 1921 (at a completely different price level). You swapped a glass with them and we all agreed that the Caillou was less exciting.'

As we left the restaurant, flushed with pride at the success of my selection, I said good night to Geoffrey and Christopher and asked what they had had before the Caillou 1921. 'Lafite '58' Geoffrey replied.

'Why on earth such a lousy vintage?' I asked.

'*1*858,' came the murmured reply.

In 1979 *Gault & Millau* held a two-day blind tasting on the theme *les Olympiades du Vin* / the Wine Olympics. The Académie was involved in sourcing the bottles to get the widest spread possible, and then helped to arrange the flights in which they would be tasted. They were grouped by grape varieties and price band. International tasters were invited, including fellow Masters of Wine Michael Broadbent, David Peppercorn and Serena Sutcliffe from the UK.

The first morning I was on a table with Jacques Seysses of Domaine Dujac in front of a range of Chardonnays. Michael was on a nearby table with the ebullient Jacques Manière, *chef cuisinier* of Le Pactole on the Boulevard St-Germain, who served his house champagne from Legras in Chouilly *en carafe*. I love this idea, not only because the decanting reduces the bubbles a fraction, but also because the simple carafe was so much more relaxed than a champagne bottle. At the mid-morning break, Michael came over, quite agitated, to say that Manière wasn't spitting out anything, which unnerved him, and could I please intervene. Before the next group of wines was served I said hello to Jacques, who knew me well from his restaurant, and said that Monsieur Broadbent was concerned and that perhaps the spittoon might be useful. His reply was clear: *Ecoute, mon petit, si je crâche, je perds mon equilibre* / Listen, my boy, if I spit I lose my balance. His place was empty for the afternoon session.

That evening I introduced the UK tasters to Alain Dutournier's superb restaurant Au Trou Gascon in the 12th *arrondissement*: a marvellous place for the best food and wines from Alain's native southwest France.

No doubt there were many surprises from these tastings, but one upset made the headlines: the Torres Black Label Cabernet Sauvignon from Penedès in north-east Spain was placed first in its group ahead of first growths Haut-Brion and Latour. It was not long before the tasters on that panel (including me) received a single line from Jean-Paul Gardère, the manager of Latour, asking: *Vous n'étiez pas victime d'un embuscade*? You haven't been conned, have you? No, and Miguel Torres didn't think so, either; the Black Label went onto justify the award year after year.

That summer, again thanks to David Fromkin, I spent two weeks across France filming what was planned to be another ground-breaking idea for the Académie and the Spurrier brand. The production was to be recorded on a 'video disc', the brainchild of Bill Connell, a good friend of David's from Washington DC. Bill was convinced in those early days of video tapes that the 12-inch disc would be far superior in terms of image- and sound-quality, so would be the future. And what better idea than to have on disc a complete tour of French vineyards with a well-known figure meeting the producers? The flip side was to be more of a structured tasting course: right up the Académie's street. Setting off from Paris, we started in Vouvray with Prince Poniatowski on his Clos Baudoin vineyard; moved to Bordeaux for a few days at Château Loudenne with Martin Bamford, taking in all the grand Médoc châteaux; then a long drive across the Massif Central to Ampuis to meet Marcel Guigal in his steep Côte-Rotie vineyards; up to Pierre Ferraud in the Beaujolais; to Jacques Seysses in Morey-St-Denis; to René Dauvissat in Chablis, and finally to Bollinger in Champagne.

I gave a private showing of the finished work (from a tape, as the disc software was not ready) to the participants and others on the second-floor offices of the

Académie (upstairs we could give classes for up to 40, as opposed to a maximum of 12 downstairs around the horseshoe bar. Most evenings both rooms were filled.) Wines from all the growers were served and the 60-minute movie was very well received, so this seemed to be time well spent.

Filming of the more educational part, planned for the following year, was delayed owing to technical problems with the disc. It finally took place in Lavin's restaurant in New York on W 45th Street, where I was beginning to set up the NYC Académie. On my own, without the back-up of the other *profs* I had had in Paris, this turned out less well than I had hoped, but finally it didn't matter because video discs were beaten out of sight by video tapes, and Bill Connell's brilliant idea – and the fine work of his team – never even went into production.

Certainly the most unexpected thing that happened to me at the end of the 1970s was taking part in an advertising campaign for Coca-Cola's venture into wine, under the brand Taylor's California Cellars. Perhaps seeing California's success since the Paris Tasting, Coca-Cola had been smart enough not to buy a major estate, but to purchase a New York State winemaker's brand – Taylor Cellars – and transfer it to California, hiring Richard 'Dick' Peterson, another of André Tchelistcheff's many dazzling pupils, as overall winemaker. The idea was to make mainstream wines for the popular market.

The genius in this plan was Albert E Killeen, an elegant and brilliant man who had looked after Coca-Cola's interests in Africa for some years and, nearing retirement age, had returned to the States. Al had looked at the Judgement of Paris and concluded that it provided a basis on which to challenge the contemporary rules of advertising, which did not allow direct comparisons between products. Thus, 'Persil Washes Whiter' and 'Avis, We Try Harder' could not add '…than Daz' or '…than Hertz'. Killeen's theory was that if an acknowledged authority in the particular field said that in his or her *opinion* X was better than Y and Z, this would be acceptable. He and Coca-Cola's advertising company had produced a small advertisement for Taylor California Cellars along these lines with a well-known New York sommelier, and there had been no objection. Now he approached me to ask if I would appear in a comparative tasting/advertisement for TV and newspapers along the same lines. I knew of him and respected the sommelier, so I agreed.

By 1978 the Spurrier brand had expanded well beyond its start-point in the Cité Berryer.

Once the date had been set, the advertising executives appeared in force, accompanied by US documentary filmmakers the Maysles Brothers (in addition to the Maysles' crew, a French crew had to be hired to satisfy the French union system). The tasting room at the Académie was commandeered and Killeen gave me three other brands to compare with the white, red and rosé wines from Taylor California Cellars. My brief was simple: to make a comparison and come out in favour of the Coca-Cola wines… fortunately I had made a genuine comparison and actually did find the Taylor California Cellars wines better. So the cameras rolled and I said: 'Hello, I'm Steven Spurrier, founder of the Académie du Vin in Paris. I've tasted these wines [at which point I named them and gestured to the bottles set out in front of me], and in my view Taylor's California Cellars is the best.' Killeen wanted me to say 'by far the best', but I thought that might be over-egging it.

To show that we really were in Paris, the brothers took endless traffic-stopping shots of me biking past the Café Les Deux Magots, Notre Dame, the Eiffel Tower and so on. I then had to go to New York to do the voice-overs. It was tremendous fun. The ads were shown all across the US and even in Mexico, where my voice was dubbed in a deep Mexican timbre, as opposed to my own 'Oxford English' tones. I was also photographed for print ads, and generally revelled in it all.

The advertising executives were puzzled as to why I wasn't taking advantage of their lavish hospitality offers. I did accept a car in from Kennedy airport, but otherwise generally stayed with friends or at the Knickerbocker Club, which took up a whole block on Fifth Avenue and had a 'swapping arrangement' with my own club in London. On one of my last visits, they queried this and asked what they could do for me. I suggested that they fly me back on Concorde, and the following day I was seated in 1A, a glass of Dom Pérignon in my hand, on the 1pm flight from Kennedy to Paris. I arrived in time to meet Bella for dinner at Le Moulin that evening.

As the decade drew to a close, things were still going well. Christian had enjoyed his first term at boarding school on the Kent coast and Kate was thriving in the French system. Bella was enjoying her English Trading Company and all my wine-based businesses seemed to be going to plan. It had been an amazing adventure since we had arrived in Paris in September 1970, and I had much to be proud of. But by the end of the next decade, things would be very different.

CHAPTER NINE
A NEW DECADE

The 1980s opened quietly, but trouble was already brewing. When we set up in Paris, I told Bella that we would stay about 10 years and then move back to the UK. Our London house near Chelsea's World's End had been sold to invest in the expanding business, but I had no doubt that when it was time to return 'home', something would turn up. In fact, by 1977 this something was already waiting: my father, aware that we would be returning for the children's further education and knowing that we no longer had a London base, offered to finance a house for us. He had set a reasonable budget, but prices had risen steeply while we had been away, so I began looking around in north Clapham.

I was pleased to find a large Georgian house that had been sloppily converted to rent out as a 'rooming house' and was being sold as such with vacant possession. The survey showed that it was in good shape and could easily be converted back into a single residence. My father approved of the house and our plans for it (if not its SW4 postcode), and the deal was signed. As Bella and I were non-residents for tax purposes, we could not own property for our use in the UK, so it stayed in my father's name.

Once re-converted, the house was wonderful, with huge windows, spacious rooms, a separate flat in the very light basement and even a cellar with stone-built bins. It was finished by mid-1977 and I moved some furniture and wines there from storage. After a break-in, however, I asked the architect to find a house-sitter to stay there and make the place look lived-in until we came back. He replied that one of his girlfriends from the distant past had recently gone through a divorce and was looking for a place to live while she re-set her life. She was called Anne; she and I met on one of my quick visits to the UK and I asked her to let my father know that she would be moving in to look after the house. This she did and, and having had a brief conversation with her, my father very correctly offered her a temporary lease. All seemed set fair... but it was not. The very presentable divorcée, now paying a peppercorn rent to live in an expensively converted five-bedroom house, acquired a boyfriend who happened to be a property lawyer. Under the terms of the contract my father had set up, they were legally allowed to stay, and stay they did for the next four years, no matter what measures I took to encourage them to vacate.

The stress of this impasse started to affect my health. I was becoming more and more tense and, although physically fit, I began to have back problems. In early 1980 I seized up: able to walk but not to bend, even an inch. Medical care was so good in Paris that I was not hospitalized, instead I was put on the strongest medication, given a neck brace and prescribed a lengthy course of physiotherapy. As my friend Bob Baker said at the time: 'You should listen to your body, it knows more about you than you do yourself.' I didn't, of course, and plunged back into my role as Steven Spurrier *Marchand de Vin* in an effort to distract myself from my disrupted plans.

My investments in the early and mid-1970s had all made some kind of sense, once one accepts the stupidity of expanding away from one's core base of action. Those in 1979 and 1981 did not. One of my regular suppliers told me of a shop that was coming on the market in the 16th *arrondissement*, owing to the ill-health of the owners. This was *Caves Copernic*, in a not-very-busy street of the same name. There was simply no reason for me to buy it, since residents from that rather snobbish residential part of Paris could order from the Cave and we could deliver, but it was a going concern, the price was not too much and I had extra staff to run it, so I went ahead. I rejuvenated it as a mini wine market, but in this dreary location the shop proved to be a struggle as well as a waste of my time. Finally it had to go.

While I could brush off *Caves Copernic* as an error of judgement, the next venture was a blend of pure folly and fantasy. Le Chemin des Vignes, the vaulted cellars that Lucien Legrand and I had opened together, was going well. Legrand's son Yves was in charge, having taken over from his younger brother. Yves had been on the shop floor at Renault and I could sense that he wasn't on the same wine wavelength as his father, but he was a good manager. Nonetheless, I still began to look around for other storage cellars that could be run as a wholesale warehouse. Curiosity took me to Bercy, behind the Gare de Lyon on the other side of the Seine in the fifth *arrondissement*. Here, there were Victorian warehouses beside wide cobbled streets and 100-year old plane trees creating the atmosphere of a bygone age. This should have been enough to warn me, but the romantic idea of re-creating a true wine centre in the area (it had once been Les Halles aux Vins) was too strong to resist. I took over the lease on a 40 x 20-metre warehouse and moved my entire stock from Le Chemin des Vignes into what became Le Chai Steven Spurrier. Gilbert Winfield, a new recruit to the Cave, was put in charge, the beaten-earth floor cemented over to accommodate a forklift truck, and we opened for business in late 1980.

The following summer, at the marvellous 10th-anniversary party I gave in Cité Berryer, there was a modest Press release that listed my endeavours past, present and future, the last including: (1) Close involvement in the renovation of Bercy to maintain business there and make this Le Centre Parisien du Vin, with fêtes, visits, tastings and wholesale wine warehouses. (2) Opening an Académie du Vin in the centre of New York City.

Sadly, both these exploits were expensive mistakes. My heart was certainly in the right place for Bercy, and the local officials were encouraging – until the mayor of Paris decided to evict everyone in order to build modern blocks of flats. I and one other merchant, Fantin Frères (whom we nicknamed les *Frères Fantômes* / the Ghost Brothers, since their *chai* was always so quiet) held out longer than the others, but it was no good.

Fortunately, a solution was at hand for the delivery and storage of wine stocks, in the form of DIVO-France. This was the small *Défense et Illustration des Vins d'Origine* mail-order company run by Bernard Bourquin, whose uncle Constant had created the original branch in Switzerland. Bernard was spending a lot of time in Canada involved in mining pursuits and had passed the name and the company over to me; I in turn had passed it on to French sommelier Jean-Pierre Civilise, who was using it and his very good palate to supply restaurants in Paris. He was pretty much a one-man band but had storage space, and since I still had shares in the company, he took over that side of things. This worked well at the time.

As far as the Paris businesses were concerned, both Le Bistrot à Vin and Le Moulin du Village were full. Steve Steede was in total charge of the former now, buying the wines directly, with the Cave supplying just a few of the more expensive bottles. I kept control of the list at Le Moulin, although Chuck wanted to go direct.

In late 1979 I had received a visit from the chef, who informed me that because 'le patron' Chuck had his hand in the till, he did not wish to remain there. I said I would look into it, and called David Fromkin in New York to inform him. David said that Chuck would never do this to us. I changed tack and said that the chef was becoming unhappy and would not stay unless 'things were tightened up a little', but this wasn't enough, and the chef left. We replaced him with a young pastry chef from Maxim's named Nick Gill, who turned out to be a real star with a fresh, modern take. He, too, left in due course to run his own restaurant in London based around a menu of several small plates at once, pre-dating the trend for tapas and dim sum.

By now Chuck was married and had a small child, but as far as I could see the family's lifestyle far exceeded anything he could possibly have been earning. I asked Christian Vannequé from La Tour d'Argent, who had been a judge at the Paris Tasting and was a regular lecturer at the Académie, to join Le Moulin, both to up its game and to keep an eye on Chuck. The game was certainly upped: Christian ordered smart shirts with Le Moulin logos and the place became more fashionable at a stroke.

The frustration of not being able to move back to London – that is, of not pursuing my 10-year life plan – was increasingly taking its toll. I was still busy, but was also looking for a change. The Académie was doing well – hardly making any money but then the Cave, despite good sales, low rent and a low wage bill never seemed to make a profit either.

Friends were encouraging me to open a branch in New York, where I thought things might be different. By coincidence I had been contacted by someone who was planning to open a wine school in what seemed to be a closed-down brothel on West 52nd Street, and he had asked me to join him in setting it up and running it. So Bella, Kate and I moved to New York in September, leaving Isabelle Bachelard, then in charge of the Académie, to make sure things were being run properly at Le Moulin. We rented a fine triplex on the ninth floor of an early-1900 building on 28th and Broadway. We had enrolled Kate, then eight years old, in the French Lycée on East 80th Street to continue her French education, but soon after arriving, were persuaded to transfer her to The Fleming School on East 60th, the best (and certainly the most expensive) prep school in the city. The decision to turn down an excellent, if strict, education in favour of an unknown one was to discombobulate Kate's future schooling for some years, but that was only one of the many horrendous mistakes I was to make. Owing to another prima donna decision of unbelievable short-sightedness, not long after settling in I decided to turn down the offer for gainful employment on 52nd Street, and to set up my own wine school instead in the basement of Lavin's Restaurant. This would end badly.

The worst episode of all, which only by a miracle did not turn out to be fatal, concerned Christian. We had spent Christmas in the UK and he had returned with us to New York for the rest of the holidays. It was his first visit to New York and he was, at almost 11 years old, very excited. He had had a cold when he left and after a few days this got much worse and he started to complain of splitting head-aches. We had a marvellous doctor for Kate, an ancient lady from Eastern Europe, who took one look at him and dispatched him immediately in an ambulance to one of the city hospitals. Apparently the pressure on the flight over had pushed all the mucus from his cold up behind his eyes and into his brain. If we had left it one more day he would have risked severe, possibly fatal, brain damage. Specialists set to work and for a week he was in intensive care. It was two months before he was well enough to be discharged and returned to school. As if in sympathy for Christian, the day after he went into hospital, Kate contracted scarlet fever.

While we were in New York, Bella took up camera work again, this time with Margaret Hunnewell, one of David Fromkin's friends from a grand Boston family who was making short advertising films. There were some good times in the US, especially a weekend spent with Bob Haas of Vineyard Brands and his wife Barbara at their place in Vermont in October, when the famous fall colours were at their peak; Thanksgiving with Digby Bridges (whose bushy eyebrows had given our Briard sheepdog his name) and his wife in Key West in Florida; and a short visit to California when we stayed at the Jordan Winery. My friend Melvyn Master was in charge of the launch of their iconic Cabernet Sauvignon. Then there was a fancy-dress party given by Michael Aaron of the Madison Avenue wine merchants Sherry Lehmann, the theme being 'famous couples'. Michael in a gorilla suit went as King Kong with his wife as Fay Wray, and the tall and imposing Peter Morrell of Morrell Wines and Spirits and his equally tall and imposing wife went as Tsar Nicholas and Tsarina Alexandra of Russia. Bella wore a long 1930s dress and a string of fake pearls, and with me in a double-breasted cream suit, a wide knot in my tie and slicked-down hair, we were recognized as Mrs Simpson and the Duke of Windsor.

Competition from the 52nd Street wine venture contributed to the ultimate demise of the New York Académie du Vin, which closed its doors by the end of June. Bella and Kate returned to London, our squatters having at last vacated our house in Rectory Grove. My last appearance on American soil that year was at a Society of Wine Educators Symposium on Rhode Island, where I was one of the lead speakers on 'How to be successful in Wine Education'. *Quelle ironie.*

I went back to Paris, where Isabelle had made a fine job of managing the school. She had also kept a tighter rein on purchases than I had at the Cave (something I was immediately to reverse), but she was concerned about Le Moulin, which was slow in paying its suppliers – including the Cave. She said that she couldn't control what went on there, but was certain that things weren't right. I had been too weak to confront Chuck directly, but by now had totally lost confidence in him. David agreed that I should do what I thought best. I approached Christian first, who astounded me by saying that 'a little had been taken off the top, as always happens in the restaurant business'. To my shocked question: 'Where is your sense of honour?', he replied '*Je m'assieds dessus*' / I'm sitting on it. Very French. I relayed this to Bella who, exasperated, said I should have sacked Chuck ages ago and that if I didn't do it now, she wouldn't stick around much longer.

The following week I confronted both Chuck and Christian, and told them I would have a professional accountant from the Restaurant Association go over the books for the last two years (it turned out that Le Moulin's part-time accountant was also in on the game), and they would have to face the consequences. Within

Tenth-anniversary celebrations. In front: Michel Dovaz, Muriel de Potex; standing: Me, Jon Winroth, Isabelle Bachelard, Patricia Gallagher, Christopher Mitchell-Heggs, Mme Fougères, Mauricette and friend; behind Mauricette: Doreen Winroth.

And the party gets going: *left*: artist Anthony Palliser, who first introduced me to the connoisseur and some-time sculptor Michael Goldman (*centre*); *right*: top taster Martin Bamford MW of Château Loudenne assesses the refreshments.

a week all three were gone, but not before Chuck had pocketed the takings on the last day and, having a key to the Cave in case the restaurant was short of anything, cleaned out my till on his way out. The hole in the final accounts was horrendous, and the company faced a *dépôt de bilan* / bankruptcy, as neither the VAT nor the rent had been paid for some time. My accountant advised me to take this route, but I had the crazy idea that debts should be honoured, so I bought out David Fromkin at a low rate and carried on with a new team. They were at least honest, but the early spark had gone, and Le Moulin reverted to its rather lacklustre former self.

The Cave's 10th anniversary was approaching and we set about planning a celebration. It was due to take place on June 18th – I did not realize that that was the date in 1940 when Général de Gaulle had given his rallying speech to France from London until Jean-Claude Vrinat of Taillevent replied that he was 'happy to accept *l'appel du 18 juin*'. Long tables were arranged outside both the Cave and the Académie to show 63 of my favourite wines and a few bottles of 1981 Gewürztraminer from Nobilo Vintners in New Zealand that Drew Harré had sourced (her brother worked there). Thanks to the Paris Tasting, California and New World wines were now becoming known in Paris, and, of course, the vintage in NZ is in the spring. Being able to show Parisians a 1981 wine in June of that year was quite a coup. The *charcutier-traiteur* / butcher-caterer opposite, Albert Lucas, provided a splendid buffet, the weather was perfect and the evening truly memorable. it marked the peak of what my life in Cité Berryer had achieved. But in the archives there is a photograph of me talking to my anxious-looking bank manager, to whom I would give increasing concern as the decade wore on.

CHAPTER TEN
BETWEEN LONDON AND PARIS

Fourteen-and-a-half years after we left England for a new life in France, we were back on home turf. The only concession our tenacious London 'tenants' had made was to release the basement flat to our old friend David Langlands. David had a brilliant brain: he had won a scholarship to Winchester and passed the exams effortlessly to Trinity College, Cambridge, which is where I met him on one of my visits. He passed the time following horse racing, about which he knew everything; taking his Staffordshire Bull Terriers – first Fred, then Boswell and finally Montrose – for walks, and drinking. He could quote whole passages from Shakespeare and the classic Scottish authors from memory and was unfailingly charming, but 9pm was about his cut-off point.

Once we had regained possession of the house, David and Fred the dog moved upstairs into the main part where there was plenty of room, allowing us to sub-let the basement, and over the rest of the summer we moved in. I was still commuting from Paris, but with Christian and Kate settled in their schools, I was ready for a new challenge. Happily, this had already been proposed by Michael Broadbent in a letter he wrote to me on New Year's Day 1982:

> Dear Steven
> An idea:
> I somehow heard that, despite your New York flirtation, the fading charms of Paris were turning your thoughts again to London.

It occurred to me last night that you might just be interested in setting up and running an academy of wine in conjunction with the Christie's Fine Arts Course which operates successfully from excellent premises tucked behind Christie's South Kensington in the Old Brompton Road.

For some years I have toyed with the idea of running high-grade lectures on wine, but the pace I have set myself is finally coming home to roost and I now intend to reduce my commitments despite the endless temptations. Nevertheless, I am sure my original idea would work.

As the Wine & Spirit Education Trust does such a comprehensive job I think that whatever we do should complement and extend those activities, but with far more emphasis on keen amateurs, company executives – moreover with some courses concentrated in time and of the highest level, to attract overseas students.

I would of course take part and, again for some time, have had the intention of mounting 'Michael Broadbent's Masterclasses' (rather pompous, but meaningful and would sell in the right quarters).

Any interest?

Yours

Michael

How could I not be interested? Of course I jumped at the chance, and during my visits to London later that year I met Michael to discuss format and content and with Robert Cumming, director of the Fine Arts Course, to see how we could fit in. It was all so simple: the arts course terms were 10 weeks long, during which the premises were fully staffed. There were occasional evening courses, but Tuesday evenings were always free. The Tour de France course at the Académie was a six-week course which would not be difficult to compress into five, so we could offer two courses a term, six a year, with the occasional extra evening for masterclasses.

The five sessions were to cover Alsace and the Loire Valley, Bordeaux, Burgundy, the Rhône Valley and Provence, champagne and sweet and fortified wines. The premises were superb: a large, well-lit room that could accommodate 45 students and three student helpers, and there was more-than-adequate storage for wine and for the 400 INAO tasting glasses needed for each session.

On October 5th 1982 – my 41st birthday – Robert introduced the Christie's Wine Course, the first session to be taught by Michael, with me in attendance. Thirty years later in 2012, after 150 courses and a good many masterclasses, I introduced Michael to take the first session of our three-decade anniversary. Michael was by then a very sprightly 85 years old.

In Paris, we had a different session most evenings and the students were taught by the same *prof* throughout the course, but at Christie's I proposed that each session be taken by somebody different. The roll-call of lecturers was impressive. From the beginning we were able to take the pick of the Masters of Wine; throughout the course's history it was taught almost entirely by MWs, the exceptions being Hugh Johnson and Pamela Vandyke-Price, both prolific authors on wine, and me. In the early days we had David Peppercorn and Serena Sutcliffe, known as the 'Peppercliffs', who were the first husband-and-wife team both to earn the MW qualification, Serena being only the second woman ever to hold it. They taught with us until Serena was named Head of Sotheby's Wine Department and opted to launch her own course.

The ebullient Christopher Tatham, main buyer for The Wine Society was another lecturer. Christopher, known as 'Monsieur Tat-tam' throughout the French vineyards, had endeared himself to me by remarking, while wrapping up his positive description of Vincent Delaporte's excellent Sancerre: 'Gosh, I do love wine!' For many years we also had Clive Coates MW, another prolific author and owner of Laytons; Remington Norman, author of definitive books on Burgundy and the Rhône Valley, whose private cellar was one of the greatest ever sold at Christie's in the late 1980s; and in more recent years Jasper Morris, Peter McCombie and Nancy Gilchrist, who took over the running of the course from me in 2013.

From the start, the Wine Course, or Christie's Education as it became, was a great success. The Fine Arts Course took a comfortable fee for rental of the room and staff costs; the lecturers were adequately paid and if they had books to sell, had ready takers. The wine merchants realized that it was good to have wine lovers actually pay to taste their wines, so they offered us a low price and lots of helpful information. Student helpers were queuing up to set up the room, serve the wines and clear up afterwards. I was there every Tuesday evening to introduce the lecturer, taking one of the five evenings myself, and then I left for Paris on the first flight the following morning, returning for the weekend. Much like the Académie, we were the only non-trade course available for many years, and we had good support from the London merchants who often enrolled their own staff because our lecturers were so highly regarded. Johnny Goedhuis of Goedhuis & Co booked in his wife and a couple of her friends on one course. They sat right at the back so they could exchange whispered remarks about the wines. I was on the burgundy session this time and, explaining the system in the Côte d'Or whereby the name of the village adds the name of its most famous wine to bolster its image, the village of Gevrey thus becoming Gevrey-Chambertin, I illustrated by saying that 'if you were just called Smith and you married a Bingham, you might call yourself Smith-Bingham'. This produced hoots of laughter from the back row, since unbeknown to me Mrs Goedhuis was indeed a Smith-Bingham.

The Fine Arts Course had never made a profit but the Wine Course put it into the black. I had a share in the net gains and have to confess that, when things went so badly wrong at the end of the decade, it was one of my few remaining sources of income. But more to the point, it worked for all the right reasons and was something to be very proud of.

Back in Paris, things were under control. Mark Williamson had left in 1980 to open a wine bar, which he had planned to call 'McCready's' after a wine-loving ancestor. I told him that this would mean nothing to Parisians, but that Colette's husband, 'Monsieur Willy', had lived just next door in the Palais Royale, and suggested Mark should play on that, allied with his own name. (Colette, author of *Gigi* and *The Tendrils of the Vine*, was married to author Henry Gauthier-Villars who used the pen name 'Willy'.) Mark offered me a half-share in the new venture, 'Willi's', at a modest price and I replied that if I took this up he would never escape me, but I did agree to supply him with wine on easy terms until he was properly up and running. This was another of my commercial mistakes – but it was made for the right reasons.

Isabelle was still in charge of the day-to-day running of the Académie. Because of my commitments with Christie's and a small export business I had built up, I had hired a new staff member for the office upstairs, but the shop was still staffed by Mauricette and a manager. When President Mitterand began to nationalize the finance industry, many of Cave's banking clients left for New York,

Frankfurt or London. IBM moved its vast offices from the Rue Boissy d'Anglas to La Défense, and while this may have brought more clients to Le Bistrot à Vin, it left fewer needing the Cave's wine supplies. I didn't immediately realize, since there seemed to be so much going on, that the shop's peak time had passed and would not return.

As I was in London during the first half of each week, I accepted a request from Graham Chidgey of Laytons that I oversee the Malmaison Wine Club. Since leaving school, Graham had worked for Tommy Layton at his shop/cellar/tasting room, and had bought the business in 1965. When we met, he had long been installed in vast railway arches in Midland Road below St Pancras Station.

I had heard of Laytons' classical yet innovative wine selections, based on quality and value for money, and was impressed by Graham's creative approach to wine buying. I shared that, but not his hard-headed business sense. He had recently absorbed the huge stocks built up by Clive Coates as a wine investment for the British Rail Pension Fund, and had created the Malmaison Wine Club to offer the wines on a retail / mail order basis. My experience of the London Wine Trade having till then been fairly limited, I found it fascinating to be part of the real thing. James Radcliffe, one of my co-trainees, was Laytons' top salesman and took over when Graham sold up in 1997 and moved away to Tuscany. Many of the people passing through Laytons in the three years I was there are now top of their respective professions, and I learnt a lot in what was very much a changing world.

In 1981 I received a visit from Ueli Prager, the founder and major shareholder of Mövenpick, a chain of fast-food restaurants that was becoming a big player in the wine world, especially in Bordeaux. Prager, an intelligent and charming man about 10 years my senior, had had the inspiration for Mövenpick while walking around the lake in his home town of Lausanne. He had watched office workers on their lunch breaks sitting by the edge of the lake, and figured that if he opened a café conveniently situated so that they could dash in and have a quick bite before going back to the office, it would work. It did, with huge success, attracting all kinds of clients. The concept evolved quickly from fast food to casual and then to sophisticated dining. This is where I came in – on the wine side – becoming a partner in the venture. Until then wine tastings, if they took place at all in Geneva, were always behind closed doors.

In Paris, the Cave was by now being managed by James Lawther, who had started with me as delivery boy/van driver and was the best pair of hands I've ever had. He went on to greater things, becoming a Master of Wine and moving to Bordeaux. Isabelle was also managing the Académie courses well, but it was Patricia who created the extraordinary annual tasting-dinners we held from 1982 to 1985 at Gaston Le Nôtre's Michelin-starred Le Pré Catalan in the Bois de Boulogne. The inspiration was *le Baptême du Millésime* / the baptism of the vintage, that focused on wines from top Bordeaux châteaux one year after the vintage. By then the final blend is well and truly made, and the wines destined to be bottled the following summer.

For many years, the Union des Grands Crus de Bordeaux (UGC) had held tastings around the world for the vintage once it was in bottle, but in the early 1980s they had not thought to take their show on the road pre-bottling. Our dinner was preceded by a tasting of perhaps 30 wines, then six or seven from much older vintages were served, the owners always there to present them. They were black-tie events, fittingly formal for the wines, food and august surroundings. The guest list grew to 120 on 12 tables, a château owner or member of the Académie on each table. Menus were set out as a 12-page booklet with full descriptions of the young and older vintages. At the 1983 dinner we welcomed the owners of Champagne Gosset, Châteaux Laville Haut-Brion, Haut-Bailly, Léoville Barton, Gazin, Figeac, Léoville Las Cases and d'Yquem, also Domaine Boingnères from Armagnac.

These were great evenings of a kind I would not have been able to hold in London. However, we did hold a Baptism of the Vintage at Christie's for the 1981–84 vintages and had planned to launch the very good 1985s, but the 10th-anniversary re-match of the Paris Tasting in New York in summer 1986 saw the California wines do even better against the Bordeaux crus classés, and the publicity that this attracted across the US annoyed the UGC so much that they refused to take part.

The Académie was in good health despite the failure in New York, and we had associate schools in both Switzerland and Canada. The Canada branch was in Montreal, where British lawyer Alan Mills and his French-Canadian wife Louise had converted the first floor of their house in the old part of the city into a tasting room. I visited in the summer of 1982 and made at least one visit a year thereafter. Young Bartholomew Broadbent (Michael's son) moved to Toronto in 1983 and opened a branch of the Académie the following year, holding tastings of Lafite Rothschild, d'Yquem and – with me as co-host – the first ever vertical tasting outside the USA of Opus One. When Bartholomew moved to San Francisco three years later, the Académie's management was taken over by wine lover and businessman Marc Nadeau, who immersed himself into the role, nurturing Canada's position on the global wine stage. He has since introduced many winemakers, wine lovers and personalities to the Niagara and Okanagan Valley regions.

The premises next door to Le Moulin housed a seedy-looking furrier business called *Le Renard Bleu*. No business seemed to take place there and it eventually closed its doors late in 1982. I thought I would liven up Le Moulin a little by taking it over and turning it into a wine bar, offering simpler food but the same wine list. It was separated from Le Moulin by an archway, but the first floor above the arch could be annexed with the first floor of the restaurant, adding much-needed space. Mary Blume, whose interviews with people in or passing through Paris appeared in the Saturday *Trib*, suggested we call it The Blue Fox, a simple translation of its previous name.

There were many cafés, large expensive ones and smaller simple ones, around the Place de la Madeleine, but we opened with a bang and were always popular. *Rendez-vous au Fox* / Let's meet in the Fox becoming a familiar local refrain. At first it was run by Tim Johnston, who had previously managed a vineyard in Provence, but he left to join Mark Williamson at Willi's and then opened his own place, Juveniles, around the corner in the Rue de Richelieu. Then, the Bistrot à Vin having been sold, Steve Steede took over. At lunch our main clients were young women from Hermès and other boutiques on the Faubourg St-Honoré, who loved the food but didn't order wine. My solution was to offer a glass of wine to match the plat du jour at a modest extra price, which went down well and sometimes a second glass was ordered. Le Fox was fun, but it never made much of a dent in Le Moulin's pile of debt.

My next venture was to turn myself into a writer. For this I owe thanks to Clare Howell, a perfect example of the English bluestocking at its best: erudite, cultured and charming. In 1981 she had taken a short course at the Académie du

Vin, seen the Cave at work and told me quite directly that what we were doing should be turned into a book. She was not a publisher but a packager, someone who thinks of an idea for a book and finds someone to write it, secures a publisher, then puts the together the book for the publisher. Her partner in the then-fledgling venture, Quintet Publishing, was Robert Adkinson, and they were both wonderful to work with. Only when deadlines loomed did they show a certain strictness. I remember that for the final version of the *Académie du Vin Guide to French Wines*, which had been accepted by the UK's top wine-book publisher Mitchell Beazley, they insisted I spend the last 10 days in their offices in Soho to be sure that the manuscript would be finished on time. I agreed, so long as they would fund my lunch every day at l'Escargot, a wonderful place that had recently been re-vamped by restaurateur Nick Lander, and they agreed.

The next book, *Académie du Vin: La Dégustation / Wine Course* came out simultaneously in French and English in 1983. Michel Dovaz, our head lecturer at the Académie for some years, covered vinification and many of the regional profiles, and his then-partner Muriel de Potex wrote the wine-with-food chapters. Ian Jamieson MW contributed the profile on Germany, Fenella Pearson that on Italy and my friend Geoffrey Roberts on California, Australia and New Zealand. This was the first 'How To' book since Michael Broadbent's *Wine Tasting*, which had inspired my wine teaching career in the first place, and Michael kindly agreed to write the introduction. The book, which I am immensely proud of, was re-issued many times, translated into several languages including Japanese, sold more than 150,000 copies and was the handbook for many future Masters of Wine and Master Sommeliers including Gerard Basset OBE MS MW.

The work after that – the one I most enjoyed writing – was a 175-page handbook called *Guide des Vins Régionaux de France* / French Country Wines, published in 1984. From my early days in Paris I had seen the sea of *vin ordinaire* slowly replaced by *vins de pays*, literally 'country wines' and, for people wishing to upgrade a little, the *vins délimités de qualité supérieure* (VDQS) led up to the highest level of wines at *Appellation d'Origine Contrôlée* (AC). I defined a country wine as wine drunk by locals and tourists where it is made, which has certain defined regional characteristics and is not too sophisticated or expensive. A country wine is not always cheap, but should be considered everyday wine at some level. So St-Emilion is a country wine, but grands crus classés St-Emilions are not. Champagne is also drunk by locals and tourists in massive quantities, but the image that champagne producers had built up for it excluded it from the book.

Throughout the 1970s I had travelled to every wine region in France, I sold many of the wines in the Cave and knew most of the rest by name. To get the facts right, I surrounded myself with all the reference books from the Académie's extensive library. Hugh Johnson wrote the foreword, quoting at the end that 'the scene Steven has mastered so thoroughly has not been a static one… over the last 10 years the backwaters of French wine have been bootstrapping themselves into official and unofficial notice. Vastly improved technology has been stimulated by foreign competition to raise standards at a rate nobody believed possible. And who was it who orchestrated the foreign competition, bringing France's best names face to face with California's best wines? It was Steven Spurrier, and I bet it has postponed his Légion d'Honneur by a good few years.'

The fourth book, *Les Vins Fins Français* / French Fine Wines, was a companion volume to *French Country Wines*. In it I say that a fine wine may be described briefly as 'a wine of quality', but Hugh later offered a better definition, that a fine wine is a wine 'worth talking about'. The aim of this book was to list the better French wines by appellation and by region (adding those which in my view had potential quality), describing their tastes and characteristics and listing the finer producers. This book, like *French Country Wines*, could therefore be used both as a source of information and as a buyer's guide. The two handbooks were merged in 1985 to become the *Académie du Vin Guide to French Wines*.

The early editions were such a success that Clare and Robert persuaded me to write the Académie's *Wine Cellar Book*. The final book from this burst of writing – five books in three years – was a joint effort with American Joseph Ward entitled *How To Buy Fine Wine*. Ward was at that time based in London and wrote about fine wines and wine investment for *The Wall Street Journal*. The preface was, of course, by Michael Broadbent. Many of the producers from around the world whom we recommended are still, one or two generations later, the same names we would recommend today.

I was still travelling to California once a year, and in September 1983 was asked to be a judge at the Sonoma County Wine Fair, the first of scores of judging positions I undertook over the years. Before it started I was invited once again to Jordan Winery, where Melvyn Master was in charge of marketing. On the way I decided to call in at Grgich Hills, the winery that Mike Grgich had set up with Austin Hills. I pushed open the large oak door to the barrel cellar and there was Mike, one of the great heroes of California wine history, telling a group about the Paris Tasting. As he mentioned my name he saw me at the door and was so surprised that he even took off his signature blue beret.

Melvyn had told me that since Jordan was near to Healdsburg north of Sonoma, I should drive to the local bar and wait for him there. I found it easily and at the appointed time swung open the doors to find myself in a saloon from an early 1950s Western: dark and smoky, full of tall, burly men in big boots and Stetsons. I was smartly turned out in a suit, as usual. I moved to a corner of the bar near the doors and felt I ought to order something manly, so went for a Jack Daniels on the rocks. As it was served, two of these huge men approached me and stood uncomfortably close, one on either side. One asked me what 'a city fella' like me was doing in their bar. Without thinking, I replied that I'd come there 'to get picked up'. Luckily Melvyn and his friends, like the cavalry coming over the hill, chose that moment to burst in through the doors.

I made my first trip to Australia in May 1985, flying to Melbourne where there was a vibrant wine scene headed up by James Halliday, an outstanding wine writer and founder of the great Coldstream Hills Winery in the Yarra Valley. I had gone out with the idea of opening a branch of the Académie, but by the time I got there, the two potential partners in the venture had already fallen out. I still co-hosted the planned tastings and, more importantly, spent time with James at Yalumba, owned by the Hill-Smith family.

I had already met the senior of the two cousins, Robert Hill-Smith, in Paris. He was very much into horses, and a regular at le Prix de l'Arc de Triomphe at the Longchamp racecourse on the edge of the Bois de Boulogne. The Prix was the final flat race of the season, held on the first Sunday in October. Since my birthday is on the 5th, it was always a good excuse to give a cocktail party for friends and visitors the evening before, and to set up on the grass on the 'common' side of the course for a picnic during the day. Robert, whom I first encountered at the course, would often join us. He introduced me to his cousin Michael, who the following year was to come to London for the final period of study to emerge as Australia's first Master of Wine, and whom I was to see much more of in the future.

Most of the Australian wines I tasted in Melbourne were good, but on the robust and rich side. In the mid-1980s it was only forward-looking merchants such as Averys of Bristol who were importing from specific growers. The Australian Wine Centre in Soho did little to show what was going on and nobody was prepared for Australia's dramatic arrival on the UK wine scene just a few years later, virtually taking it over by the end of the 1990s. The excursions I made during the full week I spent there would barely have scratched on the surface.

During the summer I had been introduced to Terry Dunleavy, an indefatigable supporter of the nascent New Zealand wine industry. He invited me to be a judge on the New Zealand Wine Competition he chaired. Flying into Auckland via Los Angeles in late October (their spring) was a long haul, but worth it to be taken to the Brajkovich family's Kumeu River estate outside the capital. I tasted their Chardonnays which did – and still do – beat many a premier cru from Burgundy.

We then drove down to the middle of the North Island to The Chateau, a vast pile of a hotel below an extinct volcano, where the tasting was to be held over three days. Apart from the Nobilo 1981 Gewürztraminer that I had presented at the Cave's 10th-anniversary party, New Zealand wines were new to me. As usual, John Avery had been the first merchant to import New Zealand wines to the UK, in the mid-1970s.

Terry had gathered a panel of the country's top wine people. One of my favourite wine books is *The Wines and Vineyards of New Zealand* by Michael Cooper, which the author presented to me, signed by all my fellow judges, as a memento of the competition. Its early modern history notes that in 1960 there were only 387 hectares planted, but by late 1972 this had expanded to nearly 6,000. (By 2020 the producing area was 39,935 hectares.) There is a full-page photograph of legendary wine writer André Simon looking deeply unimpressed by a sample of dessert wine tasted during his tour in 1964 – Simon noted later that 'most of the dessert wines lacked any trace of bouquet or breed'.

Things had certainly improved two decades later, for of the 662 wines judged, 31 were awarded Gold, 136 Silver and 231 Bronze medals. Apart from the

Gault & Millau Olympiades du Vin in 1979, this was the first 'team judging' I had attended. It was rigorously organized but relaxed, and I could not have learnt more nor had a better time.

Jean-Marie Picard was an amusing, artistic type who ran his Paris wine bar and shop, Le Petit Bacchus, very much as a 'salon'. I spent many enjoyable times there. In 1985 Jean-Marie said he was off to open a hotel and restaurant near to Tricastin in the Rhône Valley, and he offered me his shop at a reasonable price based on its turnover and location. I accepted, and in September moved my wines in – we had many suppliers in common – keeping the name, but adding 'Spurrier Rive Gauche'.

Le Petit Bacchus was right at the start of the Rue du Cherche-Midi in the sixth *arrondissement*. This was a smart residential neighbourhood with many attractive little clothes, shoes and perfume shops, but most importantly it was right opposite Poilâne, Paris's most talked-about bakery. The only inconvenience was that it was in a narrow one-way street, and if a car halted to collect a loaf of bread, it stopped the traffic. Père Poilâne, as he was known, had created a round sourdough loaf or *miche* with a dusting of flour on top called le Pain Poilâne, which even by then was famous enough to be a registered description in the French language.

An astute businessman, Père Poilâne personally delivered his bread to Maxim's in the Rue Royale, making sure photographers were there to see him carrying in the loaves piled on top of each other, and emerging with his work apron covered in flour. His younger son Lionel was even more astute and took this to an international level. I am very happy to say I was responsible for his opening in Elizabeth Street in Belgravia in the early 2000s. Jon Winroth had introduced us, and kept telling Lionel that he really must open in London. I heard of premises coming up for sale and told Lionel that they would be perfect for him, as cars could double-park on both sides of the street. After due diligence with the Grosvenor Estate, London's wealthiest landlords, permission was granted for bread ovens to be built in the basement, and I was there for the official lighting of the fires.

When I left Paris, Lionel presented me with a facsimile of the rectangular blue, white and green plaques that signpost every street and square in the city, emblazoned with 'Passage Steven Spurrier', to remind me of the days when I occupied much of the sunny side of la Cité Berryer.

Always on the look-out for something new in the wine world, I became interested in an opened-wine-bottle sealing system. The owner of a château in Entre-Deux-Mers had invented a system called Le Cruover. This kept multiple opened bottles under argon gas so that wine poured a week or so after the bottle had first been opened would be as fresh as the first glass had been. The system has now been perfected under the name of Enoteca and today no wine shop or wine bar can be without one (the Coravin system, which is used on single bottles, is better for private cellars). David Langlands, our lodger in Rectory Grove, had been a restaurant critic for Egon Ronay and knew the London scene well. He suggested that if I were to import Cruovers, he could sell them to restaurants. A modest uptake soon got us into the Savoy, into David Levin's new bar Le Metro near Harrods and a few other places, but the orders were not followed up, and before long I relinquished the importing contract.

It was thanks to David that I began to write my first series of articles on wine. An old friend of his, Simon Courtauld, had recently been made editor of *The Field*; David took over the restaurant column and suggested me for the wine. As I remember my columns were bi-monthly, and from February 1985 to December 1987 my diary is full of increasingly urgent '*Field* article!' reminders. By 1987 I was also wine correspondent for *Tatler*. My pieces mostly reported on trips I had made, people I had met and wonderful tastings I had attended. I was happy to write them, but the work was an additional distraction from the core business of selling wine in Cité Berryer. A further note in my 1985 diary, on the spread dedicated to financial planning, managing overdrafts and so on, is underlined in red: 'Essential no more cash goes out of Vins Fins!' (my holding company). This was a pious hope.

In summer 1986 I was in California at the time of the Napa Valley Wine Auction. Michael Broadbent, as auctioneer, said that I should attend this lavish affair, and gave my name to the organizers. When I turned up and asked for my ticket, they asked me my profession to add it to my badge. I replied 'wine merchant', which would have been fine had I been a US merchant, but a merchant from France didn't cut the mustard. My second choice was 'wine writer' which went better, plus I was now 'Press', which qualified me for a limousine and a driver, lunch at a winery, front seats at the auction and a drive home.

The lunch was at Phelps Winery. I had already met Joe Phelps, one of the pioneers from the early 1970s, and he had just launched his Cabernet Sauvignon 'Insignia' to instant acclaim. The auction, held under vast marquees, was full of drama and excitement and the wines fetched some astronomically high prices. When afterwards my limousine arrived to pick me up, I noticed Robert Mondavi and his wife Margrit waiting for a shuttle bus to take them to the parking lot. I of course offered them a lift and much enjoyed their company for the short ride, afterwards reflecting on the enormous advantages of being a member of the Press.

By now Pamela Vandyke-Price, the doyenne of British wine writing, had proposed me for membership of the Circle of Wine Writers, founded in 1962 by Cyril Ray. In time I was to serve two terms as chairman and two as president (following Hugh Johnson), and watch it grow from a bunch of cheerful 'scribblers' to an important organization with members worldwide.

Cyril Ray was a splendid character who had a brilliant, puckish sense of humour. He was also a committed champagne socialist, living in the Albany Hotel when in London, and in a large house in Brighton when not. He was an habitué of many of the best clubs – he sometimes lunched as my guest at Boodle's – but his left-wing views, nurtured since his time at Manchester Grammar School, remained firmly embedded. For many years he wrote a wine column for *Punch*; he also wrote many wine books. The Circle of Wine Writers hosts the annual Cyril Ray Lunch in his memory. An extra attraction for me was his love of limericks: he produced in 1979 *Lickerish Limericks*, which was considered quite risqué at the time, but which I found highly amusing.

David Campbell, publishing director at Hachette, asked the Paris Académie to oversee many of the tastings for the first edition of *le Guide Hachette des Vins*. This was flattering, though it amused me to dig out from my files a proposal for a wine guide that I had presented a few years earlier to the editor of the *Guides Bleus*. The format of the *Guide Hachette* was much the same as I had suggested – it could hardly have been otherwise – but at that time of my proposal, there had been little interest.

The Académie du Vin had one or two Japanese students, the Japanese Embassy being nearby in the Rue du Faubourg St-Honoré. One of these students, Mr Yasuhisa Hirose, went on to open the Enoteca wine shops (unrelated to

Frank J Prial and I discuss matters of moment over lunch at Le Moulin in 1987.

Enoteca open-bottle stoppers) in Tokyo, and one of our former clients at the Cave, Mrs Fumiko Arisaka, founded *Vinothèque*, Japan's first specialized wine magazine. She asked me to host some tastings for her friends, suggesting the connection could perhaps develop into a branch of the Académie, so on April 7th I boarded an overnight flight to Tokyo for a week of total immersion in a culture about which I knew nothing, but which I have appreciated ever since.

My hosts owned a lovely old building in the historic part of the city where up-market tastings were held under the supervision of sommelier Mr Kimura. I was introduced to sake and taken to the best restaurants. At one, the speciality was Kobe beef, which comes from the Tajima strain of Japanese Black cattle. The meat is a delicacy, highly prized for its flavour, tenderness and texture. A young translator was present and I asked how much my dish cost, since there were no prices on the menu. 'About a month's salary,' came the reply.

Arrangements were soon made for a school to be opened, and I am happy to say that in September 2017 I co-hosted a reception for its 30th anniversary, which featured eight wines selected from my favourite producers at that time. We celebrated three decades of continuous wine education, which had grown to four schools in Japan: two in Tokyo, one in Osaka and one in Nagoya.

By now Bella and I had decided it was time for a move to the country. Neither of us wanted to go back 'up north' to Derbyshire, nor did we want to live in the crowded commuter counties in the southeast, so that left us with the southwest. Michael Broadbent's wife Daphne, a great organizer, brought her considerable expertise to bear on the matter and told us that since I needed a base in London this should be Baron's Court, which was convenient for Heathrow Airport; and since we wanted a place in the country, we should call her and Michael's friend Micky Caruth who lived in south Dorset, because he might soon be selling his house there. We duly called, but Micky told us he wasn't intending to move just yet, so we spent some time hunting around.

We hadn't found anything by the time Micky got back in touch two years later, so we went to visit. For me it was perfect: a classic early-Victorian building with large rooms, a proper cellar and a pleasant garden. It wasn't quite right for Bella as there was no land for the horses she planned to ride, but we were told that there was a farm for sale on the edge of the village which could remedy that problem. This turned out to be an 80-hectare sheep farm with steep slopes and marvellous views to the sea just four miles away. Negotiations for both properties were successful, and on July 6th 1987 one large removal van set off from Rectory Grove to south Dorset, and a smaller one to Queen's Club Gardens in Baron's Court. Daphne had been spot on, and the Spurrier luck, so helpful in the 1970s, had come up trumps again.

CHAPTER ELEVEN
AU REVOIR PARIS

Back in Paris, sommelier Jean-Pierre Civilise who had been organizing delivery and storage of my wine stocks at DIVO-France said he no longer had room to handle my reserve stocks, and asked me to look elsewhere. I found space via Jean-Pierre Bloud, who had started up in Paris selling direct from a warehouse the year before I took over the Cave. Our paths had crossed from time to time in Paris and occasionally in Beaujolais, where his mother owned Château du Moulin-à-Vent. By that time, he was working out of a converted apple-storage warehouse in Feucherolles, one of the smart, leafy suburbs west of Paris. He was retiring from direct selling, had heard I was looking for space, and offered to sell me the business. The price seemed fair so we did the deal and I moved my stocks over before Paris went quiet in August, asking the reliable Steve Steede from Le Moulin to run things there.

Once installed, we realized that M Bloud had retained his business telephone line and so was continuing some sort of commerce from the premises, but the warehouse was just what I thought we needed and, under Steve's direction, 'Spurrier Distribution' seemed set fair.

I had never proposed Bordeaux 'futures' (buying the wine En Primeur, 12 months before bottling) at the Cave and, while not being as critical towards the 1982s as Robert Finigan was, neither did I see their fantastic future as clearly as Robert Parker did. The 1983s were also good, especially in Margaux; the 1984s were dull and hard, but the 1985s were very good, volumes were high and prices reasonable. It was the 1985s that changed my mind: I began to understand that the En Primeur system was quite simply an invitation to the buyer to 'get in early at a good price, and if you sell later, make a profit on the way out'. Having space in the new warehouse also made it a feasible proposition.

Spurrier Distribution was very successful with the 1985s, from little-known but attractive Médocs, Graves and St-Emilions, right up to the crus classés, and by mid-summer 1987 these were all in bottle and needed to be stored in customers' reserves. I had also tasted a wide range of 1986s at Vinexpo in June 1987 – there wasn't such a rush for prices to come out in those days – and had already sold on quite a few of those. Although the volumes of everyday wines being made were substantially lower in the 1970s than they had been in previous years, finer wines from Burgundy and even the Rhône had to be purchased on release from the estates, so storage was necessary.

By now the number of grand cellars with wines to be packed up and sold in London had dwindled to the extent that my Christie's contract as their Paris agent was cancelled. It had been a fascinating association and very profitable: I or my staff could charge a 'per diem' for the work and my office shared in the commission. The kinds of cellars I had been involved with ranged from those of superb restaurants such as Darroze, Le Coq Hardi and both Pruniers in Paris, to converted garages in the suburbs and grand townhouses in the centre of Paris, where white-gloved butlers would hover, pretending to assist. The cellar of one such 'hôtel particulier' consisted mainly of forgotten bottles from the late-18th and early-19th century, and there were a few ancient examples of liqueurs and spirits from which I was invited to take my pick. I chose a bottle of Pernod which, with its iconic label and foil-covered neck, could have come straight from the bar at the Folies-Bergère. I was keen to see what the real thing was like and opened it one evening in my Paris flat, pouring it over a lump of sugar on an 'absinthe spoon', as was the custom at the time, and adding water. After a few slow sips, my head began to spin… and the rest of the glass and bottle went down the sink.

Since the mid-1970s I had been building up quite a large business sending my mostly American clients back home with several cases of wine. The US rules then permitted people to return with a quantity of wine that they 'might have acquired during their time in Paris'. This was often up to 20 cases, which were packed up with their household goods. They could even reclaim the TVA / VAT as the wines were not being consumed in France. One client accumulated a serious collection, but had no cellar in his New York apartment building, so stored the wines in huge closets in his bedroom, keeping them at a constant low temperature. (His wife later left him and moved to Florida.) By the mid-1980s, since most of the American companies left in Paris had moved to La Défense, this business fell off dramatically and I was obliged to let go the very efficient woman who had run this side of the office. That in itself proved a drawn-out and costly business.

Attendances were also declining at the Académie. Patricia had proposed an ambitious expansion programme, but the timing wasn't right; she moved on to create a wine programme for Le Cordon Bleu instead. Steve Steede oversaw the creation of a fine tasting room at what was now Spurrier Distribution, however, and we were successful in holding wine courses there.

The businesses in Cité Berryer were becoming more and more reliant on overdrafts guaranteed from my bank in London, which held my flat as security. In the early 1970s I had been buying so much wine that for a few years I paid no TVA / VAT (tax not being payable if more wine is bought than is sold). Now, however, I was selling stock and getting a bill for TVA every quarter, which sometimes I couldn't pay, so incurring a fine of 10 percent plus interest. I was even occasionally behind with the rent. On top of this, since I was only in Paris two, at most three, days a week, I had stopped claiming even a modest salary. So following a quite good 1987 Christmas period (although it wasn't a patch on the old days), I decided it was time to sell up.

But none of this prevented me from travelling when I had the chance. September 1987 found me in the Douro for the vintage, staying at Taylor-Fladgate's Quinta do Vargellas where I had spent an instructive week in rather rustic comfort 22 years earlier. Alastair Robertson and his wife Gillyanne were wonderful hosts. She had poured her skills as a decorator into the house and one of their daughters, Natasha, was working on her first steps to become head winemaker for the family brand. One morning, after a particularly long night that ended with many glasses of Old Partners' Wine, the aged Tawny reserved for private consumption, I appeared at breakfast to find the guests' plates and cups untouched and a questioning, amused look on my hosts' faces. Apparently my last words before going to bed had been 'I'll swim the Douro before breakfast', and they were waiting for this to happen. The Douro, once a rushing torrent, had been dammed a little further downstream to ease navigation and produce electricity, so the stretch in front of Vargellas was relatively calm. I liked swimming, but said that if they were going to wait for me to swim to the opposite bank and back again they wouldn't be breakfasting until lunchtime, so Natasha offered to get the boat out and ferry me back once I had reached the other side. Of course everyone was well into their breakfast by the time I returned.

In February 1988 I was in Montreal to host tastings at Alan and Louise Mills' Académie du Vin, and to take part in the selections of the Societé d'Alcools du Quebec (SAQ), Canada's largest wine and spirits distributer. Wine distribution in Canada was controlled by the state monopolies, the Liquor Control Board of Ontario (LCBO) being second only to the SAQ. They collected a good deal of money in taxes, but also did a good job in selecting, promoting and distributing, and were highly regarded by both their suppliers and their customers.

From Montreal I went to Toronto as a guest of Clayton Ruby, a civil rights lawyer and great wine collector, who bought wines from Lafon, Leflaive, Guigal and Chave via the Cave as they were not available through the LCBO. He had asked me to speak at a couple of wine dinners, a role quite new to me then, but which I was to play increasingly in the next decades. It is interesting that knowledgeable collectors, who have wines in their cellars way out of the price range of most people in the wine trade, like to have someone independent to discuss them with. Such dinners have given me the opportunity to taste some of the most wonderful wines imaginable.

In March I went to Tokyo, where the Académie was spreading its wings, and was introduced to the chairman of Lumière SA, one of the major wine importers to Japan. Mr Tskamako wanted to translate the Académie Wine Course into Japanese. It had been one of the first real 'How To' books in French, English and other European languages, and to think of it appearing in Japanese was an honour.

My father died in April 1988. My mother was a strong woman, but his loss was a terrible blow to her. She let it be known that she wished still to be addressed as Mrs John Spurrier, not as Mrs Pamela Spurrier, her widowed name.

On one of my later visits to my father, he had written down a quotation for me: 'When they are young, children love their parents; as they get older they begin to judge them; seldom, if ever, do they forgive them.' If he felt some kind of guilt, he should not have, for he and my mother were wrapped up in each other and I had left home mentally as well as physically after Rugby to grow up in London. What I remember is his social ease, his looks and charm: nothing to judge, still less to forgive.

The funeral was at Marston. My father joined many generations of Spurriers in the cemetery of St Mary's Church, where he had been church warden in an unbroken family line since 1628. Nicky was to be the last to be associated with that church, since neither of his children wished to live in Derbyshire. They had the choice my father never enjoyed.

Back in Paris, I was introduced through Drew Harré to one Philippe McGarry – French despite the name – who had been director of sales at Nicolas and was now managing the fine foods firms Foie Gras and La Comtesse du Barry. He was interested in what might be done with the Spurrier brand. In his early 40s, tall, good-looking and quite brilliant, he impressed the accountant I had inherited from Mme Fougères, Gerard Jongis, but behind his charm, McGarry was tough and had never lost a business negotiation. Since he was known as having *les dents longues* / sharp teeth, Drew found a lawyer to represent me in the negotiations, a very bright woman who had come up against McGarry twice before. On both previous occasions her clients had lost, so this time she was determined to secure a good deal. I just wanted to sell, and should have made this plain.

Discussions began on open terms, McGarry meeting and liking Steve Steede and the Spurrier Distribution concept, and McGarry's partner Valérie Gans, herself from a wine family, meeting Isabelle Bachelard and appreciating what might be done to broaden the Académie's appeal.

By this time I had already agreed to sell Le Moulin du Village and the Blue Fox Bar to Mark Williamson, with their debts, for *le franc symbolique*, and despite the heavy financial loss it was a relief to see the back of them – although there was eventually an upside. The debts proved so huge that in 1997, when Mark arranged to buy le Mercure Galant, a once-fine but fading restaurant two doors down from Willi's Wine Bar, he bought it with the Le Moulin du Village company in which

I still retained one share. Having become Mark's partner almost by default, I built up my share bit by bit and, when I needed funds 20 years later, cashed in at a good profit. Mark Williamson is a brilliant all-rounder and Paris is lucky to have him.

McGarry's offer was that I should retain 25 percent of the company, he would take over the rest with 75 percent of the debts, and I would receive a good salary for the two or three days a week that I could commit to Paris. His aim was that the Spurrier brand would become *La FNAC du Vin* (FNAC then being France's go-to store for all electronic products) with outlets in all the major French cities. What could be better?

Discussions continued during May, my lawyer pushing hard to improve the deal before the end-of-the-month deadline. I had the impression that McGarry was not fully funded for the project, although he had already advanced Fr100,000 to cover some of the Cave's pressing debts. The last weekend in May was one of the Académie Internationale du Vin's summer symposiums, this time based in Chinon in the Touraine region. I had a meeting with Valérie at midday on Thursday 26th and felt that an extra effort on my part might help lubricate the deal. That evening I called her in St-Emilion to offer to keep my bank guarantees in place for a few months; she said she would pass this on to Philippe, and that I should call him on Friday evening.

The following morning I set off to Chinon. The first day's meetings went off well, with a tasting of Chinon at Couly-Dutheil going back to 1964. I called McGarry that evening as requested, but there was no answer. The next day, Spurrier Distribution was holding an 'open day' of tastings with discounted prices to bring in clients, and I left early to be there, getting back exhausted to Chinon for the dinner that evening. I called McGarry again; still no answer. Sunday morning wrapped up the AIV conference and after lunch I drove back to Paris, this time with another old friend. I poured out my problems to him, and his advice was that if the deadline had passed, I should cancel the deal. I put this to my lawyer who agreed, so, having heard nothing from either McGarry or Gans, I wrote a registered letter calling the whole thing off.

What I did not know was that McGarry had been talking to Steve Steede to plan the takeover, having realized that while my name and palate would be what he was buying, Steve would actually be running the business. When I had been at Spurrier Distribution the Saturday before for the open day, Steve hadn't thought to mention this – just as I hadn't thought to tell him that I was going to cancel the deal, thus leaving my trusted lieutenant with a fait accompli. McGarry immediately, and quite correctly, removed Fr100,000 of my best stock from Spurrier Distribution, and that was that. It was deeply dispiriting afterwards to reflect that, had this deal gone ahead, it could have validated two decades of work in Paris as well as providing financial security and hope for the future.

From that moment it was a rush for the lifeboats. I was reminded of an exchange in Ernest Hemingway's *The Sun Also Rises* when the protagonist is asked how he went bankrupt. 'Two ways,' he replies. 'Gradually, then suddenly.'

I approached Jean-Michel Cazes of Château Lynch-Bages, whose Compagnie Médocaine had expressed interest in the Paris market, but their brief researches told them my businesses were too far gone. I contacted Corinne Richard of Les Cafés Richard, a company that owned or supplied most of the cafés in Paris and had substantial vineyards in Beaujolais; Corrinne had taken courses at the Académie and I thought a couple of retail shops and a well-known wine school would add an interesting element to Les Cafés' portfolio, and she said she would discuss it with her father.

By this time it was late June, when the Fête de la Fleur celebration dinner for the flowering of the vines was to be held; that year at Château Coufran. Ewan Fergusson, then British Ambassador in Paris, and Michael Broadbent were guests of honour, and invitations were hard-sought. At the dinner I met the owner of two shops in Paris called Le Repaire de Bacchus. The shops, smarter than those of Nicolas and less pompous than Fauchon and Hédiard, my neighbours in the Place de la Madeleine, were marketing-driven: they reached out to customers rather than waiting for them to push open the door. We got on well, he showed interest in a merger though he had no money to invest, but we continued to talk.

Meanwhile Corinne Richard got back to me to say that her father was interested in the Académie, but once again I was stupid enough not to hive off this business and follow up. I even received an offer that would have seen my investment back for the wine shop/bar on the Left Bank, Le Petit Bacchus, but I stubbornly stuck to the idea that the Spurrier Brand should be kept together, and refused to let the businesses go piecemeal.

A decision had to be made before France shut down for August, and the Repaire de Bacchus owners, having estimated my debts at around three million francs (which excluded debts to suppliers but included my overdraft – then running at an impossible 17 percent) offered to take the whole lot off my hands. They offered a *franc symbolique* for each of the three companies, proposed to take two years to absorb it all, then pay me four million francs from mid-1990. They said that their fledgling company could not take on the fiscal debts, which they would renegotiate but would have to remain in my name. Gerard Jongis, having seen the McGarry deal disappear, thought this was a bit stiff, but I accepted it. After spending the first week of August assuring the change of ownership, I took the family for a much-needed holiday on Lambay Island in the Irish Sea.

Returning to Paris in September, I could only admire the energy that Le Repaire de Bacchus were putting into the Cave, but I was concerned to see them sell Le Petit Bacchus to become a shoe shop, so realising for themselves the money I should have been bright enough to accept from the earlier offer. They also closed down Spurrier Distribution, moving all my stock and customer reserves into their own warehouse south of Paris. Warning signs increased when my clients asked for delivery of their 2005s only to find that they had been sold... luckily we had full records of the reserves, so the clients were fully compensated.

I was still, at that stage, playing an important role in wine selection and my best suppliers remained to take pride of place in Le Repaire de Bacchus shops, which were growing in number; still, I was beginning to feel uncomfortable. Early the following year the long-planned renovation of the old-fashioned Cité Berryer got under way and it emerged as luxury little street called Village Royale. The Cave de la Madeleine was eventually relocated in smaller premises, and the three floors of the Académie were returned to the real-estate developers for considerable financial compensation. I can't say that this was an easy period for me, but I was at least receiving a small salary, the fiscal debts had been renegotiated and I was still involved, looking forward to the eventual pay-out.

Earlier that year I had met David Banford, an entrepreneur who asked me to be wine adviser to his latest idea, The Wine Society of America (WSA). This was a mail-order company based in Millbrook, a smart suburb in upstate New York, that sold direct to customers in all but the dry states. David had raised substantial funds on the money market, and in early October I hosted tastings for a large crowd of members in New York, Chicago, Washington and Boston. These were successful, but before too long our venture fell foul of America's established three-tier (importer, wholesaler, retailer) wine-distribution system, and had to close down.

Things were on a more even keel at the start of 1989: the Christie's Wine Course was doing well, I was enjoying writing for *Tatler* and there was also an occasional speaking commission. I was in Paris mid-week and in Dorset at the weekend. Bella and I had made our first visit to South Africa at the instigation of Simon Barlow, whose family owned the superb Rustenberg estate in Stellenbosch, and had enjoyed a wonderful week there. It had been John Avery, once again, who had launched wines from the Cape into the UK and, while the country's politics were still uncertain, there was optimism in the air.

I was to return the following year as a judge on the South African Airways panel, organized by the ebullient and energetic Peter Devereux, and afterwards became a regular visitor. My fellow judges on the 1990 SAA panel were Pamela Vandyke-Price, Piero Antinori from Tuscany, Robert Drouhin from Burgundy, James Halliday from Melbourne, and local growers Gyles Webb of Thelema and Tony Mossop, who made very good port-style wines. It was a fabulous introduction to the people in the Cape and the wines they produced, which were good then, and are extremely good now.

Around Easter I was contacted by John Chua of Singapore Airlines, who had been one of the Cave's clients on his visits to Paris, and had attended tastings at the Académie. He told me that SIA was looking to change its wine consultants: a new director had been named and a whole new team was to be appointed. The plan was to hire three consultants, one for Europe, one for the Americas and one for Australia and New Zealand, and he encouraged me to apply. A few weeks later I was summoned to the SIA London offices to be interviewed by Miss Wu, the new commercial supplies director, and Miss Chan, director of customer service.

I recognized a couple of the other applicants, one a Master of Wine, the other a top wine writer, and didn't think much of my chances. My CV had already been pored over and I was asked just one question: 'If you were to be taken on as one of the SIA wine consultants, how would you expect to fly?' My reply was that if I was expected to taste the following day (the flights were 12 hours overnight), in

Business Class; if not then in Economy with a window seat. It appeared that the previous consultants had insisted on First Class during their tenure, often at the expense of paying customers, so this was a valid question. Apparently no other applicant had suggested Economy, and I got the job. Miss Wu, who was to be my boss for 10 years, came to Vinexpo in June to be introduced to the châteaux owners.

So began a dream job: two weeks a year in Singapore, with its wonderful food, people and culture, and a more-than-adequate 'all found' salary. From the start, my co-consultants were Anthony Dias Blue from San Francisco and Michael Hill-Smith MW from Adelaide; both good friends. Anthony's wine knowledge – he was wine editor for *Gourmet* magazine – was impressive, but his dedication to the world's cuisine was even more so. During the years of our co-consultancy, I never had to look at a menu. The three of us had the most tremendous time together with late nights and – I admit – some quite bad behaviour in the early days. When I finally retired in 2014, I had spent a full calendar year in Singapore, my fees increasing as Sterling lost value, and I had enjoyed every minute.

If the SIA job was the best thing to happen to me in 1989, by far the worst was a demand from the tax authorities of the eighth *arrondissement* for Fr1.5 million which they deemed I owed for tax evasion. *La Direction générale de la concurrence, de la consommation et de la répression des fraudes* (DGCCRF) presented me with a dossier that set out my losses over the past seven years (as far back as they could investigate), which amounted to three million francs. They accused me of having falsified the accounts, asserting that I had not lost, but in fact made this sum as profit, which I had then illegally taken out of the country.

This was completely untrue but I had to prove it. Gerard Jongis declared that his accounts were correct and that I had made genuine trading losses, and there ensued many stressful months of correspondence back and forth, the DGCCRF upping their demands by charging interest, my accountants continuing to maintain that I was the victim of a false claim. This went on at some considerable expense via a series of *lettres recommandées* / registered letters that had to be delivered within 15 days. Things were by now not going well for me at Le Repaire de Bacchus and I was gearing up for a confrontation there, so it was with unimaginable relief that I received a call early in February 1990 to say that the DGCCRF case had collapsed due to *un vice de forme*: essentially, a technicality.

Meanwhile, I was integrating myself more into wine life in London and, while still being part of the wine scene in Paris, was looking forward to the end of my two-year contract and to receiving the settlement that would deal with the fiscal debts and leave a tidy sum over.

There was a big event to open one of Le Repair de Bacchus's new shops in early October, during which they honoured several of my old suppliers such as Guigal and Château de Beaucastel. The following day I told them that I had enjoyed my two years and felt I had contributed a good deal to the expansion of the business, and asked them to make arrangements for the contracted four-million-franc payment. I was told that they were sorry to see me leave, but that the money would not be forthcoming. They said our formal agreement concerning the debts and future compensation over and above the *franc symbolique* had never been signed and legalized. Technically, this was correct: I had no recourse in law. The fiscal debts I had agreed to take on when the agreement was made remained firmly on my shoulders. This was a devastating blow.

In October 1990, shortly after my 49th birthday, I returned to London. Steven Spurrier Marchand de Vin, the brand that I had created over two decades, had ceased to exist. I was not only broke, but also deeply in debt, and the future looked unimaginably bleak.

CHAPTER TWELVE
THE ROAD BACK

Once I had returned to London, it wasn't obvious what my next step should be, although clearly it was essential to cut back on expenses. An early positive sign came courtesy of my good friend Georges Lepré, sommelier of the Paris Ritz, through whom I was commissioned to write a short report on the Harrods wine department. I visited the shop a few times, checked the labels and bought some of their branded wines; I also visited competitors such as Fortnum & Mason, Harvey Nichols and Selfridges to compare products. The resulting report was not entirely complimentary, concluding that changes could well be made for the better, but nevertheless some months later I was asked if I would be interested in the position of Harrods' wine consultant. Of course I would. I was duly summoned to meet Mr Mohamed Al Fayed, who was very much in the news then, as he had been for years – and would become even more so when his son Dodi began a relationship with Diana, Princess of Wales. Mr Fayed Senior was a dramatic character, quite explosive in manner and fond of punctuating his short sentences with expletives. He told me to come in for a couple of days a week to 'sort out the wine department'.

I started in early July, meeting the department head Hugh Cochrane MW. The wine shop was on the ground floor, adjacent to the splendid food halls. Hugh took me down to the cellar where his office was, among racks and racks of wine, bins full of bottles, cases piled high; and as we entered he said: 'Better take your jacket off, it's warm down here.' What about the wines? I wondered.

Having been shown around, the first thing I did was buy a Polaroid camera and an industrial-size thermometer, find an old and prestigious bottle and take a photograph, which clearly showed the temperature of 23°C (74°F). This I sent up to Mr Al Fayed's office with a note saying that if this state of affairs ever came to the notice of a wine journalist, the department's reputation would be destroyed. By the end of the week, air-conditioning was being installed.

By September, both MWs in the department had moved on, leaving me with a free hand. I set about expanding the French range under the Harrods brand, which had previously been just claret and white burgundy, and soon added red and white Graves, Mâcon-Vinzelles, Meursault, Chablis and red Côtes du Rhône. In my research a few months earlier, I had discovered that Fortnum & Mason had a superb range of 'own-label' wines, and these were just the start.

Early in the autumn, I was interviewed by Anthony Rose of the *Independent*, whose long article was headed 'Château Harrods', noting that 'the top people's store is giving its wine department a welcome facelift thanks to Steven Spurrier'. I was quoted as preparing 'for the moment when Mo moves us downstairs', referring to Mohamed Al Fayed's intention to turn the basement into 'a purpose-built wine department, the greatest in the world, with its own bar'. Mr Al Fayed had a right-hand man named Michael Cole who was responsible above all for the Al Fayed image. He called me in and reprimanded me strongly for referring to the boss as 'Mo'. I probably shouldn't have used the name all staff knew him by, and I apologized.

My 50th birthday was coming up, so I suggested to Mark Williamson, now owner of both Le Moulin and The Blue Fox, that I take over the restaurant for a big dinner to celebrate. Nicky and my mother came over (it was her first visit to Paris since she came to see the family on the barge in summer 1972), and both floors of the restaurant were filled with friends from our time in France. Mary Blume from the *Trib*'s 'People' column interviewed me, and the write-up appeared on October 14th under the heading 'The Rise and Fall and Rise of a Wine Guru'. The article ended with a description of me jumping onto a table at the end of dinner to thank everyone for coming and announcing: 'I never thought I'd have the nerve – or the money – to give this party. Now the whole game starts up again from my point of view!'

Georges Lepré sent me a note of congratulation from the Paris Ritz – but Mr Cole once again was not amused. Since it was owing to Harrods that I could afford to give myself the party, he told me (and this much was true) I should have talked to the reporter more about Harrods and less about myself.

Meanwhile there was work to be done on the list, which hadn't even been produced the previous year. I put together a magazine-like brochure that included articles on the various regions and, in exchange for sponsorship, particular focus on major names and suppliers. On the first page I wrote a brief introduction and signed my name as head of the wine department. This was what Michael Cole had been waiting for. The heads of departments referred to each other on the shop floor as Mr Meat, Mr Fish, Mr Cheese, Mr Wine and so on. Apparently, in line with the Harrods 'code', no head of department had ever drawn attention to his individual identity in this way. Accordingly, in the third week of January I was told to clear my desk and leave that evening. My replacement was to be Alun Griffiths MW, the man behind the Fortnum & Mason wine department I had held up to Harrods as an inspiration only seven months earlier. I spent the weekend writing a report for Alun on everything that was in the pipeline for the coming few months, and when he took over he did an excellent job.

My brief spell at Harrods had at least put me fairly and squarely back in the London wine trade. The optimist in me was just waiting to see what would turn up next. My debts had been reduced, Nicky's management of the family investment company was helping, and I was ready to accept anything that came my way.

Diner's Club in South Africa was looking for a 'name' to hold wine tastings for their members, and in late February I returned to the Cape, this time with Bella, to conduct these before spending a wonderful three days in Kruger National Park. My regular spring and autumn weeks in Singapore continued, and Anthony Dias Blue asked me to be a judge at his San Francisco Wine Competition, which took me to the city for four or five days and gave me time for a catch-up visit to the Napa Valley.

In mid-July I was contacted by Arblaster & Clarke, travel agents specializing in wine tours who were recreating the Bordeaux-to-Bristol sea voyage that used to bring claret to England. This voyage was to be Weymouth–Bordeaux–Weymouth on a fine dual-masted square-rigged tall ship, STV *Astrid*. The tour was co-organized by Bordeaux Direct, a mail-order wine club founded by Tony Laithwaite, which Hugh Johnson chaired. There was a double cabin to spare, and Bella and I enjoyed this in exchange for my being the resident wine guide and hosting visits in Bordeaux. Hugh joined us for a dinner at Château Latour, where he was a director. Bella and I also helped crew the ship, climbing up and down the rigging to unfurl or re-furl the sails and keeping night watch for four hours on, four hours off, which was instructive – and exhausting. After a five-day voyage out of the Channel and into the Atlantic, mooring often along the way, we entered the Gironde Estuary and I waved to Château Loudenne as we sailed slowly past. Hugh and Judy Johnson took the return journey to Weymouth, hitting two days of heavy storms, after which they had to stay with us in Dorset to recuperate.

This first connection with Arblaster & Clarke led to a regular job, once or twice a year, as a wine guide on their well-organized trips to the wine regions. On these trips I was generously fed and housed, and much enjoyed re-visiting the vignerons – by this time the children, even grandchildren, of those whom I first met when we lived in Paris.

My friend Christopher Shaw introduced me to Jean-Louis Masurel who had bought, with colleagues, the historic Hédiard, *Epicerie Fine*, the great food and wine store on the Place de la Madeleine. I had known the store well in the 1970s and '80s and was delighted when Masurel offered me a position as consultant. Naturally, I accepted. I was back to a couple of days a week in Paris, working with inspiring people on a good salary, so it seemed that the Spurrier luck, so absent in the late 1980s, was about to return.

And return it did, emphatically, when I met Sarah Kemp from *Decanter* magazine. I already knew a good deal about *Decanter*, which had been created by Colin Parnell, a bookish and talented musician, and Tony Lord, a young Australian journalist. I had bumped into Colin from time to time, who was always rather reserved, and Tony, who was anything but. Tony was massively competitive and also a heroic drinker. Early one morning when we still lived in Clapham, I was passing the north side of the common on my morning run and saw, way ahead of me, a figure who looked like Tony. I had seen Tony late the previous evening in a restaurant where he was rather the worse for wear, and was amazed that he was now on his feet at such an hour. It was indeed him, and since we seemed on a collision course on the narrow track. I swerved out of his way, to hear him growl 'You're in England now, Spurrier, so run on the f***ing left!'

While Colin was a rather formal Bordeaux-lover, Tony supported the world outside France, and it was this that gave the fledgling magazine its international flavour. The first edition in June 1975 revealed 'How to buy Bordeaux and keep your bank manager happy' for the very modest price of 40p.

In early 1993 Sarah Kemp, *Decanter*'s publisher, and I met at a charity dinner. I was regaling her with an account of my adventures at Harrods when she said 'You're well out of that – come and write for *Decanter*.' I did just that, my first column appearing in October that year. Alongside my monthly column I was commissioned to write regular feature articles and had a place on the tasting panels. My other activities continued, but after a few years I decided not to order any more 'Steven Spurrier Wine Consultant' business cards, but instead use my *Decanter* card, since it meant much more to everybody.

In 1994, I visited Helsinki to attend the state monopoly's version of Vinexpo. This was the second of my many roles as understudy to Michael Broadbent. Over the years I received numerous phone calls along the lines of: 'Steven, I've accepted an invitation to go to XXX and find I'm too busy, so have recommended you.' Such calls took me on my first visit to Santiago in Chile, to represent Christie's; to a weekend's wine tasting in Nashville, Tennessee, and to an Office Internationale du Vin tasting in Madrid's Ritz Hotel. At one point, Michael and I were contracted to a small luxury cruise line to be the wine guides on seven-day cruises. One of the cruises was Plymouth to Bordeaux; the other toured the South China Seas. Michael took the latter and I assumed my allotted role as Number Two.

The following year I was in San Francisco as one of a panel of judges taking part in a tasting organized by Robert Finigan, comparing the top Red Bordeaux

Decanter publisher Sarah Kemp, here with Eric de Rothschild at a Royal Opera House Gala dinner.

from 1990 and 1986. In his book *Corks and Forks*, under the heading 'Bordeaux Redux', Robert suggested that the 1855 Classification had not completely stood the test of time and that, if we convened an expert panel to compare two recent vintages in a blind tasting, a more up-to-date ranking might emerge. He approached his friend Gordon Getty, a committed opera fan and owner of a winery called Plump Jack, to sponsor the event. Getty agreed to underwrite it, asking that any profit from the subsequent tasting, which was to be open to the public and followed by a black-tie dinner, would go to the San Francisco Symphony orchestra.

The two vintages selected were 1990 and 1986, the former rich and robust and later acknowledged as the best vintage of the decade, the latter more classic and perhaps overshadowed by the 1982 and 1985. Sacha Lichine, then in charge of Prieuré-Lichine, and Bruno Prats of Cos d'Estournel strongly supported the endeavour. All the wines were sourced from the châteaux and forwarded in good time to recover before the tasting took place.

Robert chaired the panel of judges, which he had selected as having 'diverse professional palates'. They were: Alexis Bespaloff of *The New Yorker*, Michel Bettane of *La Revue du Vin de France*, Anthony Dias Blue of *Bon Appétit* magazine, Mary Ewing-Mulligan MW, director of the International Wine Center in New York and author of *Wine for Dummies*, David Peppercorn MW, noted

English author specializing in Bordeaux, Frank J Prial of *The New York Times*, Serena Sutcliffe MW, by then head of Sotheby's wine department, and me. We tasted the 60 classed growths of the Médoc and the 13 from the northern Graves, now known as Pessac-Léognan. This is the ranking of the top 15 wines, 1990 and 1986 vintages taken together:

Ch Pichon-Baron, second growth Pauillac (90.5)

Ch Léoville Las Cases, second growth St-Julien (90.2)

Ch Haut-Brion, first growth Graves (89.4)

Ch Pichon-Longueville Comtesse de Lalande, 2nd growth Pauillac (87)

Ch Margaux, first growth Margaux (86.7)

Ch Cos d'Estournel, second growth St-Estèphe (86.3)

Ch Latour, first growth Pauillac (85.8)

Ch Lynch-Bages, fifth growth Pauillac (85.1)

Ch La Mission Haut-Brion, classed growth Graves (85)

Ch Léoville-Barton, second growth St-Julien (84.4)

Ch Mouton Rothschild, first growth Pauillac (83.6)

Ch Léoville-Poyferre, second growth St-Julien (83.5)

Ch Ducru-Beaucaillou, second growth St Julien (82.4)

Ch Montrose, second growth St-Estèphe (82.2)

Ch Lafite Rothschild, first growth Pauillac (81.6)

The 16th wine was third growth Margaux Château Palmer scored at 80.5, so judging by this exercise at least, the 1855 Classification stood up pretty well. The tasting required two full days of constant attention, tasting at a certain rhythm, the judges giving their marks on each wine before moving on to the next. Anthony Dias Blue, next to me, was always first to deliver, while Mary Ewing-Mulligan was always last.

In late February, I was in Athens for Greece's own Vinexpo. In the mid-1970s and early 1980s, Bella and I had spent a week or so every summer as guests of David Fromkin on crewed sailing boats known as *gülets*, touring the Greek and Turkish islands. David maintained that 'the best Greek wine is worse than the worst French wine', and had lavish supplies of Dauvissat Chablis, Leflaive Puligny and Pousse d'Or Volnay were shipped out from the Cave to the boats' owners. Our host, Nico Manessis, strongly disagreed and would, in 1995, produce the first edition of his *Greek Wine Guide*, a book that helped to launch Greek wine onto the UK market. Our visit to the mainland was an eye-opener, and the following year Nico arranged for a trip to Santorini, whose volcanic soils produced superb bone-dry white wines from the Assyrtiko grape.

In July, I was part of the *Decanter* contingent in Seattle attending a wine conference that concentrated on West Coast wines. Pinot Noir from Oregon, already much admired, was where Joseph Drouhin had made the first Burgundian investment, and he had been followed by many others. The wines of Washington State were totally new to me; they represented a breadth and complexity that astounded me when I thought back to the wine world I'd entered 30 years ago.

I was beginning to spend more time in Asia, not only for Singapore Airlines and the occasional judging, thanks to John Avery, but also in Hong Kong, due to my association with Ronald Brown. Ron had founded a company called La Languedocienne (he and his wife had a vineyard in the Midi) and he was a serial entrepreneur, which appealed to me. I became a junior partner in his fledgling business, combining my trips to Tokyo with tastings at Japan's now flourishing Académie. A few years later, Ron created the Japan Wine Challenge, and even later the China Wine Challenge, based on London's International Wine Challenge that had been founded by Robert Joseph.

I have Ron to thank for many fascinating trips all over Japan from this time and have to confess that many of the building blocks I put in place for the *Decanter* World Wine Awards (DWWA) in 2004 were based on my experiences over many years with John Avery as my co-chair, at these competitions. As Asia was such a significant emerging market we were able to invite judges from all over the world, and the reputation of both competitions benefited accordingly.

Once I became chair of the DWWA some years later, however, I felt there could be a conflict of interest so resigned from the Japan and China challenges and was replaced by Lynne Sheriff MW. From 2010, having started Bride Valley Vineyard, I asked Ron Brown to buy me out of La Languedocienne, which he did.

I enjoyed two different but very special trips in 1996. The first in May was to Washington DC, to attend the opening of an exhibition and a conference on the theme 'Red, White and American' at the Smithsonian Institution of American

History. The exhibition of wine artefacts included a bottle each of Stag's Leap Wine Cellars 1973 Cabernet and Chateau Montelena 1973 Chardonnay, winners of the Judgement of Paris exactly 20 years earlier. The title of the Paris exhibit was 'Doubtless as Good: Jefferson's Dream for American Wine Fulfilled.'

The second trip was to the Tokaji vineyards in Hungary, a country that was just emerging from communist rule. Hugh Johnson, always ahead of his time, had established The Royal Tokaji Wine Company (RTWC) to revive these great sweet wines. The vineyards had been demarcated in 1700, making them the first officially classified vineyards in Europe. Under the communists from 1945 to 1990, the classed vineyards on the higher slopes that could not be farmed mechanically had been abandoned in favour of those on the plains. Production of Tokaji Eszencia died out, since the required concentration of 70 percent residual sugar could not be achieved using grapes grown on the plains. The RTWC's 1993 vintage was the first Eszencia to be made in 50 years. By mid-1996 other investors were in evidence, including AXA Millésimes Disznókő estate, Vega Sicilia's Bodegas Oremus and a branch of the Habsburg family that had gone back to their imperial roots by reviving one of their old estates.

My visit was organized by Ben Howkins, a great expert on port, RTWC's commercial director. We were joined by three stalwarts from San Francisco: Jack Daniels and Win Wilson of Wilson Daniels, the RWTC importers, and Anthony Dias Blue. Before our flight to Budapest the following day, Ben had arranged a lunch for us at Waddesdon Manor, the magnificent home of Jacob, Lord Rothschild, whose wine cellar Ben looked after. Our summer lunch in the converted dairy came, Jacob told us, 'all from the garden', and since he was a shareholder in Château Lafite Rothschild, it was accompanied by splendid wines.

The contrast between Waddesdon and Budapest in 1996 could hardly have been more striking, but the four-hour drive to the village of Mád in the Tokaj took us back into a more romantic world of vineyards and timbered farmhouses, ancient castles dotted here and there. In the past, Tokaji wine had only been sweet. It was made by taking late-picked, super-concentrated botrytized or *aszú* berries, crushing them into a paste in small tubs called *puttonyos*, and adding them to the high-acid white Furmint wine after fermentation. The sweetness increased with the number of *puttonyos* added, and wines that had more than six were labelled

Eszencia. For Peter Vinding-Diers, co-founder with Hugh of the RTWC, the five-*puttonyos* wine 'combines sweetness and elegance, a nose of honey and violets with richness supported by chords of acidity... like an étude by Chopin: listen to it and you hear the world turn around.' Certainly we tasted enough for the world to turn under our feet: I have a framed photograph of us all standing in the sun outside the cellars with the caption 'The Tokaji Aszú Experience – It's a Mád, Mád, Mád, Mád World'.

The year ended with three lavish days at Raffles Hotel in Singapore for the second Wine and Food Experience event. My subsequent *Decanter* article, 'Life on the Middle Palate', was inspired by the owner of Napa Valley's Far Niente Estate, Larry Maguire, remarking: 'What we are looking for [in Chardonnay] is life on the middle palate.' Some years earlier, Frank J Prial had written an article entitled 'Death on the Middle Palate', suggesting that if one was unsure what comment to make about a wine, one might hazard: 'A magnificent bouquet, but it dies on the middle palate', or 'It dies on the middle palate but comes back strongly on the finish.' A number of top producers agreed that the middle palate was the key.

Georg Riedel was also at the event showing a new range of glasses. When asked when he thought a wine had reached maturity, he replied, 'when it tastes better than it smells'. Confirmation came from Dr Ernesto Illy, food scientist and founder of IllyCaffè, who gave a tasting of three espressi brewed at different temperatures. He maintained that the correct brew will extract only 25–28 percent of the caffeine but 60 percent of the beans' flavour. Dr Illy's concern with flavour rather than extract extended to the perfect coffee cup which, he told us, should be in the shape of an egg cut in half and filled no more than 35 percent full. At first the flavour is trapped by the foam – as the taste of champagne is trapped by the bubbles – then the aroma appears and is released onto the palate. Even two decades ago coffee lovers were looking for increased pleasure from balanced flavour, just as they were in fine wines. All's well that ends well on the middle palate.

At Vinexpo that year I took part in a unique scientific experiment. Under the banner 'Les Palais du Monde', 43 tasters from 14 countries and four continents gathered to test the influences on tasters of their geographic and ethnic origins, with their acquired memory of tastes and flavours, at the moment of tasting each wine. We were all asked to strap a *cardiofréquencemètre* around the chest to monitor our heartbeats, and a smaller, watch-like object around the wrist. The difference that morning was that while we were judging the wines, the computer was judging us. It came up with three families of tasters irrespective of ethnic origin:

(1) The permanently unsatisfied: negative tasters looking for faults before searching for pleasure. Most of this group came from countries with a history of wine.
(2) The modest ones: these people tasted with a blend of confidence and humility, leaving the last word to the wine itself.
(3) The enthusiasts: this group was interested in a wine's personality, and approached each one as though they had never tasted it before. They tended to come from countries where wine-growing was rare.

When there were four or more tasters from a specific country, the computer came up with the ethnic profile: the French showed knowledge by reference (all the wines were French), the Belgians were convivial, the Swiss methodical, the Germans looked for aroma, Scandinavians preferred robustness to delicacy, Canadians looked for balance, the Japanese showed emotional reactions to high acidity, while the British were reflective and did not waste words. At the end of the day we received printouts of our reactions to each wine in the form of a hospital-style cardiogram. Robert Joseph's was all over the place, an expression of intensely varying emotion, while mine was flat as a board, perhaps the vinous equivalent of the stiff upper lip.

The first *Decanter* Fine Wine Encounter, the brainchild of Sarah Kemp, was held in 1997 in November at The Landmark hotel in London. Two vast rooms were filled with producers from all over the world, each with just a 2 x 1-metre table to set out their wares. Sarah insisted that either the owner or winemaker be present, often both; never just a salesperson. This gave readers the opportunity to meet characters as diverse as Al Brounstein from Napa Valley's Diamond Creek, Henri Lurton of Château Brane-Cantenac and Simon Barlow of South Africa's Rustenberg estate. Masterclasses of first growth Bordeaux or grand cru burgundy were sold out. I was pleased to be part of a project that put producers in touch with the people who buy and enjoy their wines.

Two more ventures in 1998 saw me spreading the word again: one in Rome and one in London. Roberto Wirth was the owner of Hotel Hassler, a grand hotel at the top of Rome's Spanish Steps. He owned another tall, narrow and long-abandoned building abutting the steps, in which he wished to open a wine school. Classrooms were duly fitted in the ground- and first-floor rooms, a restaurant was established on the third floor and two suites of rooms – which could be accessed from the hotel – on the fourth and fifth floors. Thus was formed the Académie du Vin di Roma, for which I set a tasting programme, also visiting twice a year. The venture was wound up in 2005, but not before Ian D'Agata, an Italian-Canadian with a brilliant mind, palate and a passion for wine, had become involved. D'Agata is now one of the leading experts in Italian wine.

The London venture, Vinopolis, was on an altogether different scale. The idea was conceived by Duncan Vaughan-Arbuckle who, after retiring from the army, had gone into the wine trade and been the first person to bring cheap Bulgarian wines into the UK in vast quantities. I learnt that he had come up with an idea named 'Wineworld' and had found a hectare of unused space under the railway lines leading into Cannon Street Station. Duncan had outlined plans for a 'total wine-tour experience', and now he had a huge space under soaring brick arches to put it in. This was too good an opportunity to resist, even with the Paris debts still not totally paid off, and once again my bank manager came through for another roll of the Spurrier dice.

My early contribution, apart from the investment (a drop in the ocean compared to the £26 million that had been spent by the time the doors opened late that year) was to suggest a change of name from Wineworld to Vinopolis – City of Wine. The finished project offered 18 different 'rooms', spaces devoted to each wine region or country. Beginning with Georgia, where wine had been born in 8000BC; the tour moved on through Greece and into France, which had four rooms, including a reproduction of the Roman Arena in Orange for the Rhône Valley. There was a marvellous space for Italy where four Vespas were set up with screens in front of the handlebars; visitors could jump on board the scooter and imagine they were careening through the vineyards and villages that streamed in front of them. Champagne was on an upper floor, with bubbles beside the lift that took you there; the New World was represented in all its glory and exciting potential; the Judgement of Paris took pride of place in the California room; South Africa was a mass of flora and fauna; 'pipes' of port stood in the port room... and much, much more.

Vinopolis served 150 wines by the glass and had three restaurants, which were themselves very successful, as well as housing the Vinopolis Wine Academy – this was my baby. It became a sought-after venue for brand launches and publicity parties since we could cater for hundreds of guests in an attractive, highly original space. It was quite extraordinary – but sadly a little before its time. We needed 250,000 visitors a year for the tours to make money; alas we never had more than 100,000. Vinopolis continued to trade until 2014, with regular injections of capital to keep it going, but is now sadly just a memory.

What is not just a memory, however, is Borough Market on the south bank of the Thames, which had been a food and produce market since the 12th century. The market had run down to almost nothing, but the opening of Vinopolis gave it a new lease of life and it is now one of the most-visited attractions in London. A debt is owed to the vision of Duncan Vaughan-Arbuckle and Tony Hodges and the courage of the investors: Vinopolis was not only good while it lasted, but it also left a permanent impression on the area.

Another positive influence from Vinopolis's 'before-its-time' optimism was on the huge *Cité des Civilisation du Vin* wine museum/cultural centre that opened in 2016 at the far end of Bordeaux City docks. Sylvie Cazes, sister of Jean-Michel Cazes of Château Lynch-Bages and many other Bordeaux estates, visited Vinopolis twice as a director of the budding Bordeaux venture to see how the visions compared. When the latter finally opened after long delays (and vastly over budget), I bet Véronique Sanders of Château Haut-Bailly a bottle of her wine against a bottle of Bride Valley that it wouldn't work but, seen as 'too big to fail', would survive un-loved, supported by the city of Bordeaux. My view was that the locals wouldn't visit, and that tourists would prefer either to be in the beautiful city of Bordeaux itself, or up in the increasingly tourist-friendly vineyards. I am happy to say that after the first year, I had resoundingly lost my bet.

In the spring, I visited Burgundy, which had rolled through the 1990s with continuing increases in quality and vineyard definition, many winemakers having turned their attention from the cellars back to the soil. Some years earlier, the agronomist and later AIV-member Claude Bourguignon had shocked the region by remarking that there was 'less active life in the soil of the Côte d'Or than there is in the Sahara Desert'. Already Domaines Lafon, Leflaive and Leroy were farming according to biodynamic principles, as was Aubert de Villaine of the Domaine de la Romanée-Conti, who described his winemaking technique as 'picking the grapes when they are fully ripe and then doing as little as possible'. If burgundy was good then, due to the increasing health of its vineyards, it is a true benchmark today. The problem even in those days was a shortage of stock.

In 1999 I attended for the first time the En Primeur tastings organized by the Union des Grands Crus de Bordeaux (UGC). At these events, merchants and journalists taste wines from the previous vintage, sometimes at the châteaux but more often in tastings organized by the UGC to show its members' wines. Tasters choose whether to taste blind or open. In Bordeaux I prefer not to taste blind; the label gives me the information I need about the estate, its style and its track record. I am often asked how wines can properly be judged at just six months old, and the simple answer is that they are judged for potential.

Some of the greatest non-blind tastings I have taken part in over the years have been organized by Los Angeles-based nuclear physicist Bipin Desai. In early February that year I had spent three days in Los Angeles tasting every single wine ever produced by Paul Draper of Ridge Vineyards in California's Santa Cruz Mountains. I had first met Bipin in the 1980s in Paris, where he was collecting wines from Domaines Lafon and Leflaive and also the 'La-La's from Guigal, some of which I could supply him with. I describe Bipin as a 'collector' even though he dislikes the word because of its connotations of possessive hoarding. He preferred to define his passion as 'a search for knowledge, a continual pursuit of greatness in wine. The purpose is to experience greatness, and my tastings allow many other people to do the same'. I became a regular guest at his Paris tastings, which were always held at Restaurant Le Taillevent.

The AIV's Spring Symposium that year was in Austria, venues ranging from Schloss Seggau in Styria, a historic bishop's palace on the borders of Slovenia, to the Esterházy Palace in Eisenstadt, where we were treated to a concert by the Haydn Quartet (Joseph Haydn had lived at the palace for 30 years, and part of his salary was paid in wine). We went on to Rust, whose Ausbruch sweet white wines

Hugh Johnson has compared to the Hungarian *aszú* wines from Tokaj, and finally to Kamptal in the Wachau region, home to the Bründlmayer Estate at Langenlois. With 50 hectares and every vintage from 1947 in his cellar, Willi Bründlmayer blends tradition and innovation. He produces wines from his magnificently sited Grüner Veltliner and Riesling vineyards that combine ripeness and finesse – 'the tenderness of wine' – to a remarkable degree.

At the end of 1999 *Decanter* asked its columnists to choose their 'six best wines of the year' before the magazine updated to a different format. My choice for the year's six best fought to the top through stiff competition. They were: Haut-Brion Blanc 1948, Vouvray Le Haut Lieu 1947 Domaine Huet, Haut-Brion 1966, Hermitage La Chapelle 1961 Paul Jaboulet Aîné, Fonseca 1983 and Yalumba Old Four Crowns Port 1889. Each wine was extraordinary; Haut-Brion 1966 was simply beautiful. What is it that made those wines so special? For me, the answer lies in a combination of acknowledged quality, probable rarity and an element of surprise. They will all have surpassed my expectations, combining total satisfaction, a touch of mystery and an undeniable sense of privilege, and left a certainty that I could never again drink the same wine with so much pleasure.

The Spurrier family welcomed the new millennium in Dorset with some very good wines, starting with champagnes from the 1990 vintage (my favourite being Pol Roger) and ending with a 1900 Madeira. I then embarked on one of the best, though far from the most comfortable, trips of my life. We went to Georgia, where the National Museum in Tbilisi has evidence of grape pips and vessels for winemaking that date from 8000BC. The visit was organized by Georgian Wines & Spirits (GWS), a company benefitting from a substantial investment by Pernod-Ricard which is spearheading a crusade for quality in the world's oldest wine-producing country.

The once-famous wines of Georgia had almost ceased to exist. Although Georgia had supplied the imperial Russian court, after the country's brief period of independence (1918–21), the Bolsheviks invaded and the wines were lost to the outside world. Production and distribution were centrally planned; quality plummeted. When the USSR collapsed in 1990, Georgia found itself with ruined vineyards, little awareness of modern international tastes, and just two functioning wineries.

Our party for the trip was in the hands of Levan Gachechiladze of GWS, who was setting up a wine institute that would impose regulations from vine to wine with support from the Office Internationale du Vin (OIV) in Paris. The aim was to form the basis of a system of *Appellation Contrôlée*, and I am happy to say that this has been achieved.

At that time, most of Georgia's vineyards were in the Kakheti Valley, which begins an hour's drive northwest of Tbilisi. Only a dozen of the 500 or so indigenous grape varieties were then planted. Rkatsiteli made a fragrant crisp white, while Mtsvane was fuller and fruitier, the best white being Tsinandali, a blend of the two. Saperavi virtually monopolized red wine production, its grippiness reminding me of Sangiovese, while the less-planted Matrassa was more plummy with lower tannins. GWS's top brand was Tamada ('toastmaster').

Our lengthy lunches and dinners were served à la Russe, the tables loaded with dishes that were presented in no discernible order, and many toasts were proposed and enjoyed. After four days I concluded that with the Saperavi grape the Georgians had created a 'hangover-free wine', for however much I drank, my head was quite clear the next day. At a late breakfast on our final morning deep in the countryside, carafes of Saperavi accompanied the usual jugs of fruit juice and I thought – despite my companions' raised eyebrows – that a glass would do me no harm. This was a mistake: an hour later I was smitten with the accumulated result of four days of trying to keep up with the Georgians.

My first visit to Slovenia in late May was organized by Robert Gorjak, a young wine educator whom Bella and I had met in Montalcino a couple of years earlier. I had not set foot in this country since 1965, when it had been part of Yugoslavia under the control of President Tito. Two days of tasting were held in Slovenia's grandest hotel on the shores of Lake Bled, formerly President Tito's personal residence, and before that one of the Habsburg family homes. I was offered President Tito's suite, which could have housed several families in comfort. There was a trip to Movia, a wine estate on the border between Slovenia and Italy, run by the charismatic, slightly eccentric Aleš Kristančič. Because the estate had produced Tito's favourite wine, it was the only one in Yugoslavia that had remained in family hands. The quality of these wines – and of the less famous wines I tasted – were a revelation of natural fruit and purity of expression.

In late July, Bella and I were in Seattle for the biannual World Vinifera Conference, afterwards hiring a car to drive down Route 1 through Oregon and into Napa, where we stayed with Warren Winiarski at Stag's Leap Wine Cellars. The wine country was hardly recognizable from our first visit in the mid-1970s, Napa being, in Warren's words, 'at the stage the Médoc had reached in the late-19th century: we are turning wine into art and it is now a cultural phenomenon.' In earlier days he said that wine had to have 'the three Gs: Ground, Grape and Guy/Gal', but he had now progressed to the three Vs: Vineyards, Vision and Vitality.

The high spot of 2000 was a three-day event hosted by Rhône expert John Livingstone-Learmonth in and around Gigondas. For some time John, author of *The Wines of the Rhône*, had been planning a dinner at Les Florets in Gigondas to celebrate his 50th birthday. A substantial bet on Sinndar at 16/1 to win the Derby, topped up by unpatriotically backing France to win Euro 2000, persuaded him that the celebration should be extended over a weekend – his personal version of *les Trois Glorieuses* – to which he asked 60 willing participants.

The most interesting trip of 2001 was to New Orleans, and later to Nashville, in May. At the 10th New Orleans Wine and Food Experience there were many grand tastings held over two days, the Best of Show Award going to Beaulieu Vineyards' Georges de Latour Private Reserve 1997, which harked back to the superb wines made by André Tchelistcheff. Bella and I took a break afterwards to see some of the country for the first time, driving off on a roundabout route via the cotton town of Natchez, with its marvellous antebellum houses; on to Jackson, Oxford, home to the University of Mississippi, and to Memphis to visit Graceland and eat vast slabs of ribs in the downtown Rendezvous restaurant.

We reached Nashville for *Un Eté du Vin*, a wine weekend designed to raise money for the American Cancer Society. Wine critic Homer Blitch and local businessman Tom Milam had put on the first of these events in July 1980, when a tasting had been followed by an informal auction that raised $3,000. When I had visited Nashville in one of my Broadbent-understudy roles, the top lot was a private collection of Château Mouton Rothschild in magnums spanning 100 years – the 1945 at the gala dinner prompted a spontaneous ovation – and over $600,000 was raised. In 2001, the auction catalogue was bursting with once-in-a-lifetime lots put together by wine collector Tom Black. They included 50 vintages of Petrus from 1924 to 1998 and a bottle of every vintage of Stag's Leap Wine Cellars Cask 23 from between 1972 and 1995 – Warren himself was of course present. The evening raised $1.2 million.

Two things fuel such remarkable events: the passion and generosity of the donors and spenders, and the US tax system. Donors can write off the cost of their donations at open-market value, and buyers can write off every cent above this value. Guests attending the $5,000-per-couple dinner can write off all but the cost of the food, the wines being offered by patrons and written off accordingly. Imagine how much more fun and successful fundraising events would be in the UK if Her Majesty's Revenue and Customs followed suit.

I turned 60 in October 2001 and spent the weekend celebrating, first with a lunch at the Chelsea Arts Club. (The Arts Club, 'founded by artists for artists' in 1891, is a splendid example of bohemian life that London has almost entirely lost, and a complete contrast to Boodle's, my other club in St James's Street. Fortunately, I am now a life member of both, so neither of them can throw me out for bad behaviour.) We enjoyed scallops with pea purée, rack of Welsh lamb, English cheeses and a fine chocolate birthday cake along with suitable quantities of Pierre Gimonnet Premier Cru Blanc de Blancs, Bernard Morey Chassagne-Montrachet Premier Cru Les Caillerets 1995, Château d'Angludet 1982 and Foreau Domaine du Clos Naudin Moelleux 1990, all of which were drinking superbly as I had hoped. Bella had booked us and two of our closest friends on a late-afternoon Eurostar which, after we had enjoyed a few glasses of champagne and a short sleep, deposited us at the Gare du Nord in Paris. From here, we crossed the street to the Brasserie du Nord for oysters and Sancerre.

In late 2001, I spent a magical day at Louis Jadot in Beaune to celebrate 30 years of inspired winemaking by Jacques Lardière, which ended with a 90-year old wine. The morning tasting concentrated on the Jadot holdings in Bonnes-Mares and Corton-Pougets; Lardière remarked that 'only a great terroir permits a wine to age properly, and it is only by ageing properly that a wine can express its terroir.'

Time not travelling in 2002 was still well spent: Oz Clarke's publisher Adrian Webster had commissioned the *Clarke & Spurrier Fine Wine Guide*, and my remit was to cover all of France. This gave me an excellent excuse to bring myself back up to speed on facts and figures – while remaining just as subjective in my opinions.

Thoughts of wine were suspended by the death of my mother in August. She had been in good health at 86, and on her 85th birthday all the family had gathered at the Jockey Club at Wincanton Racecourse for lunch in her honour. There was a funeral service in her village of Wick St Lawrence near Bristol, and then we followed the coffin to Marston where, after a further service, it was lowered into my father's grave. As she requested, the only inscription added to the stone above her dates was 'and Pamela, his Wife'.

A long-planned visit to the Douro in October began as a 'Symington sandwich'. Only a cup of coffee on the early flight from Gatwick to Oporto had separated the splendid magnums of Graham 1970 presented by Clare Symington at the Michael Broadbent Tribute Dinner the evening before, and Dow's Midnight, the Symington's newest port, which we were treated to on arrival at Vila Nova de Gaia. This and the 28 other ports and seven table wines that followed made up the British sandwich of Symington and Taylor, with a slice of Quinta do Noval in the middle.

In the Douro, older vintages are traditionally brought out to accompany plainly cooked local dishes. Of the many superb wines we tasted, four stood out for me at that time: the nectar-like Taylor 1966, the amazing Quinta do Noval Nacional 1963, the indestructible Dow 1945 and Noval's ethereal wood-aged Colheita 1937. Nor should I ignore the raisiny-sweet Taylor 30-year old tawny, two bottles of which appeared, with a candle, to celebrate my 61st birthday with Alastair and Gillyanne Robertson at Quinta do Vargellas. Rather than signing the visitors' book to record your thanks for their wonderful hospitality, the Robertsons prefer their guests to write a poem. They have amassed a collection ranging from perfect pentameters to downright doggerel. My effort falls into the latter category:

> To have one's birthday at Vargellas
> Is not the luck of many fellas,
> Where Gilly's hospitality dims
> Two days of supping with the Syms,
> And Alastair's infectious charm
> Convinces me that there's no harm

In thinking that the vines *en face* [belonging to Cockburn]
Make wine that's only good, alas,
For putting in a standard blend,
While all the grapes around us end
In Vargellas, or the *Nec*
Plus Ultra of the Taylor deck.
And if such thoughts help make me merrier,
They're further helped by Laurent Perrier.

One of the guests a few pages before me had been Len Evans, the great Welsh-Australian wine impresario, who had conceived several stanzas in praise of port, ending each with the lament: 'But port makes me fart!'

Back home, I headed up one of the Gidleigh Park Hotel wine weekends that I had been hosting off and on for a few years, this time based on the wines of Piedmont and Tuscany. American ex-banker and wine lover Paul Henderson and his English wife had taken over this rambling hotel deep in Dartmoor two decades earlier. They had built it up to be one of the finest of the English country house hotels,

The label might have disintegrated but the promise remains: Quinta do Noval Nacional 1963, once described by Serena Sutcliffe as 'Nirvana'.

with a Michelin-starred cuisine, comfortable rooms and the lovely moors on the doorstep. Between two splendid dinners, Paul had raided his cellar for a Saturday-morning tasting of 18 Super Tuscans from 1997 to 1985, focusing mostly on Ornellaia, Sassicaia, Solaia and Tignanello. Ornellaia, a 135-hectare estate near to Bolgheri, was part of the Antinori inheritance from the della Gherardesca estates of Piero and Lodovico Antinori's mother. It was Lodovico's brainchild, and there is general agreement that it has equalled – even surpassed in some vintages – the wine of their cousin's Sassicaia estate.

Two years earlier I had taken part in a vertical tasting of Ornellaia's Masseto from the six hectares on which André Tchelistcheff had insisted, against the advice of Bordeaux's Professor Peynaud, that Lodovico plant 100 percent Merlot. In the early years, Lodovico found that Masseto was behaving more like Cabernet Sauvignon, retaining a certain leanness and grip. Michel Rolland took overall charge from 1995, reducing yields by 30 percent and selecting French oak specifically for the blend. The 1995 proved to be the turning point and now, although the ownership of Ornellaia has passed into the hands of the Frescobaldi family, Masseto, thanks to Lodovico's vision and flair, is one of Italy's greatest wines. At Gidleigh Park I rated the first growth-style Ornellaia above Sassicaia, while the 1999 vintages of Tignanello and Solaia were nothing short of sensational.

The major Spurrier event of summer 2003 was our daughter's wedding. Kate arrived with me in a horse-drawn carriage to be married in the village church to Andrew Richards. That evening 150 people gathered under a marquee for dinner and dancing, and the following day there was a Sunday brunch for as many guests again. Bella and I took ourselves off to Naples to relax afterwards, before I set off in early June to Tokyo for a week of the Japan Wine Challenge.

Vinexpo that year took place in a heatwave that preceded the hottest European summer on record. Temperatures edged above 40°C. The exhibition halls had no air-conditioning and bottles were literally popping their corks as you walked by. But the heat was nothing to the storm that exploded over St-Emilion the evening of the Dîner Millésimes de Collection held by the premier grand cru classé châteaux. When we arrived at Château La Gaffelière, torrential rain was falling and something like a tornado was buffeting the car. Turning into the drive we were met by a scene of utter devastation: rain had broken through the middle of the marquee, elegantly-set tables had been overturned like skittles and the kitchen tent was flattened, spoiling the entire dinner but for the cheese. Happily, no one had been hurt. Our quick-thinking hosts marshalled us down to the cellars and before long, standing among the barrels with glass, napkin and bread roll in hand, we began to enjoy wines from the 12 different châteaux from 1998 down to 1953. It was the kind of party that stays in the memory long after other Vinexpo evenings have faded.

The most memorable tasting of 2003 was at a pre-sale dinner at Christie's that celebrated three centuries of Château Latour. It was a little under nine years since François Pinault had bought Latour from Allied Lyons, thus returning this first growth Pauillac to French ownership after a hiatus of 31 years. (When the Pearson-Harvey consortium bought control of Latour from the de Beaumont and Contrivon families in 1962, President de Gaulle commented: 'They can hardly take the soil with them.')

Latour had now emerged from a period of quiet renovation. Small quantities of 'library stocks' had been made available, covering 64 vintages from 1863 to 1996, and the wines at dinner, served from magnums, ranged from 1961 back to 1881. Younger vintages were available at the pre-sale tasting, and the nine older wines had all been re-corked at the château between 1990 and 1992. From the oldest trio of 1909, 1890 and 1881, the 1890 stood out as being full of life, flavour and grip, quite stunning for a 113-year old wine, while the 1881 had kept a truffly fragrance. The next three were a solid and rich 1952, a rather medicinal 1937 and – the revelation of the evening – the 1924, which had huge warmth and depth of flavour. After this the 1917 failed to shine, but the evening ended with two blockbusters: the 1961, whose intense colour revealed the purest concentration of Cabernet Sauvignon, and the historic 1945 that showed the energy and power of one of the greatest vintages of the 20th century.

As if to confirm the rivalry between Bordeaux and Burgundy, another extraordinary wine experience took place in 2003 in Bouchard Père et Fils' 13th-century cellars in the centre of Beaune during the Hospices de Beaune week-end. Champagne's Joseph Henriot had bought this grand Burgundy name and its stock of ancient vintages a decade earlier. The very early vintage in this heatwave year began on August 21st and finished just one week later. It was the earliest harvest since 1731, the same year that Bouchard Père et Fils was founded. Henriot celebrated this coincidence by showing early vintages back down to 1846. His theory that such vintages rely on fruit rather than acidity to keep them going was borne out by a Meursault-Charmes 1953 (harvested September 14th), a Corton-Charlemagne 1952 (September 18th), a Meursault-Perrières 1947 (September 7th) and a remarkable Meursault-Charmes 1846 (September 16th). This last was the oldest wine in the Bouchard cellars, thrice recorked, and it resembled a dry amontillado that grew and grew in the glass.

The reds were equally extraordinary, beginning with Savigny-lès-Beaune Les Lavières 1976, another heat-wave year (September 8th), followed by Beaune-Marconnets 1959 (September 14th), Beaune Grèves Vigne de l'Enfant Jésus 1947 (September 7th) which was the nearest vintage in style to 2003, Beaune Clos du Roi 1929 (September 25th), a magnificent Romanée-St-Vivant 1906 (September 22nd) and even the Chassagne-Montrachet Morgeot 1893 (August 30th) from pre-phylloxera vines, which still showed strength and vitality at 110 years old. The final wine of the dinner was Beaune Grèves Vigne de l'Enfant Jésus 1865, acknowledged to be the greatest burgundy vintage of the 19th century: still deep in colour, clear and limpid, fresh and sweet, marrying delicacy and power. Eight years previously I had attended a dinner where Joseph Henriot had ended with a Volnay-Santenots from the same year, but the Beaune, drunk on home ground, was even more memorable.

CHAPTER FOURTEEN
FREE AS A BIRD

By 2004 the Paris debts had at last been paid off, and I was back to buying the odd work of art, keeping up the cellar in Dorset and continuing to travel for wine-related events. In January I had organized a dinner to celebrate 40 years in the wine trade at Ransome's Dock, chef Martin Lam's restaurant just south of the river in Battersea. This was known as 'the wine trade restaurant' since, although there was a long, varied and good-value wine list, Martin was also happy for people to bring their own bottles for a moderate corkage fee. Thank heavens it was moderate, for 45 guests managed to get through 59 bottles, made up of Pol Roger Champagne 1995, Jean-Noël Gagnard Chassagne-Montrachet Premier Cru Les Caillerets 1999, Château Léoville-Barton St-Julien 1989, Château de Beaucastel Châteauneuf-du-Pape 1990, Willi Haag Brauneberger Juffer-Sonnenuhr Riesling Auslese 1985 and Fonseca vintage 1966.

Perhaps not every glass was drained to the dregs, but the impressive roll-call does illustrate my belief that when the wine is good and the dinner leisurely, one shouldn't skimp on quantity. The most agreeable statement I heard regarding *consommation à table* came from Georges Thienpont, owner in the 1960s and '70s of Vieux Château Certan in Pomerol. He said: 'A magnum of claret is suitable for two gentlemen dining together, provided they have had a bottle of champagne beforehand.' It was a very jolly evening.

When I accepted an invitation later that month from Eduardo Chadwick to attend a tasting of his top Chilean wines – Don Maximiano, Seña and Viñedo

Chadwick – at the Ritz-Carlton in Berlin, little did I think that the event would find me travelling around the world with him for the next 10 years.

I had never been to Berlin, nor had Bella, so we booked in for a long weekend. Only when we arrived the afternoon before the tasting and met up with Eduardo did I realize that his wines were going to be compared in a blind tasting with similar vintages of first growth Bordeaux and top Super Tuscans, the common theme being that all the wines were Bordeaux blends. About 30 of the best European palates and wine writers had been invited, and that evening Eduardo hosted an informative overview of the wines of Chile.

The following morning René Gabriel, Switzerland's renowned wine expert from Geneva's Mövenpick, and I flanked Eduardo at a table in front of 40 guests. There were 16 wines, and once the results had been annotated it fell to me to read out the results, in reverse order starting with the 10th wine. Eduardo smiled and visibly relaxed when he heard that Seña 2000 had tied for fourth place with Château Margaux 2001. Having already received the recognition he was after, Eduardo was hardly paying attention when I then announced that Seña 2001 was ranked second and Viñedo Chadwick 2000 was first. Perhaps nobody in the room was more surprised than he was, and this event was immediately dubbed the 'Berlin Tasting', tipping its hat to the Paris Tasting of 1976. The full ranking was:

1	*Viñedo Chadwick* 2000
2	*Seña* 2001
3	*Château Lafite Rothschild* 2000
4=	*Château Margaux* 2001
4=	*Seña* 2000
6=	*Viñedo Chadwick* 2001
6=	*Château Margaux* 2000
6=	*Château Latour* 2000
9	*Errázuriz Don Maximiano Founder's Reserve* 2001
10=	*Château Latour* 2001
10=	*Antinori Solaia* 2000

What Eduardo was looking for in 2004 was recognition that his wines, and by extension the best wines of Chile, could measure up to the benchmarks of the

European wine world. This was just what I was after in 1976 for the Chardonnays and Cabernet Sauvignons from California and, like Eduardo, I was not expecting such a startling result, the 'upstarts' beating the benchmarks. Tastings such as these certainly have relevance, but they also bring surprise, even criticism and disbelief. It is therefore important to repeat them with the same wines in different places with different palates, but always blind. During the next decade I accompanied Eduardo to São Paulo, Rio de Janeiro, Toronto, Beijing, Seoul, New York, Chicago, Los Angeles and Moscow between 2006 and 2012, ending with the 10th-anniversary celebrations in Tokyo, Hong Kong and London in 2014. Eduardo held 22 events across 15 nations and his wines were placed among the top three in 20 of these: a remarkable success rate.

On our last evening in Berlin in 2004, I took Bella to Borchardt, a brasserie that had been famous in the 1930s and had recently been renovated. To do my bit for German wine, after a carafe of Riesling I ordered a bottle of a red from the Lemberger grape. The young sommelier frowned and said: 'Sir, I may be a German patriot, but not for our red wines. I would suggest you take the Chianti.'

The Berlin visit meant that I missed out on the annual Southwold claret tasting, an event that had begun about a dozen years before, hosted by Simon Loftus of Adnams Brewery along with wine merchants in the seaside town of Southwold,

Eduardo Chadwick (*centre*), wine critic and journalist Igor Serdyuk and I celebrate Chilean wines' success (again) in Moscow in 2012.

Suffolk. The guests origianally comprised UK importers from Bordeaux such as Berry Bros & Rudd, Justerini & Brooks, Corney & Barrow, The Wine Society and specialist independents plus a single journalist, Clive Coates MW. The Press contingent now included Jancis Robinson MW, Neal Martin and me. The wines we tasted were dry and sweet whites and reds from all the crus classés, and many crus bourgeois and 'second wines' from the Bordeaux vintage four years back, the wines having been in bottle for about two years. This allowed for a 'proper' judgement of the year in question, as opposed to the En Primeur tastings from the barrel that were made just six months after the harvest. Initially, two bottles of each wine – even from the first growths – were sourced directly from the châteaux, but some châteaux (and even some of the Super Seconds) later declined to provide them. In those cases if members of the Southwold group did not have the specific wines in stock, the tasters clubbed together to buy them in.

The blind tastings, in flights of 12 wines grouped as far as possible by appellation, cover almost 200 wines. They last two full days and are conducted under the 'Chatham House Rules' which bar participants from using or referring to any scores but their own and those of the group. These scores are 'topped and tailed', meaning that the highest and lowest are eliminated. (One of my wine-writing colleagues, a prolific and very serious author of books on all aspects of Bordeaux and its wines, ignored this rule on the one occasion he attended, and has not been invited back.) Apart from giving our rankings – still using the now old-fashioned 20-point scale – we comment on the wines, and the results are transmitted to the châteaux. This is all handled with the utmost discretion, and most of the châteaux find it very useful to have the combined, un-biased opinions of such a qualified bunch of tasters.

In 2017 when both the Adnams hotels were under renovation, the group re-located to Farr Vintners, the UK's biggest dealer in Bordeaux, so was re-named the Southwold-on-Thames group. That year we looked at the 2013s, a vintage everyone would prefer to forget, and from which I didn't buy a single bottle.

An added benefit of being part of the group is that we are asked to dig deep into our cellars for bottles to share in the evenings. The late, very great Bill Baker, who died at just 53 years old (and whose girth was so impressive that doors of Wells Cathedral were too narrow to accommodate his coffin with its 10 pallbearers), gave us straightforward advice on this point: 'Don't bring crap.' It is an opportunity to share one's very best in the very best company.

My project with Sarah Kemp for the *Decanter* World Wine Awards (DWWA) came to fruition in April 2004. Although the proudest achievement of my life in wine is the creation of the Académie du Vin, the DWWA runs a pretty close second. I had been pushing Sarah to create a *Decanter* competition for some time and she always pushed back: '*Decanter* does events, not competitions.' Then, a month or so before Vinexpo 2003, she agreed that the time was right and asked me to set the rules. They are simple: tasting at tables of four with a senior judge per table; flights of not more than 12 wines, presented like-with-like in price brackets; full information given except the name of the wine.

We wanted a regional chair for each country or major wine region, and by the time we unveiled the plans, the original 14 had been selected and contracted to taste only for *Decanter*, and several dozen more lined up with a year's contract. The rules have been refined since the first competition, but not changed.

In the first year we received 4,500 samples to be judged on the 20-point scale. Medals were awarded to four categories: Commended (14.5–15.4), Bronze (15.5–16.9), Silver (17–18.4) and Gold (18.5 and above). In the early days the percentage of entrants receiving each award were 25 percent, 25 percent, 12 percent, and under two percent respectively. Numbers of entries rose steadily from this first year to reach 16,534 in 2019. For some time the DWWA has been the largest and most influential wine competition in the world, but not in our wildest dreams did Sarah and I expect to see such a volume. In 2019 wines came from 56 countries, some of which did not even produce wine when we started. The judges, including 65 Masters of Wine and 23 Master Sommeliers, came from 29 different countries.

Judging has now moved to the international 100-point scale, which works out at Commended 83–85, Bronze 86–89, Silver 90–94 and Gold 95 and above. My instructions to the judges are simple: recognize and reward quality. Quality all over the world is getting better but the judging remains strict.

On the last day, all the Golds within each category are re-tasted and a Platinum medal awarded to the best wine in each category. A week later, the three chairs are joined by two other judges and all these wines are pitted against each other in defined categories to arrive at the Platinum Best of Show.

Any competition is only as good as the validity of the results, the results are only as good as the judges. The judges, for a large part, are only as good as the organization that surrounds them. The role of wine competitions, particularly for emerging markets, comes down to just two words: information and trust. An award represents an accolade for the producer, and if it helps the consumer to make a good-value, pleasing purchase, that's a win-win situation.

I very nearly didn't make it to the 2004 South African Airways Wine Selection judging in August that year. Immigration at Cape Town airport refused to let me into the country since I did not have a clean page in my passport on which they could affix the temporary entry visa. They were not impressed when I showed them my invitation to the competition and, when I helpfully peeled off a defunct US visa to provide the requisite blank page, the official informed me that not only was I an illegal immigrant, but I could now also be charged with defacing an official document.

At this point, SAA Food & Beverage Manager Owen Jullies, seeing one of his judges about to be deported, began to call in some favours. The British Consulate declined to help, saying that a wine tasting was not a matter of life and death. The head of Chancery agreed to call the official and authorize him to issue the visa, but the official said he required that authorization in writing. John Platter, whose wine guide is the bible of South African wines, called the Minister of Agriculture, but it was a Saturday and the minister was on the golf course. Meanwhile, Lynne Sheriff MW, who had organized the international judges, was pulling strings from London. She eventually contacted President Mbeki's personal wine adviser and, after I had been detained for five hours, the official returned my passport complete with the visa, muttering that powers greater than his had authorized my illegal entry. From that moment, things improved mightily. Bella came to collect me and we spent the evening with friends from London, celebrating my release.

SAA is a proud flag-carrier for the country's wines. Lynne joined the judges the following day to team up with Annegret Reh-Gartner and Egon Müller, both top producers from Germany's Mosel region, and Geoff Merrill from Australia. Local judges were Cape Wine Masters Dave Hughes, Allan Mullins and Tony Mossop. On the last morning we visited the Rustenberg estate outside Stellenbosch, where owner Simon Barlow remarked that the Cape was becoming 'a vinous Eldorado', his newest neighbour on the slopes of the Simonsberg being May-Eliane de Lencquesaing of Château Pichon-Longueville Comtesse de Lalande.

A conference in Paris on 'The Future for Emerging Wine Markets' opened 2005, the focus being on Asia. I had been to China a few times and often to Japan and Singapore, and at the time felt that consumption was beginning to flow down to the middle classes. I was surprised, then, to hear Canadian Don St-Pierre Jr, co-founder of China-based importer ASC Fine Wines, the largest importer/ distributor in the country, announce that 'given everything we have to deal with, the traffic lights for wine are still on amber'. He was followed by Rajeev Samant, a bright young man who had recently moved from Silicon Valley to Nashik, four hours by train from Bombay, where he was planting vineyards to create a vision of Napa Valley in his home country. By the next decade, Samant's brand Sula had 50 percent of the local market and was set to become India's largest winery. He said: 'For India, the traffic lights are on green!'

Over the years Bella and I have spent time at Fattoria Nittardi near Castellina in Chianti. This is one of the most beautiful of many such small estates. It dates from the 12th century, and in the early 16th it was owned by Michelangelo di Lodovico Buonarroti Simoni, who assigned its management to his brother Leonardo while he was busy in Rome painting the Sistine Chapel ceiling. A few *fiaschi* were requested for the pleasure of Pope Julius II, who proclaimed it 'nectar Dei' (hence 'Nittardi'). In 1983 the property was acquired in a pretty run-down state by Frankfurt art dealer Peter Femfert and his Venetian wife Stefania, and since that vintage Peter has asked his artist friends to design not only a label for the wine, but wrapping paper as well. Philippine de Rothschild chose HRH Prince Charles to design the label for her 2005 vintage; Peter's choice fell on Yoko Ono.

I had met Peter at various wine tastings in London and we got on well, so when he offered us a week in one of the apartments in the original house, I was very happy to accept. We discovered that the English school he had attended for a couple of years while in his teens had been founded by my great-grandfather George Herbert Strutt. There cannot be many of my ancestor's pupils who own an internationally renowned art gallery, or indeed who have created such a beautiful estate in Tuscany. Fattoria Nittardi is now part of my life, the family connection giving me a connection to Peter that adds something personal to our joint passion for wine and art. It is also the most magical place to visit.

Peter has installed a series of large sculptures in the grounds and the vineyards. After one visit we stayed in Lucca, where there was a huge antiques fair. In the main square, one of the dealers had a pair of vast bronze lions, taken from a palazzo in Naples. I knew that Peter liked lions so I asked the dealer to email him a photo. Peter took the bait, bargained down the price, and now these splendid animals, known as 'the Spurlions', guard the entrance to the Nittardi cellar.

Peter owns a few hundred hectares here but, because of the zoning in and around Chianti, he has only a dozen hectares of vines. Being unable to expand at home, he bought 30 hectares of unplanted land in the Maremma, near the coast in the hills around Scansano overlooking Monte Argentario. His first vintage produced two red wines, Ad Astra and Nectar Dei, to which he has added a white Vermentino named Ben.

Two dinners stood out for me in the first half of 2007, the first being for Michael Broadbent's 80th birthday at his club, Brooks's. I have the classic English menu: spiced brown potted shrimps, roast rack of lamb, poached pear en cage with sauce Anglaise, Colston Bassett Stilton and farmhouse Cheddar; accompanied by Pol Roger 1998, Chassagne-Montrachet Les Champs-Gains 2000, Château Haut-Batailley 2000, Château Lafite Rothschild 1996, Michele Chiarlo Moscato d'Asti Nivole 2006, Cockburn's 1967 and Cockburn's 1927 vintage ports.

The second dinner was a grand affair at Chatsworth in Derbyshire, where 45 guests had paid handsomely to enjoy white burgundies presented by Anne-Claude Leflaive and Right Bank clarets by Christian Moueix, preceded by Champagne Salon 1996 and rounded off with a splendid Lot 53 (ie 1953, but at that time cognacs could not carry a vintage) cognac from Tesseron. The beautiful surroundings were matched by the simple grandeur of the wines, which stood out for me as exemplars of their appellations. Christian Moueix remarked modestly: 'Our only talent is to be respectful of terroir', but he then went up a gear to describe his Château Magdelaine 1961, commenting: 'Here is elegance that goes beyond appreciation, that takes one to another level, that shows we are part of history.' Such wines do not happen by chance, however unique the terroir. They need dedicated perfectionists to practise good husbandry and avoid the temptation to exaggerate. Such people are by definition risk-takers. This was summed up by host Adam Brett-Smith, with regard to Anne-Claude Leflaive: 'Her greatness lies in being courageous… transforming the estate's viticulture, philosophy, yield, quality and perception, when the instinct might have been to do nothing.' The same could be said of the custodians of Chatsworth, each generation taking its inheritance into the future with intelligence and vigour. Benchmarks are essential in all walks of life.

In September 2007 I had a serious bicycling accident. I have always ridden a bike wherever I lived (except in New York), and had had the odd minor scrape, but was never minded to wear a helmet. That year, *Decanter* had taken the Victoria and Albert Museum as a venue for its awards party, and I had had great pleasure in presenting one of the top awards to John and Janet Trefethen of Napa Valley for their Cabernet Sauvignon. We arranged to have lunch the following day with Michael Broadbent. I set off on my bike a little after noon on a sunny day, knowing the route by heart. I would have reached the pavement outside the V&A at around 12.30pm, but the next thing I knew, 45 minutes later, I was in an ambulance. I had been knocked off my bike by a speeding motorcyclist, and (I learned later) gone head-over-heels across the handlebars, smacking the back of my head on the pavement as I landed.

When I came round, I was asked if I remembered anything about what had happened, but at the time it was a blank. The motorcyclist stayed nearby until the ambulance set off, the police having taken his details, and I was whisked off to the Charing Cross Hospital to have my head stitched up.

I had been knocked out for well over half an hour and during that time, a V&A staff member who had been at the *Decanter* evening had come out of the building, seen me face up on the ground, recognized me from the evening before and called the office. That evening I received a visit from Sarah Kemp bearing a brand-new cycling helmet adorned with *Decanter* stickers, and a visit from Bella, who had rushed up from the country on hearing the news. After five days in hospital I moved into the London Clinic to spend a week recovering. The specialist there told me he was a wine buff and that several years earlier he had looked after Harry Waugh (a connoisseur and one of the UK's most influential and revered wine merchants) who had injured his head in a car accident in Burgundy. He said that I had been very lucky, but that the damage done might affect my sense of smell, therefore my sense of taste. This could have extremely serious implications, not least to my livelihood. Had I suffered palate-impairing damages, an insurance claim would have been for substantial damages. I initiated legal action, but it was forestalled by the motorcyclist's extraordinary counter-claim that I had run into him, and so knocked myself off my bike! His insur-ers backed him up, insisting that since I was on record as having remembered nothing about the accident, I was not in a position to challenge his version of events – in spite of copious circumstantial evidence that proved it was false.

I did actually lose some of my sense of smell for a while, slowly getting it back to about 90 percent. I compensate by paying much more attention to the taste and texture of wines when I taste, but I can no longer detect the smell of TCA, or a 'corked' wine. Perhaps that is a blessing in disguise?

My physical recovery was much quicker and I was up and about for the 25th anniversary of the Christie's Wine Course. Little did Michael Broadbent know, when he gave the first 'Introduction to Wine Tasting' lecture in October 1982 at the age of 55, that he would be opening the batting again in October 2007 teach-ing 'Classic Grapes, Classic Styles'. The big change was that at the first lecture, all eight wines were French, while this time only one of them was. In 1982 New World wines were sold by just a handful of specialist merchants, but by 2007, 60 percent of all wine drunk in the UK came from six countries in the New World, and just 38 percent from the four main wine-producing countries of the Old World. Even New World vineyards were, until well into this millennium, situated firmly between the 30th and 50th parallels, but now with China, India and Brazil there is a *new* New World emerging to which the old-fashioned tenets of viticulture might no longer apply.

I escaped the 2008 Dorset winter with Bella to spend two weeks in Argentina. Of the many bodegas I visited as part of a *Decanter* tasting, the finest was that of José Manuel Ortega – 'O Fournier' – at which his wife Nadia had created an award-winning restaurant. José Manuel, whose family came from Burgos in north-ern Spain, is a former banker who made a large range of wines from what he refers to as 'cult grapes' in Maule in Chile and in Spain's Ribera del Duero. He became a great friend and involved me in his DOSS Foundation project: 100 cases selected from the best barrels in each of his wineries by Dany Rolland, Ortega himself, his winemaker José Spisso and me (hence DOSS), which were sold at $100 a bottle, all the proceeds going towards higher education for underprivileged students. Like his hero Robert Mondavi, José Manuel liked to give something back.

One of my early *Decanter* columns in 2009 was headed 'Late-bottled vintage port – back from the dead'. This now justifiably popular style of port known as LBV was launched by Taylor, Fladgate and Yeatman's Alistair Robertson with a Taylor 1965, bottled in 1970. True vintage port is bottled after less than two years in cask and is meant to mature for decades, throwing a heavy sediment which requires careful decanting. Announcing their new brand, Robertson said: 'We have been working on the idea of offering a port that could be considered vintage, yet could be poured bright and clear, straight from the bottle.' The secret is to mature the vintage in wood and then 'late bottle'.

Having been a great supporter of LBVs, which sold well in my Paris shop in the 1970s and 1980s, I began to lose patience with them in the 1990s. In the early 2000s, I put it to David Guimaraens, who had succeeded his larger-than-life father Bruce as winemaker for Fonseca and then the whole of the Taylor group, that he had colluded in the degradation of the category, which by then resembled a rough 'ruby'. No doubt the change in style was partially driven by supermarkets' determination to keep the price in single figures, and by the competition for market share, but still something needed to be done. The exchange was widely reported and must have struck a nerve, since a late-2008 tasting of a range of 2003 and 2001 LBVs at the Portuguese Embassy showed a complete turnaround. Today the quality of port has never been higher, although UK consumption is in decline. The LBVs, preferably unfiltered, and 10-Year-Old tawnies, the two styles that have made port so famous over the years, are once again a sure bet.

The high spot at the end of the year was Pierre-Henry Gagey's celebration of 150 years of Louis Jadot, the Burgundian house he took over on his father André's retirement in 1992. Just 24 of us were there to begin the tasting with red wines (as is customary in Burgundy, rather than starting with whites). Pierre-Henry announced that he had chosen one wine from each of 15 decades of the company's existence, 'not necessarily the best wine from the best vintage, but wines that Jacques Lardière (head winemaker since 1970) and I really like'. In descending order they were: Bonnes-Mares 2003, Gevrey-Chambertin Clos St-Jacques 1997, Beaune Clos des Ursules 1985, Le Musigny 1978, Gevrey-Chambertin Clos St-Jacques 1966, Chambertin Clos de Bèze 1953, Beaune Boucherottes 1949, Chambertin 1937 (with 1934, one of the only two good vintages of the 1930s), Beaune Clos des Ursules 1929, Corton-Pougets 1915, Beaune Clos des Couchereaux 1904, Clos de Vougeot 1898 (the first 100 percent pre-phylloxera wine of the evening), Clos de Tart 1887, Pommard 1878 and Corton 1865. French wine critic Michel Bettane remarked that it was 'a great Corton', to which Gagey replied 'I'm glad you liked it, as those were our last two bottles'. Experiences like these go far beyond privilege.

The burgundy theme was alive and well that April at a dinner to celebrate Aubert de Villaine, co-owner of the Domaine de la Romanée-Conti, being named *Decanter* Man of the Year 2010. Sarah Kemp made a fine speech saying that Aubert has that supremely rare gift: a profound humility allied to absolute self-belief, and she asked me to present the prize, a decanter. 'Thank you, Steven', he murmured as he accepted it, adding 'but you know we don't decant in Burgundy'.

He and I were recently reminiscing about the old days and he remarked that 'things were simpler then, money was mentioned less and we just did the best we could with the grapes we picked', thus stepping lightly over the lifetime of care he had devoted to his vineyards, and to the past, present and future of the domaine.

My first trip of 2010 was to Puglia, where I had not been since August 1965 when Bella and I disembarked the overnight ferry from Greece at Bari. Over four days I was introduced to aromatic dry whites from Malvasia Bianco, Fiano and Vermentino grapes, spending more time on the robust reds from Negromaro, Primitivo and the recently revived Susumaniello.

Primitivo, named for its early ripening, arrived in Puglia unannounced in the 1870s, some saying that it was related to Pinot Noir, others that it was a cousin of the Piedmontese Dolcetto. Research by Professor Carole Meredith at the University of California Davis confirmed in 1998 that it shared the same parents as Zinfandel and Plavac Mali from Croatia. Primitivo di Manduria – in those days wines often took the name from the train station the barrels were exported from – was made a DOC in 1974, but the DOC later risked being rescinded for 'non-use'.

By 2010 Primitivo was back, being served at presidential dinners, and since then has continued, as has Puglia itself, to conquer more markets.

A wine that has little problem conquering markets is claret, and the 2009 vintage revealed over the first week of April showed that the hype which had been building up since its harvest was justified. Prices were very high, only to be surpassed by the 2010 vintage, which was cynically held back from release until Vinexpo in June 2011. This was a mistake. Once the euphoria died down, prices declined considerably. Buying wine En Primeur suffered a crisis of confidence, and while this is still the way that Bordeaux merchants place the 60 or so top brands into markets around the world, it is nothing like as popular as it used to be.

Perhaps the most interesting wine trip that year, and certainly the one with the longest-lasting influence, was to the Domaine de la Verrière (whose wines sell under the Chêne Bleu brand) near Vaison-la-Romaine in the southern Rhône. It was for a conference on Grenache, a grape described as 'the Cinderella of the wine world'. Personally, I would give this description to Cabernet Franc, rather than to this much-planted but underrated grape, which Mark Savage MW described as 'both workhorse and wonder horse'. Grenache is long-lived and perfect for blending as well as on its own. The symposium saw the launch of a Global Grenache Association (Les Grenadiers du Grenache) and the creation of an International Grenache Day to be held annually on September 24th around the world.

If the Grenache Symposium required some intellectual effort, our last trip of the year needed only a good appetite. We were guests of Christian Seely, MD of AXA Millésimes, for a weekend at Quinta do Noval, one of the most famous port estates in the Douro. Two of the Noval pigs, which at three years old weighed 300kg each, were slaughtered and we watched preparations for what Fergus Henderson of London's St John restaurant calls 'nose to tail eating' while savouring a few delicacies and drinking a little port. Christian had also invited publisher and wine judge Ch'ng Poh Tiong, who, on a previous visit, had said that to prepare a pig properly you need 3,000 years of history, so had promised one day to bring his own cooks from China. As neither the cooks nor their history were available to travel, Christian had instead commandeered the two brothers from Au Bonheur du Palais, Bordeaux's best Asian restaurant. Another guest was Daniel Llose, head winemaker at all the Cazes family estates, who arrived with dozens of bottles.

Meals were for all 18 of us, the Bordelais pig-preparers on one long table, the guests on another. The first night brought a cascade of northern Rhônes, the best being Chapoutier's Ermitage 1999; the second day's lunch saw a large range of Languedocs, while at dinner white burgundies and second growth 1998 Médocs were served including of course AXA's Château Pichon-Baron. A mid-morning tasting of Quinta do Noval vintage ports – 1994, 1967, 1966, 1966 Nacional, 1963 – and its remarkable single-vintage 1995, 1968 and a memorable 1937 colheita, was followed by lunch which concentrated on the 2000 vintage, beginning with Roederer and continuing with another range of Médocs.

CHAPTER FIFTEEN
POACHER TURNS GAMEKEEPER

When Bella bought our farm in 1987, I noticed that the soil was full of chalk. I was still running the Académie in Paris at the time, so I put a couple of blocks in my pocket to show to Michel Bettane, France's great wine guru and then our top *professeur*, and asked him where he thought they had came from.

'Champagne, of course,' he said.

'No, Dorset.'

'In that case you should plant a vineyard.'

A little later I asked Chablis producer Michel Laroche, who was in England for a sales tour, to come down and take a look at the site. It impressed him enough to take some soil samples back with him, analysis of which suggested the soil would be a good basis for growing Chardonnay and grapes from the Pinot family. At that time I might have planted Pinot Blanc and its humidity-resistant cousin Pinot Auxerrois, but 1987's rainy summer thankfully put paid to that idea and I didn't think about it again until the early 1990s when, at the International Wine and Spirit Competition Awards ceremony, I was handed a glass of something sparkling and asked what it was. 'Easy,' I said, 'grand cru blanc de blancs, probably Cramant.' It never occurred to me that it might not be champagne – but it was in fact Nyetimber Blanc de Blancs from West Sussex.

Several years later, Ridgeview from East Sussex, whose slightly crisper style I had admired at tastings, won the 2010 DWWA trophy, beating champagne and sparkling wines from all over the world. By this time, English sparkling wines were well and truly launched, with 1,500 hectares under vine across southern England and a few pockets further north. All but a few of these new plantings were producing grapes for sparkling wines.

One of the pioneers of English wine was Major-General Sir Arthur Guy Salisbury-Jones, whose Hambledon white wine I had imported from Hampshire to Paris in 1972. The Wingfield Digbys near Sherborne, north of us in Dorset, revived winemaking in Sherborne Castle in 1982, but the estate came to prominence only much more recently thanks to its sparkling wines.

At Vinexpo 2007 I took the opportunity of presenting a dossier on our land's potential to Jean-Claude and Jean-Charles Boisset, father-and-son owners of the hugely successful company based in Burgundy and in Napa. The Boissets – especially the irrepressible Jean-Charles, who had moved to Napa a few years before – showed keen interest. His sister Nathalie oversaw the French side of the business from the family base in Nuits-St-Georges, and he had bought Robert Mondavi's former home in Oakville. An habitual acquirer of new vineyards, he was always up for something new. That autumn we received the first visit from Georges Legrand and the head viticulturalist to see what could be done as a joint venture: we had hoped to find 30 hectares or so to plant, and to build a winery with a potential production of 100,000 bottles.

There followed two more visits, the second with a representative of Pépinières Guillaume, a specialist vine nursery; analysis of deeply dug soil samples from all over the farm; studies of the sloping ground (better for sheep than for vines), exposure and wind factors, and visits to other vineyards across the south. In the end, the Boissets' advice was plain: there were really only 10–12 hectares that ticked all the boxes. He said we should buy the vines from Pépinières Guillaume, plant these in the qualifying hectares and take the grapes to Ian Edwards at Furleigh Estate nearby. If all goes well, he added, we will buy your wine. With that, we were off.

Everyone agrees that great wines are made in the vineyard, but few ask where the vines come from. *Pépinières de Plants de Vigne Guillaume* in Burgundy's Haute-Saône region, northeast of Dijon, is recognized as the world's finest *pépinière*, or vine nursery. All the top Champagne houses and the great and the good of Burgundy are the firm's clients. Pierre-Marie Guillaume's 20-year study of Sangiovese clones in Chianti caused a sea-change in what was planted where, and the quality from this historic region has never been better. He has a vine nursery in California that supplies the west coast of America, and this sends vines east to Virginia. On my travels, I find his name cropping up all the time to the extent that I send him regular emails saying, *Pierre-Marie*, *je ne peux pas vous échapper /* I can't escape you! On a recent visit, I asked him his secret and he replied: 'To do the job well, you put your boots on, walk the existing vineyards or closely examine those to be planted to get a real sense of the soil and the climate, then propose vines that will show a balanced vigour and have a long life producing healthy grapes.' Simple. Pierre-Marie Guillaume is the unsung hero of many, many great wines.

So during the winter of 2008–09, we prepared a little over two hectares and vines were planted mechanically under close supervision. The Bride River meanders close to our house; its valley and half a dozen villages within it are recognized as being of outstanding natural beauty, so we decided to borrow the name for our brand-new Bride Valley Vineyard.

In December, I was in Paris for Le Palais des Grands Crus, the greatest wine tasting I have ever attended, held at the Petit Palais. It was followed by dinner at the three-rosette restaurant Pavillon Ledoyen, which the guests accessed via a passage under the street. Served mostly from magnums and double magnums, there were 62 Bordeaux, including all eight first growths from both Left and Right Banks plus d'Yquem; 33 burgundies, from Domaine Leflaive's Bâtard-Montrachet 2006 to an Imperial (eight bottles) of Domaine de la Romanée-Conti's 1989 La Tâche; 10 Rhônes that included top wines from Beaucastel, Chapoutier and Jaboulet as well as all Marcel Guigal's grand cru 'La Las'; 16 champagnes with Cristal, Dom Pérignon and Krug to the fore. Germany was represented by Egon Müller, Italy by Ornellaia, Sassicaia and Solaia, Australia by Yarra Yering and California by Harlan Estate. Most of the owners were there to present their wines and taste everyone else's, while most of the guests were members of Le Club Ficofi.

The club is the brainchild of Bordeaux-born Philippe Capdouze, who realized that the world's greatest wine producers and the people who appreciate their wines might like to meet each other. For an annual subscription and an entry fee, members have access to stocks acquired thanks to Capdouze's relationship with the producers. In 2012 the company delivered 35 million euros'-worth of

Bride Valley takes
shape: Ernst from
Germany oversees the
planting of Pépinière
Guillaume's finest
French vines.

wine to its 150 members (the list closed at 200). Ficofi guarantees sourcing, and a concierge services allow the wines to be drunk in the best possible condition, something appreciated as much by the producers as by the members. In recent years I have hosted tastings for the firm in London, Hong Kong, Delhi and Mumbai.

In the spring I was invited to attend a discussion on cork by the Portuguese Cork Association. António Rios de Amorim, Chairman and CEO of Amorim, the country's biggest cork company, admitted that the image of cork as a wine closure had suffered badly in the 1980s, but that producers had reacted with massive investment in research and technology in the 1990s, and cork should now once again be admired as the perfect natural closure. While the Stelvin closure, a screwcap specifically designed for wine, continues to gain market share, cork was reaffirming its value for ecological sustainability, and moving closer to 100 percent security against cork taint, or TCA.

Cork trees, which are stripped of their bark every decade or so, can age more than 200 years, and I am totally in favour of it for wines, red and white, that need to be cellared. Alongside the damage that poor corks inflicted on wine as a product in the past, continuing damage is being done to the French wine industry by La Loi Evin, passed in 1991. This outlaws any advertising that even hints at the pleasures of wine. Nobody believed literally in the 'Guinness for Strength' ad designed in the 1930s (the campaign ran for 30 years) that had a Guinness drinker effortlessly carrying an iron girder, but it was cheerful and good for the brand. A meeting of the Académie du Vin de France noted recently that a country that considered its Belon oysters, Bresse chickens and Brie worthy of recognition by Unesco but refuses to promote its own viticulture was dangerously myopic, and that the damage already done would only get worse. I was reminded of this on a visit to Paris, dining with Bella at La Fontaine de Mars, one of the classic, unchanged bistros in the city, on seeing behind the bar a lovely 1930s print. A glamorous couple in white flannels appear against a map of France picked out in grapes with the caption *Buvez du vin et vivez joyeux* / Drink wine and live joyously.

In Tuscany that summer, a gathering storm was averted. Sixty-nine percent of Brunello di Montalcino producers voted against allowing up to 20 percent of 'foreign' grapes in the production of Rosso di Montalcino. There had already been a big scandal when evidence of Cabernet Sauvignon, Merlot and Syrah had been found in some Brunellos. Heavy fines had been imposed and questions asked. Plainly the producers who had planted grapes other than the accepted Sangiovese felt that Rosso was just a second label of Montalcino, and that volume could grow to satisfy a larger market. I am a big fan of Rosso di Montalcino and while I can still just about afford Brunello, Rossos are one-third the price and more approachable, and the whole point of them is Sangiovese. Permitting other grapes would be the thin end of the wedge. It is interesting to note, meanwhile, that while the rules for Chianti Classico do allow 20 percent of 'other' grapes, there is a trend back to 100 percent Sangiovese for the DOCG wines.

In October 2011 I turned 70 and a series of celebrations provided great compensation for having been born in such a poor year for wine as 1941. One of them was a large lunch that Bella and I hosted at The Seaside Boarding House near our home. The weather was wonderful (for October), and when lunch ended at around 5pm, Jasper Morris MW decided to go for a swim. He surprised our guests at the hotel by repeating the performance before breakfast the following morning.

The next day we gave a vineyard picnic for many more friends and family. With a full house to manage and further guests expected before the picnic, Bella remonstrated with me as I left for the Sunday service at our local church, saying that I should stay to help. I replied simply that I had a lot to thank God for, and went on my way. After the service I thanked our splendid Welsh vicar, Bob Thorne, who said, 'aren't I supposed to come up and bless your vines some day soon?', to which I replied: 'Yes, please; today at 2.30.' He duly appeared in his robes, raised his arms and blessed them as 'little children of God' (– and lo! They delivered just under 500 bottles from vines in their 'third leaf'). This was a great birthday gift.

The Circle of Wine Writers, of which I was then president, had a Christmas party that year that was sponsored by the Virginia Wine Board and held in the august surroundings of The Old Hall in Lincoln's Inn Fields. Just four years before, the first tasting of Virginian wines had taken place at Vinopolis, and the scattering of wine writers who attended immediately spread the word about the elegance and freshness of the wines: lemony Chardonnay, floral Viognier, fragrant Cabernet Franc, vibrant Cabernet Sauvignon-Merlot-Petit Verdot blends and even a little of Piedmont's Nebbiolo, all benefitting from the cool climate and surviving the humidity. The contrast in style between these and wines from the much warmer US west coast is marked, not least for the balanced alcohol that sees them reach 13.5% as a maximum. If 'preppy' is a positive description for wines, Virginia produces the preppiest in America.

Bella and I snapped up an invitation in 2012 from Andrea Franchetti to attend the Contrada d'Etna, a tasting he organized on his Passopisciaro estate in Sicily. Even in spring there were still traces of snow among the vines planted at 1,300 metres on the volcano's blackened-earth slopes. Etna's local grapes are Nerello Mascalese (which shares characteristics with Nebbiolo and is mistakenly thought to be related to Pinot Noir) and the softer Nerello Cappuccio for the reds, and Carricante, which Peter McCombie MW describes as like 'drinking liquid oyster shells' for the whites. The dry summers and long ripening time have encouraged Franchetti to plant Chardonnay and Petit Verdot, while his neighbour Marco de Grazia of Tenuta delle Terre Nere stays with the local varieties. He makes a stunning Calderara Don Peppino from 140-year old pre-phylloxera vines – which he openly admits has been influenced by Chave's Hermitage.

The biggest event of the year was the AIV Symposium in London in early June. Having proposed the UK visit at the previous meeting, I had to come up with a programme for the 40 attendees. The welcome dinner was at Boodle's in St James's, which had opened especially, the chef preparing a menu of the best of British produce to go with wines which (except for the Graham's 1980 port) came from my cellar. Two evenings later, thanks to fellow member John Salvi, the dinner was at Vintners' Hall, the heart of the country's wine trade since the 14th century, where members' wines were poured and guests shared the traditional loving cup. On the intervening two days, we visited English vineyards and gardens, Nyetimber and Ridgeview on the first day, Great Dixter Gardens and Hush Heath Estate on the second, both in equally traditional English summer rain.

Bella and I spent the New Year in Rio de Janeiro, where my niece and her family live. We saw in 2013 with a stunning firework display (and Bollinger 2002) on Copacabana Beach, before flying south to Porto Alegre for a three-day visit to the vineyards. Brazil is the fifth-largest wine producer in the southern hemisphere, behind Argentina, Australia, South Africa and Chile, with five vineyard regions, the most important being Serra Gaucha, north of Porto Alegre. The vineyards include the country's only DO, Vale dos Vinhedos, and the area is known as 'Little

Italy' since many of the estates are still owned by third- and fourth-generation Italians who came from the Veneto at the end of the 19th century. Our visits were to wineries that export, the UK being one of their target markets. The high spot was an eight-course wine-pairing exercise at Pizzato, a 42-hectare estate run by œnologist Flavio Pizzato and his family. Further visits to Lidio Carraro, whose wines I had come across on my first visit to São Paulo a few years before, and the sparkling wines from Casa Valduga, Miolo and especially Cave Geisse, convinced me that Brazil is a wine country to watch.

Late in January I was back in Southwold with the usual crowd to taste the highly rated and very highly priced 2009 Bordeaux in the worst weather imaginable. (The 2010 prices went even higher, leading to the inevitable collapse.) But not even the deepest snow could keep more than 100 guests away from the memorial banquet held by Bristol's Commanderie de Bordeaux for its founder, wine merchant John Avery MW, who had died in late 2012. An empty chair had marked his absence on our first day in Southwold.

Aidan Bell – who had worked many years with John – and I pushed through sleet and fog across deserted roads after the final morning's tasting to arrive in time. We changed into dinner jackets to enjoy Avery's Champagne Rosé before sitting down to a series of wines that showed Bordeaux at its best: Domaine de Chevalier 2003 white from Graves, Château d'Angludet 1995 and Château d'Issan 1985 both from Margaux, Château Canon 2000 St-Emilion from the Right Bank, returning to the Médoc with a superbly fragrant Château Margaux 1988, then a gloriously rich Château d'Yquem 1989, finishing on 1983 Graham's port, which allowed us to raise another glass to John's memory. A month later the wine trade filled St James Garlickhythe opposite Vintners' Hall, a Wren church known as the wine-trade church, for his memorial service.

A mid-March visit to the Rhône Valley began at Domaine Georges Vernay in Condrieu and ended at the Clos de l'Oratoire des Papes in Châteauneuf-du-Pape, each visit confirming that this region is the best in France for wine lovers, be their pockets shallow or deep. Rhône expert John Livingstone-Learmonth said that he has never seen such energy and optimism and that even in 'old-fashioned' appellations such as Châteauneuf-du-Pape, the younger generation is bursting with ideas.

Georges Vernay, who sadly died in 2017 at the great age of 92, was revered as 'the Pope of Condrieu'. As mayor in the late 1960s when the area under vine in this appellation had fallen from its pre-war 200 hectares to just seven, he refused to give up, or to make easier money from fruit-growing or even house-building. By the early 1970s the hectare total had crept into double figures and by 1984 to the low 20s. But more important than saving this historic wine, Vernay saved Viognier for the entire world, since this capricious grape was known only in Condrieu; nowhere else. Wine occasionally needs heroes like this.

April found me in Russia, my third visit in as many years, but this time in the southern city Krasnodar on the Black Sea, one of Catherine the Great's favourite summer watering holes. I had been invited to judge the Southern Russia Wine Competition and to attend the Vinorus Vinotech trade exhibition. The other guests were John Salvi from Bordeaux, the much-travelled Brett Crittenden from Australia, and editor of *Wine Business Monthly* Lisa Shara Hall MW from the USA. The Russian co-chairs were assisted by nine local judges headed by Igor Serdyuk, the country's leading wine critic who was, thankfully, fluent in English.

The dry white and dry red winners were both from local grapes, the five white Golds medals included a Chardonnay and a Sauvignon Blanc and the four red Golds showed two Cabernet Sauvignons, the other two being from the Saperavi, more famous in its native Georgia. The assembled guests praised the overall quality, but heard that an increase in indigenous varieties was not assured, since there is not a single vine nursery in Russia. Wine has a low priority in Moscow, nevertheless the large and small producers we met were all passionate about their wines and open to every kind of advice. Several of them, appropriately named 'garagistes', ignore state rulings entirely, working below the radar to produce wines for a local clientele. With people such as these, Russian wines have a very positive future.

Early summer tastings featured 2011 vintage port, the latest vintage to be generally declared since 2003, causing David Guimaraens of Croft, Fonseca and Taylor to say that 'the 2011s stand out for the purity of the fruit and the quality of the tannins, which are silky and well integrated but provide plenty of structure'. Charles Taylor MW of UK merchant Montrachet was more precise: 'The best vintage since 1994, possibly since 1963.' I have bought the vintages 1994, 1997, 2000 and 2003 on release and have wines from the 1980s and 1970s in the cellar, but with a consumption in Dorset of just three bottles a year, these will see both me and the next generation out, so my two grandsons can look forward to six bottles each of Cockburn, Croft, Dow, Fonseca, Graham and Taylor, which will be reaching the magic 20-year mark by the time they both come of age.

The International Cool Climate Chardonnay Conference in Niagara, Ontario, which is based on the highly regarded International Pinot Noir Conference in McMinnville, Oregon, was sold out for the full three days. My first visit to Niagara had been in the mid-1980s, when the grapes planted were mostly hybrid, and it was hard to be encouraged by the wines. Now, with hybrids being a thing of the past, it is hard *not* to be encouraged by what Ontario produces.

The wine country is situated between the 41st and 44th parallels, on the same latitude as Oregon and central Burgundy, being a little warmer than both during the growing season and having cooler nights during the harvest. Viticulture here is 'green'; many vineyards are organic and a few biodynamic. I was the keynote speaker and moderator on the second morning over an extensive Chardonnay tasting, aided by an impressive panel of Chardonnay producers from France and California as well as Niagara. My top vote went to winemakers in Oregon and Burgundy as well as to Thomas Bachelder's Niagara Saunders Vineyard 2011; second place went to Louis Jadot's Puligny-Montrachet Les Folatières 2010 and third to François Morissette's Twenty Mile Bench 2011. Niagara's cool-climate Chardonnays are very good, especially if they benefit from outside experience.

Another cool climate is Tasmania, so cool indeed that Jean-Claude Rouzaud of Roederer gave up trying to make sparkling wine there, preferring to 'lose a hand before losing an arm'. His son, Frédéric, has dismissed England as being 'too windy' to plant, and he has a point. At the DWWA in September, the International Chardonnay trophy went to Josef Chromy's 2001 from Launceston and – though Tasmania has less than one percent of Australia's vineyard area – the island picked up Regional Trophies for sparkling and Pinot Noir, plus additional Golds for Chardonnay, Pinot Noir and Riesling.

Australia's most famous Chardonnay – in my view the white equivalent of Grange – is Eileen Hardy from Hardys, the historic dynasty winery established in 1853 by Thomas Hardy, a young émigré from Devon. Later that month his great-great-grandson Bill Hardy presented a vertical tasting of the Eileen Hardy

Chardonnay, named after his grandmother, who travelled to London aged 84 years old to receive an OBE from The Queen. Since the 2008 vintage, fruit sourced from Tasmania has dominated that from the Yarra Valley in the 'Eileen' blend, and the 2012 was really quite superb.

My mentor Michael Broadbent's last *Decanter* column, appeared in 2013. He opened it with: 'However arbitrary, 433 consecutive monthly articles is enough.' That is 36 years and one month without a break. I was pleased to celebrate my 300th column in October 2018, and retired after my 318th in April 2020, but nobody can ever rival Michael's figure. His first columns appeared under the title 'Michael Broadbent's Tasting Notes' about which he remarks, 'it was so much easier in those days. I used to sit up in bed on a Sunday morning, open my current tasting book, find a theme and write. Sometimes it took me as little as two hours.' (After which Michael and his wife Daphne would have their traditional Sunday morning Buck's Fizz.)

It was his first employer in 1952, the 'irascible but innovative' Tommy Layton, who told him to take a note whenever he tasted a wine. Michael goes on: 'My first tasting note, a modest Graacher Riesling, was made on September 17th and, being a creature of habit, I now [July 2013] have roughly 100,000 tasting notes in 150 identical red books.' Those in possession of his *Great Vintage Wine Books* I and II, with notes beginning from mid-18th-century wines, know the debt that wine lovers owe to him. He has certainly had a greater influence on my life in wine than anyone else inside or outside the trade.

His last column was celebrated in *Decanter*'s dining room at the Michael Broadbent Tribute Lunch, where he was presented with a book containing his first and last columns, photographs from across the years and dozens of memories from readers. It also included a limerick each from Simon Berry and Hugh Johnson:

Simon Berry:
The one thing you know about Michael:
Any wine that he says you will like'll
Be complex and complete,
Taste just like Lafite,
And make you go fast on your cycle.

Hugh Johnson:

The great thing about Michael B

Is his utter disdain for PC

How come all the girls

Prick their ears for his pearls?

(I wish it could happen to me.)

To which I could add:

The aura of Michael, my mentor,

Transforms rooms he happens to enter,

His erudite charm

Spreads vinous balm,

While attention 'round him seems to centre.

Of the many memorable quotes from the tribute book, two stand out. First, Michael's own on the frontispiece: 'Wines are like people. Some are perfect but boring, some are precocious but fail to live up to their promise and some may be flawed, but the way they develop is endlessly fascinating.' And Christian Moueix's recollection of Michael describing one of his wines as 'a marvel, like making love in a hammock', something which, 20 years later, Moueix admitted was still on his to-do list.

The lunch showed some of Michael's favourite wines. As an apéritif, the Pol Roger 1996 was described as 'Churchillian', while with Loch Duart salmon came magnums of Felseneck Grosses Gewächs Riesling 2010 (steely freshness with two decades in front of it) from Prinz Michael zu Salm-Salm. Château Lafite Rothschild 1990 ('all the elements in place together') accompanied the roast partridge to perfection and Michael's favourite dessert wine, Michele Chiarlo's Nivole Moscato d'Asti 2012 lifted the bread-and-butter pudding to new heights. Graham's 1970, served from a 2.1-litre bottle known as a tappit hen, ended the meal with richness and warmth and accompanied further toasts to the Broadbents.

My last big trip in 2013 was back to India to hold tastings and dinners for The Wine Society of India in Mumbai, Delhi and Bangalore. I had founded the WSI seven years before with David Banford, a serial entrepreneur whose mail-order company, The Wine Society of America, I had at one time consulted for. That operation had eventually failed owing to fierce opposition from the US import system, but in 2004 David asked if I would help him to set up a similar venture in India. He knew a bit about the country, having been brought up in Mumbai. We launched the business in 2006, teaming up with United Spirits Ltd, the largest beer and spirits distributor in the country, a year later. The market was then growing at 30 percent a year, albeit from a miniscule base. Under the banner 'Four Seasons Wine Discoveries', we supplied our members with six bottles of wine, four times a year. David ran the business and I looked after the wine selections.

We spent much time and money launching our new baby, including giving the largest wine tasting ever held in India – 900 thirsty guests – but India's distribution channels were far from straightforward (and not cheap) to negotiate, which made the cost of doing business punishingly high. David arranged a further merger with Direct Wines, the world's largest mail-order wine company, and while they were stabilizing the company and expanding the membership, I continued to visit the major cities to host wine tastings. The membership grew to over 12,000 but in 2013, United Spirits having already given up the struggle, Direct Wines announced that India was a step too far, even for them. The Wine Society of India ceased to exist, with total losses all round. If ever the laws are changed to create even a half-level playing field for imported wines, India will become a huge market. Sadly, few believe that this will happen any time soon.

In January 2014 I presented my wines at Liberty Wines' annual trade tasting at the Kennington Oval, pouring glasses of Bride Valley Cuvée Reserve 2011 alongside the other fine non-champagne sparkling wines on this merchant's distinguished list. It was the first time in my whole life in the wine trade that I had been on the selling side of the table. I was now a producer. In my early days as a trainee, later as a buyer and even later as a critic, I would write notes on each wine tasted, occasionally commenting on and discussing it with the producer / winemaker on the other side, but presenting my own product was a brand-new and exciting experience.

When I first discussed my ideas for the Bride Valley vineyard with Georges Legrand, I told him that I intended to make only one wine, a single vintage Brut. No blanc de blancs, no rosé and certainly not a non-vintage built up from stocks of reserve wine as they do in Champagne. He told me bluntly that this was stupid and I had to make at least two wines, if not more. 'Why?' I asked, assuming that my model was simplicity itself.

'Because with just one, the only question you can ask is "Do you like my wine?", whereas with two or more, the question can be: "Which of my wines do you prefer?"'

Our tiny, vicar-blessed 2011 vintage produced only the cuvée réserve, but I was thrilled with it. Tasting it pre-release after a purposely low dosage of eight grams of sugar per litre (the average then was 10g/l or more), I found it clearly represented the vineyard's light, chalky soil. I was as proud as any father could be to present it at the tasting. In 2012 there was so much late-summer rain that we didn't bother to harvest, but then neither did Nyetimber, the benchmark producer in the southeast, who said that it was not worth the expense and trouble of sorting the healthy grapes from the rotten ones. This washout affected the very young vines and despite a normal growing season in 2013 we made only 2,700 bottles from 20,000 vines. The Chardonnay and Pinot Noir performed quite well, but we had very little from the Pinot Meunier.

I asked Ian Edwards, owner of the award-winning Furleigh Estate who takes the grapes for Rosé Bella, to macerate our best Pinot Noir for 24 hours to bleed off a little colour from the skins, then to press very slowly to obtain more colour. The resulting pink juice would be darker than we wanted, so it had to be blended with enough white juice to lighten it before bottling. Thus in 2013 we made 900 bottles of rosé and 1,800 blanc de blancs, both of which were well received.

English wine and especially Bride Valley enjoyed a bumper 2014, the grapes being plentiful and ripe. We produced 21,500 bottles from 30,000 vines, split between about 50 percent brut réserve and 25 percent each of the blanc de blancs and Rosé Bella. The brut was released in January 2017 with an 8g/l dosage, the rosé in June with just 7g/l to preserve the precision and wild-strawberry Pinot Noir fruit, as was the blanc de blancs, again with 8g/l due to the high acidity from our Kimmeridgian chalk soils.

In 2017 the wines were tasting beautifully, winning awards and selling well all over the world. That was the good news; the less good news was that the cold 2015 summer gave us only 7,000 bottles of very light wine; the 2016 even fewer but of better quality; and of the 2017, the 30,000 bottles predicted after flowering in early July dropped to just 9,000 bottles from 42,000 vines due to an attack of mildew during a rainy August. We were looking at averages of under one quarter of a bottle per vine, and not even the Domaine de la Romanée-Conti could survive on that. During the 2009 Vinexpo in Bordeaux I found myself chatting to Eric de Rothschild at Lafite and told him of the inaugural planting in Dorset. Immediately he put his arm around my shoulders, saying: 'Welcome to the Club!' At the time I thought of it as congratulation; it sometimes seems more like commiseration.

Looking on the brighter side, as I always have, Ian Edwards told me that it takes 10 years for a totally new vineyard to establish itself, and that once it is established one could look for an average of a kilo of grapes per vine. Even though this is much, much less than in Champagne, less even than in the drier and slightly earlier-ripening southeast of England where most of the country's vineyards are, it would show me 33,500 bottles a year and suit me just fine.

In February I spent a week in Mendoza as one of the 12 international judges for the 2014 Wines of Argentina Awards. From just 660 wines there were 70 Golds, 12 Trophies and four Regional Trophies. The idea of Argentina as a two-varietal country – Torrontés for white and Malbec for red – still seemed to hold true in volume and branding, but blends and other single varieties were increasingly to the fore. The welcome surprise was the emergence of Cabernet Franc, a grape that won one Regional Trophy (Bodega del Fin del Mundo, Patagonia 2010), two further Trophies and two Golds. Cabernet Sauvignon also showed well.

March saw the last of my twice-yearly weeks in Singapore, which I had been enjoying since 1989 as a consultant for Singapore Airlines. Since I was a decade older than the country's official retirement age of 62, I had had a good innings in a city state where, when I started, if you wanted to drink wine with the huge variety of Asian cuisines, you had to bring your own glasses as well as your own bottles. Now the island must be one of Eurocave and Riedel's best clients. While I knew that my co-consultants Michael Hill-Smith and Jeannie Cho Lee, respectively Australia's and Asia's first Masters of Wine, had planned a final dinner for me, I had no idea of the array of wines I would enjoy in wonderful company over five evenings. To list them here would take too long, suffice it to say that

Ausone, Canon and Cheval Blanc, all superb St-Emilion 1964s, rubbed shoulders with Domaine de la Romanée-Conti's Richebourg 1996 and Hermitage La Chapelle 1982; Roederer Cristal 2004 and Dom Pérignon 2002 represented champagne; Bouchard Père & Fils Chevalier-Montrachet 2008 and 1998 and Remoissenet Père & Fils Le Montrachet 2006 represented white burgundy; Giacomo Conterno Barolo 1964 and Ornellaia 2008 from my cellar appeared for Italy; and Australia showed brilliantly with Tyrrells Vat 1 Hunter Semillon 1998 and Penfolds Grange 1990. What a send-off. My younger friend Oz Clarke has replaced me – but I bet he won't have such great wines when he is retired.

In May it was Macedonia. I have to confess that before then I had never knowingly drunk a Macedonian wine, but after just three very busy days organized by Wines of Macedonia, I was again reminded why I am so excited by wine, even after 50 years in the trade: you never, ever, stop learning.

Vineyards in the landlocked Republic of Macedonia in the heart of the Balkans cover only four percent of cultivated land, yet wine has been one of Macedonia's cultural symbols for over 4,000 years. As part of Yugoslavia in the second half of the 20th century, the country produced bulk wine from 39,000 hectares, and while this area had shrunk to 25,000, at all the wineries I visited, including those of the lowest-priced wines, quality was the top consideration. The grapes are mostly local varieties that have been grown for centuries, but since the vineyards are on the 41st parallel, just south of Bordeaux and Tuscany, international grapes are increasingly being planted.

At the Vinexpo Asia-Pacific trade fair in Hong Kong in May, the most surprising exhibitor was Hattingley Valley from Hampshire. Owner Simon Robinson was delighted by the interest his English sparkling wines attracted, receiving more visitors on the first day in Hong Kong than he did during all three days of Germany's ProWein Trade Fair. The Gold medal he won at the DWWA just a month earlier for his 2011 rosé must have helped. The high spot at this very buzzy event was a Masseto Retrospective, a tasting of 14 vintages from 1987 to 2010 in the presence of winemaker Axel Heinz and consultant Michel Rolland.

Our August holiday took us across France to Pol Roger in Epernay, down through Burgundy to Fattoria Nittardi in Chianti, the Sesti's Castello di Argiano south of Montalcino, and to Cahors, my first visit there for 30 years. Here, a renaissance is under way. It is home to Malbec, now far more famous in Argentina than it is in southwest France. From a total of 22,000 hectares in the original appellation, only 4,500 remained under vines in 2002 when a charter of quality was proposed to classify the best vineyards into grands and premiers crus. France's appellation body turned down the proposal, and a dozen years later only 3,300 hectares remained.

Help was at hand, however, from soil experts Claude and Lydia Bourguignon (Claude a fellow member of the Académie Internationale du Vin), who have opened a local office and are replanting a long-abandoned terrace vineyard on a limestone base. While everyone agrees that good wines are made in the vineyard, people such as the Bourguignons, Italy's Alberto Antonini and Chile's Pedro Parra work all over the world analyzing soils and subsoils in extraordinary detail, advising specifically what should be planted where to produce wines of quality and character. The cru project has been reactivated, a growing number of vignerons are practising *pigéage* (punching down the cap during early fermentation) to soften the Malbec's austerity, and Cahors looks like becoming Burgundian in its emerging patchwork of vineyards.

The wine year ended in splendour in China with *Decanter*'s inaugural Fine Wine Encounter at the Ritz Carlton in Shanghai. Concerned that some local wine lovers might participate too enthusiastically, tickets were timed 9am–1.30pm and 2.30pm–6pm, the hour in between giving the staff time to tidy up, and the producers time for lunch. In the morning I had co-hosted a masterclass on Chinese Cabernet Sauvignon and Merlot, alongside wine consultant Professor Li Demei. The top producers from the Old and New Worlds were there, happy to be showing their wines to such keen tasters.

During the lunch break I found myself on a table with Jean-Philippe Delmas of Haut-Brion, Alexander Van Beek of Giscours and Peter Femfert of Nittardi among others. The menu was enticing, but there was only water to drink. The producers took just a few moments to get up from the table, go to the next room where their stands were, and return with bottles. Thus the day continued, tasting after tasting, to conclude with a dinner in honour of Jeannie Cho Lee MW, Korean-American wine critic, author, journalist and consultant whose almost rock-star reputation set the standard of the spectacular wines served.

One of the many advantages of my years with Singapore Airlines was that the remuneration package included four round-trip tickets a year. Following my retirement, we flew into Perth and then to the Margaret River, probably Australia's most beautiful vineyard region, clocking in with the Peterkins at Pierro Vineyards, Vanya Cullen, and David Hohnen at McHenry Hohnen. From there we flew to Melbourne where we stayed at the Melbourne Club. This is another of the clubs that has a reciprocal arrangement with Boodle's, which it completely dwarfs, having been built as a copy of the imposing Reform Club on London's Pall Mall. As we arrived, a wedding reception was in progress, all the ladies elegantly turned out in hats and white gloves.

Melbourne's Chinatown is close by, and a visit to the famous Flower Drum restaurant was well worth the detour. From here we drove along the coast, then headed inland to stay at The Royal Mail in Dunkeld, which has Australia's finest wine list – three entire pages devoted to its collection of Domaine de la Romanée-Conti alone. We chose the tasting menu with local wines by the glass. Then it was across country through the Coonawarra, a stunning drive, to arrive at Michael and Stacey Hill-Smith's modern and airy house in downtown Adelaide in time for tea.

Shaw & Smith, Michael's winery and vineyards, was founded with his cousin Martin Shaw who was chief winemaker at Brian Croser's Petaluma for eight years before he set up the 'flying winemakers' network in France, Spain, Chile and New Zealand. Their vision was to make refined and exciting wines that would rank among the finest in the country exclusively from the Adelaide Hills. It is safe to say that they have succeeded, and in 2012 they set their sights further away, buying the exceptional 20-hectare Tolpuddle Vineyard near Hobart in cool-climate Tasmania, where they produce Australia's leading Chardonnay and Pinot Noir.

After a day of tasting, Brian and Ann Croser came to dinner. The Crosers had put Petaluma on the Australian fine-wine map 30 years before, only to see it taken over by local brewers Lion Nathan and pass into the hands of Japanese brewer Kirin. They have now regained possession of their original winery buildings, where they make the Tapanappa wines in partnership with Champagne Bollinger. The younger generation is now going for cooler sites, he remarked, small lots and total individuality. He also pointed out that the perception of Australia as a hot country (in wine terms) was misplaced, since as many as 24 of the officially designated vineyard regions were cooler than Bordeaux.

After two marvellous days at the Hill-Smith beach house at Victor Harbour, we flew to Sydney, spending our final evening there with Andrew Caillard MW at his home in the quieter residential part of the city. Andrew (British by birth, Australian by adoption) is head buyer for Woolworths, the country's largest wine retailer, as well as having created in 1990 the Langton's Classification, an independent list of Australian wines based on price, demand and supply at auction.

At the end of March it was back to Bordeaux for the En Primeur tastings, this year the 2014s, an overall good vintage and a great relief after the dire 2013s. I had been attending this event, along with several hundred wine writers, critics and merchants from around the globe, since the late 1990s.

A small band of us became known as *Le Groupe Robinson-Spurrier*, centred around Jancis Robinson and me. A number of the châteaux whose wines the group had to taste for our respective magazines and papers were part of the Union des Grands Crus de Bordeaux (UGC) but many, particularly the first growths and an increasing number of Super Seconds, were not. In order to taste everywhere, we would plan with military precision, making appointments at least two months in advance and carefully working out routes between châteaux so that no more than 30 minutes were spent on each stop.

A typical day, beginning in Margaux and ending in Pauillac, might run something like this: 8.30am d'Issan, 9.00 Palmer, 9.30 Margaux, 10.15 Rauzan-Ségla (more time at Margaux, as Paul Pontallier, the much-missed winemaker and director of 30 years always talked a lot), 10.45 UGC tasting and lunch, 2pm St-Pierre, 2.30 Ducru-Beaucaillou, 3.00 Léoville-Las Cases, 3.30 Latour, 4.00 Pichon-Comtesse, 4.30 Pichon-Baron, 5.15 Batailley, 5.45 Grand-Puy-Lacoste. Then back to whichever château was putting us up for dinner.

For years I had Robert Gorjak from Slovenia as my map reader (navigation having been never been my strong point), and there was always another passenger or two. My last En Primeur marathon was in 2016 for the 2015s, a really lovely vintage which I likened to 1985, a year from which I have never had a bad bottle. It was a pity to step away from these tastings, particularly since 2016 was another wonderful vintage, but I didn't miss the planning or the fatigue at all.

On to Paarl in the Cape to appear as one of the three international judges of South Africa's 14th Old Mutual Trophy Wine Show, which I had judged alongside Jancis a few years before. This tasting was conceived and chaired by the country's leading wine authority Michael Fridjhon, and the rigour of judging and the reputation of the results is such that the show attracts the best wines from the top producers. I admire Fridjhon's philosophy, which he sums up in the mnemonic: PAPERCLIPS: Purity, Aesthetic Integrity, Potential, Equilibrium, Refinement, Complexity, Luminosity, Intricacy, Persistence, Savouriness. He says: 'Wines that manifest these features are hardly ever the result of pure chance. Like other "created" works of art, they are artefacts of intention. Winemakers talk of how they are merely the midwives of terroir, but every decision they take moves inexorably towards the end result.' In his opinion, judging wine is 'an approval rating that quantifies how successfully the winemaker achieved what he set out to do.'

When introducing the 2017 *Decanter* Asia Wine Awards, I told the seven vice-chairs that they were 'here to judge the wines, but should let the wines judge them'. This caused a 'that's very Zen, Spurrier' comment from Michael Hill-Smith, but it is indeed the case that only by listening very carefully to what the wine is saying can one judge it correctly.

At the bi-annual Bordeaux Vinexpo Fair in mid-June, 480 guests, including 275 journalists from 37 different countries, were welcomed to Château Margaux by owner Corinne Mentzelopoulos and her family for a tour of the new cellar and winery buildings. Designed by Norman Foster to celebrate the 200th anniversary of the château itself, Bordeaux's most impressive and memorable private residence, the new buildings are in total harmony (the key element in a great wine) with the past. As Lord Foster explained at the dinner, his original idea had been to create something new – think of Frank Gehry's winery at Rioja's Marqués de Riscal or Christian de Portzamparc's winery/belvedere at Cheval Blanc – but the more he visited the estate and studied the historical records, the more he was drawn back 200 years.

The menu was conceived by the three-star Parisian chef Guy Savoy, and for the first two courses, wines from the 1855 Classification were served *au hazard des tables*, depending on who was hosting each table. I had the great good fortune to be on the table of Martin and Mélissa Bouygues, owners of Château Montrose,

The whole family toasts the 2015 vintage: Christian (*standing, left*), Kate (*seated, right*).

(who three nights later concluded Vinexpo with an unforgettable Fête de la Fleur dinner for 1,500 guests), and Frédéric Engerer of Château Latour, so we were served these two wines from the 2006 and 1995 vintages. Although such wines were hard to improve on, the Margaux 1985 (Paul Pontallier's first vintage) served in magnums did just that, a truly great, supremely elegant wine, the epitome of the château itself. The meal ended in grandeur with Château d'Yquem 1988 and the guests mingled long after dinner was over. At the Mouton Rothschild dinner two years before, there had been a firework display. It was not needed that evening.

In autumn I was back in Dorset to check on the progress of the vintage. It had suffered from a cold summer and ended up being very small and not very ripe, with the result that only a little Rosé Bella was made, three-quarters of the juice being kept back to blend with the 2016s to make a non-vintage. This was something I had never expected to be part of the Bride Valley range. My decision following the 2016 crop (better quality but also small volume) was to make a Rosé Bella and a blanc de blancs, but blend the rest with most of the 2015s to make a Crémant NV, a wine with under four bars of pressure compared to six bars for the Brut Réserve. I had high hopes that this would become the first crémant English sparkling wine, which is indeed what it became. In 2020 it was still, to my surprise, the only one.

Soon it was off to British Columbia, the only Canadian wine region I had not yet visited. While some European – even New World – countries might have a much longer history and grander wines, I had seldom encountered such beautiful scenery, such passionate viticulturists and winemakers and tasted wines of such encouraging quality that really showed a 'sense of place'. One of the many people I met was Anthony von Mandl, already known as the Robert Mondavi of the Okanagan for his formidable vision – both aesthetic and vinous. His two landmark wineries, Cedar Creek and Mission Hill, as well as two smaller ones, Martin's Lane and CheckMate (which specializes in Chardonnay), are finding their way onto the world's markets where they deserve a place alongside the well-known names. Another surprise came at the BC Pinot Noir Celebration organized by Jak Meyer of Meyer Family Vineyards. Although Merlot is BC's most-planted red grape, Pinot Noir has a better reputation, the style being more Old than New World and often distinctly Burgundian.

To conclude my visit, we staged a 'Judgement of Vancouver', comparing 12 Chardonnays and 12 Syrahs with benchmark varietals from around the world. Sadly the best-ranked Chardonnay, Blue Mountain Reserve 2013, found only 6th place, but C C Jentsch 2013 Syrah came first in its flight.

My final trip of the year, and certainly the most memorable, was to Marqués de Riscal's cellars in Rioja to taste a full century of their wines, from Don Guillermo Hurtado de Amézaga's first bottling in 1862 down to his direct descendant's splendid 1964. From these years, only 11 vintages were missing, the remaining 92 having slept undisturbed in the cellars – 'The Cathedral' – since their birth.

Very few of the wines had been recorked, as is the practice in Bordeaux once the wines enter their fifth decade; none from before 1926 had. Every bottle was opened with port tongs, which are clamped red-hot around the neck of the bottle below the cork so as to break off the top cleanly without disturbing the sediment. The wines were served in nine flights, each covering a decade or so. Everyone present was deeply moved by this journey through time, sharing a profound sense of exhilaration that the wines could so genuinely represent the vintages as experienced by their producers. Our hosts asked us to name the five wines we thought the finest. Mine were 1874, 1897, 1922, 1945 and 1964. Here are a few sample notes:

> 1874–84: *With vines (all brought from Bordeaux) maturing, this flight was exceptional, most wines showing a deep mahogany colour. 1874 was elegantly robust and full of natural sweetness.*
> 1921–31: *A superb decade, the wines having totally retained their natural warmth, depth and vigour.*
> 1946–55: *As in Bordeaux, marvellous wines from the late '40s, the truly lovely 1953 having a caressing texture.*
> 1956–64: *Quite an even flight, ending in glory, the youngest of all finding oak, richness and tannins blended together, explosive yet controlled.*

In early December the AIV annual symposium was held in Berlin, since our retiring President, Mariano Fernández Amunátegui, was at that time Chile's ambassador to Germany. As ambassador to Britain, a decade earlier, he had been a firm supporter of his country's wines, exceeded in ambassadorial promotions only by his counterpart from Portugal. Bella came with me, since Berlin is such an exciting city for art. Raymond Paccot, whose Swiss wines from Domaine La Colombe are superb, and in whose honour the AIV moved to Lausanne the following year, stressed that in wine, as in all walks of life, it was individualism that mattered, and the AIV's mantra of *le vin vrai, le vin nature, le vin noble* / true, natural and noble wine must, especially today, be supported and maintained.

In late January 2016 I attended the Naples (Florida) Winter Wine Festival, a lavish three-day event that ends with an auction for the Naples Children & Education Foundation. (Since its inception in 2000 it has raised well over $200 million.) I was there to promote a lot that offered a two-day tour with me in Napa Valley to celebrate the 40th anniversary of the Judgement of Paris. The festival opened with a presentation tasting based around the Paris Tasting, at which Bo Barrett of Chateau Montelena and Ted Baseler of Stag's Leap Wine Cellars presented their wines. Bella, who was photographer on that day in 1976;

George Taber, whose report sealed the event's place in history, and I made the link between the past and the present. Montelena showed its great Chardonnay in magnums from the 1992, 1998, 2001, 2004 (the best for me) and 2008 vintages, while Stag's Leap presented the SLV Estate Cabernet Sauvignon from 1983, 1993, 1998, 2008 and 2012, this last getting my top vote.

The dinners put even those of Bordeaux' Vinexpo to shame. No fewer than 17 Master Sommeliers were on hand to advise and pour, and more than 30 owners of wineries – from boutiques to big names – were opening their own bottles. I was proud to offer the US its first taste of Bride Valley 2013 Blanc de Blancs. On the Saturday, after a walk-around tasting of top-quality donated bottles, a few hundred people sat down under a vast tent for the auction. To help the bids flow, and flow they did, the Master Sommeliers circulated with astonishingly good bottles.

Among those offered to my table were: White – Poggio al Tesoro Vermentino 2014, Louis Latour Montrachet Grand Cru 2010, Marquis de Laguiche Chassagne-Montrachet 2010 and Kistler Hyde Vineyard Chardonnay 2008; Red – Kamen Estate Wines Sonoma 2010, Chateau Montelena Cabernet Sauvignon 1997, Tablas Creek Esprit de Beaucastel 2013, Château de Beaucastel 2010, Château La Conseillante 1998, Drouhin's Beaune Clos des Mouches 2005, Thibault Liger-Belair Nuits-St-Georges Les St Georges 2008, Fontodi Flaccianello della Pieve 2006, Sassicaia 2008 and Ornellaia 2006.

The 64 lots, all donated, were hedonistic in the extreme. I had put together a trip to Napa for two couples, with sponsorship from the Napa Valley Reserve, Meadowood Country Club, Chateau Montelena, Grgich Hills, Stag's Leap Wine Cellars and Jean-Charles Boisset's Raymond Cellars. It fetched $220,000. When I went over to congratulate and thank the successful bidder, he said he would have been happy to have paid more.

In 2016 the Arblaster & Clarke tour was on the theme of biodynamic burgundy. Biodynamism is a holistic system of agriculture based on a series of lectures given by Austrian polymath Rudolf Steiner in 1924 and is being practised more and more by producers seeking chemical-free, environmentally friendly methods of producing food and wine. In fact, it is scarcely different from the methods used centuries ago by the monks whose monasteries owned most of the Burgundian vineyards, and it is in Burgundy that it is practised most.

On our first morning Frédéric Magnien, fifth-generation vineyard owner in Morey-St-Denis, explained that biodynamism aims to 'revitalize and intensify organic life in the soil and to allow the vines to strengthen and energize themselves through the natural powers of the cosmic bio-lunar phases of viticulture'. The following morning at Château de Monthelie, the historic estate abutting Meursault and Volnay, we saw two dozen people in the courtyard on either side of a long table cheerfully knocking the manure out of hundreds of cow's horns, in which it had solidified during six months over the winter, buried deep in Burgundian soil. The resulting substance was to be 'dynamized' by being made into a solution with rainwater, spun both clockwise and anticlockwise to create a vortex, and then sprayed onto the vineyards. This application would certainly be better for the soil than the artificial fertilizers widely used in the 1970s and 1980s.

There are many detractors of such methods, notably the producer of sublime sherry and AIV member Jesús Barquín who says: 'What we see looking over the biodynamic landscape is a vista of starry eyes and good intentions mixed with quasi-religious hocus-pocus, good salesmanship and plain scientific illiteracy.' Fellow AIV Burgundians such as Guillaume d'Angerville, Dominique Lafon and Jacques Seysses would disagree, while my own view is that Burgundy is already kaleidoscopic, and biodynamics allows it to shine brighter than ever.

The buyer of the Naples auction lot made the visit to Napa with his wife and another couple in mid-May. The first evening was spent at the Napa Valley Reserve, the exclusive wine club created by Bill Harlan of Harlan Estate (as was the Meadowood Country Club where we were staying). We presented wines that pre-dated 1976 to show the history of Napa Valley. Lunch the following day was at Montelena, and in the early evening we visited Grgich Hills, where Mike Grgich, who had made Montelena's winning 1973 Chardonnay, was still wearing his French beret and flirting with the ladies in his 91st year. Dinner that evening was at Stag's Leap. The following morning, I had arranged with Jean-Charles Boisset to hold a 'Judgement of Napa' at his Raymond Vineyards: his JCB Blanc de Blancs 2012 against my Bride Valley Blanc de Blancs 2013. More than 100 guests blind-tasted the two sparkling wines and his won – but not by a landslide.

After the Napa trip, Bella met me in Washington DC for some anniversary celebrations at the Smithsonian National Museum of American History, where the original bottles of Chateau Montelena 1973 and Stag's Leap Wine Cellars 1973 were exhibited among the '101 Objects that Made America'. Once again, Bo Barrett, Ted Baseler and George Taber were there to tell the story, and we were joined by Stag's Leap Wine Cellars' founder Warren Winiarski, and Violet Grgich, representing her father. This time it was a three-day celebration of May 24th 1976, a date that the House of Representatives had voted to become An Important Day in American History.

On the second night there was a black-tie dinner for 600 people in honour of the event and the effect it had had on American wine. I was asked if I would like to say a few words at the end and, taking in the room's anticipation, said: 'It is just and fitting that we should be here at The Smithsonian to celebrate how a Croat (Grgich) and a Pole (Winiarski) made American history in Paris with a little help from an Englishman.'

The next day before our late-evening flight back home, we attended another tasting celebration in the Halls of Congress. Several senators and governors were present and at one point I was called to the podium to receive from Congresswoman Nancy Pelosi a signed and sealed document saying that the Second Session of the 114th Congress had approved Resolution 734 'Recognizing and honouring the historical significance of the 40th Anniversary of the Judgement of Paris and the impact of the California victory at the 1976 Paris Tasting on the world of wine and the United States' wine industry as a whole.' I was also given an American flag, neatly folded and boxed, which I was told had been flying above the Capitol dome of Congress for two days in my honour! A palm-reader in St Tropez who, back in May 1968, had predicted a 'possibility of lasting fame' had turned out to be quite correct.

The Cistercian monastery at Schloss Gobelsburg in Kamptal, Austria, was founded in 1137. I had first visited the monastery with the AIV 20 years earlier, and returned in June 2016 to attend a two-day symposium focused on the 19th-century wine-making styles at the monastery as well as in Georgia, Madeira and Rioja. A smaller group, dominated by members of the AIV, gathered a month later at a 'Tribute to Terroir' weekend at the historic Abadía Retuerta winery on the edge of Spain's Ribera del Duero region. Bordeaux-born Pascal Delbeck, head winemaker since

Former honorary presidents of the Wine & Spirit Education Trust Michael Broadbent, Hugh Johnson, Jancis Robinson and Gerard Basset help celebrate my taking on the role. Far right: the Trust's Executive Director, Ian Harris.

the start, opened the event by saying: 'Terroir is like music, it can't play itself, it can't even discover itself, it needs the hand of man.' The theme for the day was 'How can man influence terroir?', the answer to which was summed up by Carlos Falcó, Marqués de Griñón: 'By knowledge and desire.' Later, I reflected that, while terroir obliges us to speak of it, in the end it will speak of us.

My last trip abroad that year was to return to India to blend wines with Piero Masi at the Fratelli Winery in Akluj in the state of Maharashtra, two hours north of Pune. A partnership between the Sekhri brothers from Delhi, the Mohite-Patil brothers from Maharashtra and the Secci brothers from Tuscany, Fratelli ('Brothers') planted on sparse, elevated and rolling land and produced wine only from their own grapes, becoming number two in the Indian wine market after Rajeev Samant's Sula.

I had done some tasting and consulting for them before, but the idea now was that Piero and I would create a new label with wines made for consumers of wines in the mid- to high price bracket. I suggested the name P+S (Piero + Steven) – but

P+S already stood for Prats & Symington, wine blends made in the Douro, so we settled on 'MS', hoping that Marks & Spencer wouldn't complain. Piero and I are very different: he tall, angular, wedded to the soil; me a city boy. He didn't speak English and I don't speak Italian, so we communicated in French, generally starting our tastings of tank samples from different ends of the spectrum, but slowly coming together in agreement. From the 2015 vintage we agreed on an 80 percent Chardonnay-20 percent Sauvignon white, a 93 percent Sangiovese Bianco-7 percent Sangiovese Rosso rosé and a 60 percent Sangiovese-20 percent Cabernet Franc-20 percent Syrah red. All three have been very well received, and we continue to refine them.

In December I received two pieces of news, both great surprises which, while recognizing my past contribution, gave me a certain direction for the future. The first was the offer of the three-year term as honorary president of the Wine & Spirit Education Trust. My predecessors in this role had been Michael Broadbent, Hugh Johnson, Jancis Robinson and Gerard Basset, and I was immensely proud to stand alongside them at London's Guildhall for the Diploma presentations. The WSET teaches over 100,000 students across the world. For someone whose wine-trade life has centred around education, the presidency was indeed an honour.

Sarah Kemp and I toast our hugely enjoyable 25-year partnership in wine.

A few days later I opened a letter from Sarah Kemp to discover that I was to be the 2017 *Decanter* Man of the Year. This was an amazing surprise. Knowing there would be an awards lunch, I immediately called Sarah to say that I reckoned I could secure Boodle's, which could seat around 50. 'Don't worry, Steven,' came the reply, 'we alreaady have Le Gavroche and they can go to 70!'

I had served on the Man of the Year panel for many years, looking for individuals who have 'made an outstanding contribution to the world of wine'. The first, in 1984, was Chateau Musar's Serge Hochar. I had seen many of my candidates go through and in 2017 had pushed strongly for Eduardo Chadwick – who I am glad to say took the honour in 2018.

The lunch at Le Gavroche was truly spectacular. Michel Roux Jr created dishes that matched the eight wines, whose producers were all present or represented. Bella was there of course (so was Bride Valley Rosé Bella 2014 as the last wine) as were Christian and his partner Christine and Kate and Andrew, my brother Nicky and many, many friends, including 10 previous Men of the Year in person and a further three represented by family members. Angelo Gaja (1998) made a speech and presented me with a pair of spurs – a rather more modern pair than those featured on the Spurrier coat of arms.

The *Decanter* April issue carried a flattering survey of my career by John Stimpfig with quotes from colleagues. Patricia Gastaud-Gallagher, who had been director of the Académie du Vin from 1973 to 1989 when I sold it, wrote '…every wine lover in Paris at that time remembers the Académie du Vin and Cave de la Madeleine'. Patricia was there at the lunch and recognized so many people from the past in Paris that she decided to find out what had become of the Académie. Apart from the school I founded in Tokyo in 1987, which now has four branches in Japan, it had ceased to exist. She discovered that the name and logo had not been registered for over five years, meaning that both were free to be re-registered. This she and I put in motion in July, and we asked Canadian Marc Nadeau, who had successfully run a branch of the Académie in Toronto, and later Mark Williamson, on board. Thanks to Patricia we are now registered across the world.

On 2nd September 2017, in Tokyo, I celebrated the Tokyo Académie du Vin's 30th anniversary by hosting a masterclass that featured wines I had loved over 50 years in wine:

Dom Weinbach Riesling Schlossberg Alsace Grand Cru 2015

Dom de Chevalier Pessac-Léognan Grand Cru Classé de Graves 2012

Dom Bonneau du Martray Corton-Charlemagne Grand Cru 2006

Dom Tempier Bandol Rosé 2016

Dom Chanson Beaune Clos des Fèves Premier Cru 2009

Ch Langoa-Barton Troisième Cru Classé St-Julien 2005 (1995 in Paris)

Ch de Beaucastel Châteauneuf-du-Pape 2005 (2001 in Paris)

Dom Huet Vouvray Le Mont Demi-Sec Loire 2008

The revivified Académie du Vin was launched in the UK in October 2017 with the same wines, five of which came from my Dorset cellar. I hosted a celebratory masterclass at 67 Pall Mall – a private members' club launched in 2015 for wine lovers and fine dining which has become something of an institution in the wine industry. We also toasted the renaissance in Paris at Mark Williamson's Macéo restaurant over lunch, Patricia and Marc (who had come over especially from Toronto) acting

Max (*left*) and Maud (official vineyard dog), Bella and me on the steps of our Dorset home.

as co-hosts. Isabelle Bachelard, who had managed the Académie in the 1980s was there, as were many other colleagues from the past.

The AIV, the wine trade's think tank', holds its AGM in the first week of December. It was a pleasant surprise to learn that the 2017 meeting would be in Barcelona, and that most of the first day would be devoted to the region of Priorat, where I had never been. Priorat and Rioja are the only two *Denominación de Origen Calificada* (DOCa) in Spain (Priorat uses the Catalan version, DOQ: *Denominació d'Origen Qualificada*).

The Roman capital of the Iberian Peninsula was Tarraco, today's Tarragona. From the middle ages until Spain's division of church and state in 1835, the region was controlled by Carthusian monks, from whose priories the region's name derived. Vineyards were abandoned, declining from 5,000 hectares to just 600 in the late 1970s, when René Barbier, son of a Catalan wine merchant, and his wife Isabelle happened upon Clos Mogador. It was then a vast amphitheatre of crumbling slate with centenary Carignan and Grenache vines. During the 1980s, tiny quantities of their Clos Mogador found instant admirers, among them Riojan Alvaro Palacios and Bordeaux merchant Christopher Cannan, who swiftly took the export rights. With a few years Christopher (an AIV member) had acquired his own Priorat estate, Clos Figueras. My visit to these two estates, trailblazers in a DOCa that has grown to 2,000 hectares, was an eye opener.

This trip ended the year's travel and Bella and I spent Christmas in London seeing Christian, Kate, their spouses and the grandchildren, but we were back in Dorset for a cheerful dinner for eight, seeing in the new year with Bride Valley Rosé Bella 2013. My diary was already filling up with trips for the first part of 2018, but what was principally occupying my mind was the forthcoming publication of my memoirs – *Wine, A Way of Life*.

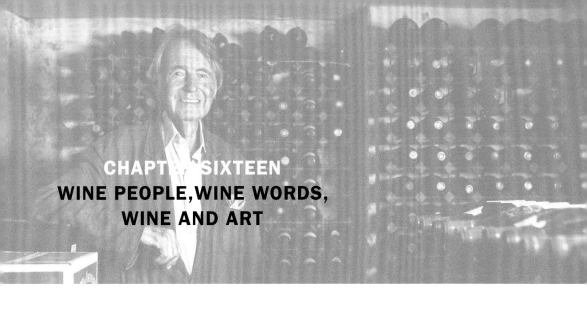

CHAPTER SIXTEEN

WINE PEOPLE, WINE WORDS, WINE AND ART

I was back in America in 2018 for the Symposium of Wine Writers held at the Meadowood resort in Napa. Two full days were spent on seminars, tasting panels, winery visits and impressive wine-pairing dinners, and if this wasn't enough to focus writers' minds, the third day was spent at the Culinary Institute of America (CIA) at Greystone, the vast late-19th-century complex once home of the Christian Brothers. Their winemaker, Brother Tim, is still revered.

We were there for the annual Napa Valley Premiere pre-auction tasting where almost 100 wineries offer tastes of 60–120 wines. The wines fetch astronomical prices the following day. Almost all were red, but I was happy to note a definite swing away from the 'fruit bombs' that had characterized the previous decade.

The following day I had an appointment to taste a bottle of Clos du Val 1972. Wine lover and collector Alan Davies had invited me to attend a dinner at which he was showing four of the California Cabernets from the 1976 tasting alongside Haut-Brion 1970, Mouton Rothschild 1970 and other treasures from his cellar. California's Clos du Val 1972 came up trumps. An American filmmaker known for his wine documentaries, Jason Wise, had contacted me some months earlier and he was there to record the tasting, which was conducted in a private room at the CIA. Jason had already produced *SOMM 1* and *SOMM 2*, films that concentrated on aspiring and successful sommeliers across America, and wanted to make a third in the series, this time looking back into history. He had also contacted Fred Dame,

Signpost to success: a tangible reminder of my role
in putting Clos du Val – and Napa – on the wine map.

the master sommelier who helped establish the American chapter of the Court
of Master Sommeliers, and Jancis Robinson, the three of us having 'seen it all
happen' in the world of wine from our different vantage points. In autumn 2017,
Jason and his crew came down to Dorset for a weekend to get some background
stories from me, and they also spent time with Fred and Jancis.

The new film's central feature would be a blind tasting at Terroirs, New
York's cult wine store, where Pinot Noirs from around the world were to be
judged by the city's top palates. The Clos du Val showed superbly, a very strong
(French owned) voice from the past, and as we wrapped up, the winery's export
director approached me to say they would like to do something to honour my
contribution to their success, along with that of Napa and indeed California wine.
Within six months I received a photo of 'Steven Spurrier Lane', which signposts
the drive leading from Clos du Val's entrance on the Silverado Trail to the newly
constructed winery. I could not have been more pleased.

Filming of the final piece of *SOMM 3* took place in late March in Paris, at Mark
Williamson's restaurant. Fred, Jancis and I were each asked to bring a bottle of the

wine that had inspired us to make our life in wine. For Fred it was Ridge Monte Bello 1968 (he brought a magnum), for Jancis it was Comte Georges de Vogüé Chambolle-Musigny Premier Cru Les Amoureuses 1959 (bottled by Averys and supplied by the family cellar), and for me it was of course the Cockburn 1908 vintage port, kindly offered by the Symington family and delivered in advance to rest the sediment.

The wines showed marvellously, and perfectly justified their roles in our lives. The tastings didn't end there, however: the New York episode had revealed three top Pinots, which Terroir's owner had brought with him for us to taste blind and make our own choice. Jancis picked what turned out to be Bloom's Field 2014 from Raj Parr's Domaine de la Côte in Santa Barbara's Santa Rita Hills; Fred's choice was the Marquis d'Angerville Volnay Premier Cru Les Champans 2015 (which I had misjudged as being too tannic), while my choice was Domaine Bachelet's Gevrey-Chambertin Premier Cru Les Corbeaux 2015. *Vive la différence!*

In May I was in Croatia at the invitation of wine producer Ivica Matošević. Having created his own vineyards and winery in 2005, Ivica had swiftly become one of Istria's leading lights and, although he had planted Chardonnay and Sauvignon Blanc, he was particularly proud of what Malvasia, Croatia's prime white grape, could do right across the board. The local wine fair was taking place in Poreč, on the Istrian coast, and my role was to conduct a masterclass of 12 Malvasias, from bone-dry sparkling through un-oaked, oaked, young and mature to richly sweet, to show the breadth of the varietal's capabilities. Chenin Blanc could match it for versatility but not, I thought, for charm.

In June I teamed up with Eduardo Chadwick again for an event entitled 'Into the Future' that started in London at 67 Pall Mall and finished the next evening at Taillevent in Paris. I was presenting three English sparkling wines – Bride Valley Blanc de Blancs 2014, Nyetimber Classic Cuvée and Wiston Estate Rosé 2014 – while Eduardo showed a fuller range from the Errázuriz stable – Las Pizarras Chardonnay and Pinot Noir 2016 from his Aconcagua Costa vineyards; Viñedo Chadwick 2015; Don Maximiano Founder's Reserve and Seña 2013; Kai (mostly Carmenère) 2010 and Don Maximiano Founder's Reserve 2009. While these wines were well known in London, they were not in Paris. In late October Eduardo and I held similar tastings at the Grand Hyatt in Beijing and at the Académie in Tokyo.

My memoirs were launched in June and there were book-signings over the next few weeks, by far the most pleasurable being in Bordeaux, over a lunch hosted by Véronique Sanders at Château Haut-Bailly, and an evening reception the following day hosted by Jean-Michel Cazes. A visit to the *Cité des civilizations du vin* on the waterfront, not far from the merchant's cellars on the Quai des Chartrons where I had trained 53 years earlier, showed me how much had changed, while a leisurely lunch with my old friend John Salvi revealed that in the Médoc some things remained just the same. Michael Broadbent once remarked, 'one always comes back to claret', and I agree. A 2020 catalogue of my Dorset cellar revealed that of the 2,988 bottles below stairs, 759 were claret. That's quite a lot to come back to.

Later that summer I attended the second of what was to become an annual seminar of Fine Minds 4 Fine Wines to be hosted by Champagne AR Lenoble at their cellars near Epernay. Everyone had brought bottles for the two-day event and I pressed the cellar master into tasting Bride Valley's Blanc de Blancs 2014 alongside his Chouilly Grand Cru. He was complimentary and direct, saying 'you've got what we've lost: acidity'.

While the sales of my memoirs were going well, I sensed that bookstores were not as interested in books about wine as they once were. What was on the much-reduced shelves were erudite, well-written tomes on countries or regions, and buying guides. Over lunch with Hugh Johnson, I wondered aloud what had happened to the literature of wine that had inspired us. Where were the equivalents of such marvellous books as *Stay Me With Flagons*, *In Search of Wine* that had entranced and taught us in the 1960s? Who now remembered the wonderful annual *The Compleat Imbiber*, edited with such flair by Cyril Ray? 'All gone,' Hugh replied. 'Maybe someone should try to re-create them.'

The two most precious books in my own library are not about wine, but about art. They are illustrated by British painter Steven Spurrier RA (1878–1961) – no relation – and Henri Matisse (1869–1954), artists as different from each other as they could possibly be. Spurrier's illustrations covered the theatre, some fashion and popular culture, and he was particularly fascinated by the circus, the famous name in the 1930s being that of circus-owner Bertram Mills (1873–1938). Spurrier had travelled with Mills's circus, researching illustrations for Noel Streatfeild's *The Circus is Coming* (J M Dent & Sons Ltd, 1938). My single-edition book is simply entitled *Circus*, and was created for and dedicated to Bertram's son, Cyril, 'with appreciation and best wishes from Gertrude and Steven Spurrier, December 1947'. It contains 14 colour drawings of acrobats, clowns, jugglers, horses and elephants dated from 1933 to 1938. Most are just sketches, but they take you into the Big Top as if it were yesterday.

Also precious to me, Matisse's *Jazz*, a 2005 reproduction of the original 1947 Téiade publication by Editions Anthèse, is a sizable boxed set of around 50 images and one of a limited edition created to coincide with the exhibition of the originals at the Musée du Luxembourg in Paris. There are parallels with wine. I have often split wines into two categories, those that are made to impress (which are not the wines for me) and those that are made to express. Matisse certainly impresses, but

Matisse's *Icarus* (1947) in free-fall, and (*in front*) Spurrier's *Baker Boys* (1934), which captures the speed, energy and danger of their virtuoso bareback performance.

via the transcendental expression of colour and form. Spurrier on the other hand allows the actors in his circus sketches to express themselves.

Encouraged by my discussion with Hugh about the dearth of good wine books, I contacted Simon McMurtrie, whom I had got to know when he was group chief executive of Laithwaite's/Direct Wines five years earlier. I knew Simon had a brilliant business brain, but didn't know that at a young age he had been publisher at Mitchell Beazley and had published Hugh Johnson and Michael Broadbent, among others. I put to him the idea of using the Académie du Vin name as the publisher of high-quality, thoughtful wine books. He liked the idea, and we started to make plans, agreeing that the first book we should publish would be a commemorative edition of Michael Broadbent's *Wine Tasting* (1968), the book that had first inspired me. Aware of my rather slight grasp of business realities, Simon's advice as co-founder of the Académie du Vin Library was friendly but firm: 'Keep having the ideas, Steven, but stay away from the numbers.'

Back at Bride Valley, Bella and I had converted part of our original stable block into an office and storeroom, the open-plan living space upstairs providing the perfect tasting room. This gradually became my 'Wine and Art' room, and now houses the scores of pictures and artefacts I have amassed over the years, including what my father called his 'spit-outs' of 18th-century glass, Michael Broadbent's wine maps of the Médoc and the Mosel, and the original metre-square logo from the Académie du Vin.

The very first picture I bought at Sotheby's in 1958 for six guineas was an original coloured engraving by George Townly Stubbs (1748–1815), after England's greatest equine artist George Stubbs (1724–1806). My second purchase that same year was a pair of still-life lithographs by the French Fauvist Maurice de Vlaminck (1906–58). Although I had a cheque book and paid for them there and then, since I was still under 18, the gallery told me they could not do business with 'minors' and made the bill out in my father's name.

The room is a sort of kaleidoscope of visual images where we can seat two dozen or so for a tasting or lunch. The gardens to the back have a stretch of water running from our farm that cascades over a waterfall and down through the village towards the sea. Here, I have a collection of free-standing sculptures by Marzia Colonna and Caroline White, and I hope to keep adding to them.

Above: my wine, art and tasting room; *below*: Bella and me with Brother Sun, Sister Moon, by Marzia Colonna ARBS.

The difference between buying art and buying wine is that the former is more immediate: you come across something you know you like, know you would like to have, and then must decide if you can afford it. If you don't buy it there and then, it might have gone when you change your mind and come back the next day. Wine on the other hand is usually bought at leisure and ends up in the cellar waiting for its time to come.

Art and wine should both represent 'value for money', but the more important value, especially of art, should be pleasure. Some say that more than half the value of a wine cellar lies in the anticipation of the pleasure it will yield. This is not particularly the case for me, although my last bottles of Taylor and Dow 1977 and Quinta do Noval 1963, which have been sleeping quietly for over three decades, inspire pleasurable anticipation as their decanting time draws near.

Art and possessions – objects, sculptures, furniture – are there in daily life all the time, reminding you of their stories, whereas wine can talk to you only once it is in the glass. I have more works by Steven Spurrier than by any other artist. I recall going to a retrospective of his watercolours at the Leicester Galleries in London shortly after his death and finding them a bit 'wishy washy', but this missed the point entirely, for although he was a prodigious, prolific and admired artist, he was above all an illustrator. His work was meant to please, not to provoke (which could seem an easy approach in art as well as in wine) and when you saw how much they pleased, the point came home.

Our vineyard is a working vineyard, but I don't work it, rather walk up and down the rows admiring it and the many hundreds of Italian Alders we planted for windbreaks. While I hope that my plan to change a loss-making sheep farm into a profit-making vineyard will still come true, it already produces wines that sparkle with purity and precision and gives great visual pleasure.

The potential of the 2018 harvest was looking great. After three very small years in 2015, '16 and '17, we needed a big crop, preferably of good quality, and we got both. After a cold spring, the summer was truly Mediterranean – I even found myself with the grandchildren swimming in the Channel for the first time since my prep-school days in Hastings. Our vintage normally starts in mid-October, a month after Champagne's, but this year we kicked off on September 28th.

I had always said, somewhat flippantly, that if ever the grapes were ripe enough, we would make some still wine. On the opening day of harvest, the tiny south-facing block of Pinot Noir had small berries and dark skins and was showing 11% potential alcohol. Off it went to the Furleigh Estate for red wine. Two weeks later the harvest was coming to an end, winemaker Ian Edwards having bought in extra tanks for what turned out to be almost 60,000 bottles – more than the previous seven vintages put together. With quite enough Chardonnay already pressed for sparkling wine, the final block, again at 11% potential alcohol, was set aside to make still wine. Thus were born Dorset Chardonnay – which on tasting Hugh Johnson took for a Montagny – and Dorset Pinot Noir: around 3,000 bottles of each. We made another Chardonnay in the lighter 2019 vintage, and some Pinot Noir Rosé, but we need a summer like 2018 to produce another red.

Meanwhile, Wines of Chile had invited me to host two big tastings for its export market in China, so at the end of October I arrived via Hong Kong airport at Shenzen in the south of the country. Wide boulevards lined with palm trees and spanking new high-rise buildings showed a bustling prosperity, and the 100+ audience at a packed seminar took to the wines. The Chilean style, fruit-forward but less robust than Australia's, is easy to appreciate and the price is reasonable. The next day a similar event was held in Beijing, and that evening my hosts met at the Chilean Embassy where we were to dine with the Ambassador and Eduardo Chadwick. The following afternoon and evening I was again sharing the podium with Eduardo, accompanied by China's top wine educator Fongyee Walker MW, for another presentation of our 'Into the Future' programme. Eduardo and I took the same tasting to the Académie du Vin in Tokyo two days later.

Back in London, the first weekend in November was the *Decanter* Fine Wine Encounter, where I had been asked to present a masterclass of 12 wines that had meant a lot to me over five decades in wine. The choice was surprisingly easy:

Bride Valley Blanc de Blancs 2014 (of course)
Pol Roger Blanc de Blancs 2008 (from the champagne house that has been my
     favourite since Paris days)
Domaine Georges Vernay Condrieu Les Chaillees de l'Enfer 2016 (from the
     man who saved Viognier for the world)

López de Heredia Viña Tondonia Reserva Blanco Rioja 2005 (an estate I
    visited in 1965 and have never forgotten)
Ch Prieuré-Lichine Quatrième Cru Classé Margaux 2010 (Alexis Lichine, who
    owned and restored this château between 1951 and 1989, was my hero)
Domaine Tempier Bandol Cuvée Classique 2011 (to remember my friends Lulu
    and Lucien Peyraud)
Marchesi Antinori Tignanello IGT 2006 (both the man and the wine epitomize
    pure Tuscany)
Viñedo Chadwick Alto Maipo Valley Chile 2000
St Henri Shiraz Penfolds 2004
Schloss Vollrads Rheingau Riesling Spätlese 2004
Hugel Pinot Gris Sélection des Grains Nobles 1989 (to remember the great
    Johnny Hugel, who masterminded the SGNs)

The wines were all marvellous, and while I spoke about the people behind them, they spoke about themselves – so eloquently that they received their own standing ovation. I was deeply moved.

A 48-hour turnaround at the end of the following week found me in the Cape, at the invitation of the De Wet family, to be one of the keynote speakers at their annual Celebration of Chardonnay event. The De Wetshof Estate was founded in the early 1970s, but ancestors had arrived in the Cape in 1634, later making their base in the Robertson Valley. One of the best-known and best-liked of South Africa's wine producers, Danie De Wet, has now passed the reins to third-generation Johann in the vineyards and Peter in the cellar. They concentrate on Chardonnays and are acknowledged as industry leaders, producing six different bottlings. We were treated to a vertical tasting of the flagship Bateleur over dinner. The estate is out on a limb, a good two hours' drive from Cape Town, and is more famous for its fruit production than for its wine. Indeed, while some fruit-growing estates have been converted into successful vineyards, many more have tried then reverted to fruit. The De Wets succeeded because they kept firmly to their vision.

As well as attending the Bordeaux En Primeur tastings in early April, I had gone to Tuscany for the Anti-Prima tastings of wines from Chianti Classico, Brunello de Montalcino and Vino Nobile di Montepulciano. Through these I had developed a great interest in Sangiovese, especially from Chianti, so it was an honour to be invited to Florence on the opening day to be named Gallo Nero Ambassador of the Year. The award comes with no responsibilities other than being seen to support Chianti Classico. The growing number of bottles in my cellar bear out my total commitment.

At the end of March, accompanied by Caroline Gilby MW, an expert on Eastern European wines, I attended the WineUp Fair in Cluj-Napoca, the unofficial capital of Transylvania in northeast Romania, a charming town with landmarks dating from Saxon and Hungarian rule. Our hosts were Ioana Micu and her husband, founders of ArtVinium, who had created this event a few years back to educate consumers and producers about Romania's wine growing potential. Held in the fine Baroque Bánffy Palace, which also houses the Museum of Art, it was an extensive walk-around tasting with a masterclass on each of two afternoons. For mine, on the second day, six 'classic wines' had been selected, and I was asked to select a further six that had impressed me from the tastings. I recall a lovely sparkling blanc de blancs from local grapes, an Aligoté-Chardonnay blend that Burgundy would have envied and a Cabernet Franc. I look forward to returning, having now decided to focus my wine trips in Europe where there is so much still to discover.

One of the most memorable evenings of the year was the combined launch of the commemorative edition of Michael Broadbent's *Wine Tasting* and the newly formed Académie du Vin Library at Vintners' Hall on April 30th. As the event coincided with the DWWA week of tastings, judges from all over the world who knew Michael were able to attend. Guests had a choice of Bride Valley Dorset Crémant, Pol Roger White Foil (from Michael's favourite champagne house) and Frescobaldi Chianti Classico to keep them going, and after a fine presentation about the Académie du Vin Library by chairman Simon McMurtrie, I presented the first copy of the new book to Michael, who, smiling, was splendidly enthroned in one of the Vintners' armorial chairs. Bartholomew Broadbent noted how appropriate it was to see this book launched just two days before his father's 92nd birthday and two days after his wedding to Valerie Smallwood.

To show how important Michael's book was, I feel it is worth quoting the opening paragraph of *Wine Tasting* in its entirety: 'The original article, upon

Fifty-one years after its original publication, our commemorative edition of Michael Broadbent's *Wine Tasting* launches the Académie du Vin Library at the Vintners Hall. Simon McMurtrie and Valerie Smallwood join the ovation.

which this book is based, was written in 1962. At that time I was with Harveys and one of my tasks was to conduct weekly tastings for the executive and sales staff in Bristol. What struck me was not only the inconsistency of the approach to tasting in general but also that, understandably, the newer recruits had very little idea what to look for when confronted with an unknown glass of wine. As for laymen, the vast majority had not the faintest idea how to proceed – this was immediately apparent at the many lecture-tastings that I, and other members of the Harveys staff, conducted all over the country in those days. In short, very few seemed to know even the first principles of wine tasting. Nor were they helped by existing writers on wine, for in the whole course of some pretty voracious reading I had come across not a book, not a chapter even, which dealt – in English at any rate – with what I considered a pretty vital subject.'

At the end of June I was in Toronto to give a presentation on 'The Future of Fine Wine' at the George Brown College of Applied Arts and Technology. This sort of theme is not simple, for at no time in history have fine wines been as good as they are now, with dozens joining their ranks each year. The future is bright, just as it is for wine drinkers looking for an everyday glass. I proposed various scenarios and left lots of time for questions which, in an auditorium of 150 or so people, came thick and fast. The previous day a busload of attendees had been taken up to

With author and
Master of Wine,
Fiona Morrison,
whose day job (with
her husband Jacques
Thienpont) is the
running of three
Bordeaux estates:
Le Pin, L'IF and
L'Hêtre.

Niagara Wine Country. Once again, I marvelled how much the scene had changed since my first visit in 1986, when my voyage beneath the Falls in *The Maid of the Mist* was a great deal more memorable than the mostly hybrid wines I tasted.

Back in London I joined a privileged crowd in Berry Bros & Rudd's Napoleon Cellar on July 10th for the launch of the Académie du Vin Library's second book, *10 Great Wine Families – A Tour Through Europe* by Fiona Morrison MW. Hugh Johnson sums it up thus: 'Fiona has written a book from a viewpoint no other writer, as far as I know, has ever possessed: a seat at the heart of the action.' Fiona is married to Jacques Thienpont, owner and winemaker of Le Pin in Pomerol. The tremendous success of their wine has seen the couple forging friendships with some of the greatest wine families in Europe – all sharing a similarly uncompromising pursuit of quality. All but one of the families featured in Fiona's book were there that evening, having sent ahead bottles from their own cellars for the celebration.

Back in 2013 I attended the three-day International Pinot Noir Celebration (IPNC) at McMinnville, a little town about two hours' drive south of Portland, right in the middle of Oregon's wine country. At that time it was as a guest speaker, this time, at the end of July 2019, I was the lead speaker; asked to choose Burgundy as the theme and make my presentation on two consecutive days to an audience of more than 400. I felt the IPNC (described by Frank J Prial as 'the most un-buttoned of all wine festivals') needed a surprise, so I chose to focus the Côte-Chalonnaise, for far too long overshadowed by the Côtes de Nuits and Beaune, under the title 'Côte-Chalonnaise – the Third Côte'. Having opened the presentation with Aubert de Villaine's Bouzeron 2017, the appellation from 100% Aligoté that he himself had brought about, we moved onto three Chardonnays: Château de Rully Rully, Domaine de la Ferté Givry and Louis Jadot Mercurey. Then four reds: A et P de Villaine's Bourgogne Côte Chalonnaise La Digoine, Louis Jadot Rully, Antonin Rodet Givry and Château de Chamirey Mercurey. The tasting went down a storm, and the wines showed great value for money as well, everyone agreed, as giving great pleasure.

Then it was time to pack up the car for our August holiday. For a decade or more the pattern has been the same: a three-day drive through France on varying routes heading for Tuscany to spend a week at Nittardi near Castellina in Chianti, and then 10 days or so at Castello di Argiano in the southern part of the Brunello di Montalcino DOCG, always being there for Bella's birthday on the 14th. At Piero Masi's small Chianti estate, he and I spent a long morning putting together the MS blends for Fratelli from the prolific 2019 vintage. Then Argiano always offers time for a new discovery, and this year it was Paradiso di Frassina in the north of the DOCG where the owner, with support from the universities of Florence and Siena and sponsorship from Bose, has installed 100 speakers that broadcast Mozart 24 hours a day over two hectares of vines. The estate's single-vineyard wine is called Flauto Magico / Magic Flute, and the regular Brunello, Moz Art Wine.

We were back in good time to attend my brother Nicky's 80th birthday at the family home in Derbyshire. Sixteen of us sat down for lunch around the very table at which, on Christmas Eve 1954, our grandfather had told me I was old enough to try the port – Cockburn 1908. Moving slowly with a walking frame, Nicky made it into the dining room, seating himself in front of his portrait, and was in good cheer throughout the meal; but sadly it was the last time we were to be together.

Ben Howkins was the first winner of the WSET Scholarship the following year, so it was appropriate that the launch of his book, *Sherry: Maligned, Misunderstood, Magnificent!* (the Académie du Vin Library's third title) took place four days after the presentation. He and I, with Beltrán Domecq, president of the Consejo Regulador de Jerez, hosted a masterclass with the following wines:

Tío Pepe En Rama (bottled 2019)

Tomás Barbadillo Single Private Cask Amontillado

Bodegas Tradition Old Fino (in magnums)

Valdespino Palo Cortado Single Cask 2000 (from its Macharnudo vineyards)

Bodegas Alonso (Sanlúcar) Single Cask Amontillado (over 100 years old
   with no younger wine added since the early 1990s)

Three half-bottles of this last wine had been drawn from the cask in early October. They left Beltrán speechless, for even he had not tasted a wine of such age that had held such vitality and vigour. The strength of sherry, which is being recognized at last, is in its diversity, from the driest of the dry finos to the sweetest of the sweet PXs.

Lunching with a friend on November 15th, I received a call from Bella to tell me that Nicky had died. I excused myself to return to my flat, and called Derbyshire to speak to my sister-in-law. The answering machine clicked in, and when I heard Nicky's calm voice saying 'You've reached Marston Hall, we're not able to take your call…' I just sat down and cried.

The funeral took place in early December. Family and close friends met for the service in the local church, where Nicky had been 'Patron of the Living' as had our father and grandfather before him. The church was overflowing, so highly had he been respected in the county. Locals who had known our grandfather (Captain Jack) and father (Mr John) as well as Nicholas had many kind words. We decided to place his ashes in our parents' grave on what would have been his 81st birthday, joining four centuries of Spurriers in the churchyard. The estate will be sold, but the memories will endure.

The launch of the *Académie du Vin* Library's fourth book took place at 67 Pall Mall. Few readers under 60 will have heard of *The Compleat Imbiber*, an annual illustrated compendium of the best writing on wine, its art, culture and history. Edited by Cyril Ray, the co-founder of The Circle of Wine Writers, it was the perfect gift, but sadly was no longer produced after 1992.

With support once again from Hugh Johnson, we re-launched it as *In Vino Veritas*, and I have high hopes that it too will become an annual. To welcome members to the launch and help with the book signing, I hosted a masterclass from the 2005 vintage with wines from my cellar.

Bella and I had exciting plans to spend the end of December and new year in Uruguay. A handful of Uruguayan producers had presented their wines at their embassy in London in the late 1990s and a few of them, particularly the Pisano family, had attended the London Wine Trade Fair ever since. Daniel Pisano always asked 'when are you coming to see us?', and this time, at the Fair in May, I was able to surprise him by saying 'in the New Year'. Daniel and his former export manager Fabiana Bracco (now with her own Bracco Bosca winery) jumped into action, as did Christian Wylie, head winemaker at Bodega Garzón, Uruguay's flagship estate, and within a few days it was all set up.

Compared to its neighbours, Uruguay is tiny, yet it has the widest river in the world – Rio de la Plata, 45 kilometres bank to bank at its broadest – and the oldest (2,500 million years) bedrock vineyard soil on the planet. It also produces top-class footballers that it can't afford to keep and makes excellent European-style wines that are more appreciated abroad than at home. There are vineyards all over this little country, which straddles the 30–35th South parallels, the same latitude as the best vineyards from Argentina, Chile, South Africa, Australia and New Zealand. Uruguay is the only wine producer in South America with an Atlantic climate, giving cool nights that lead to balance and elegance.

The main grape varieties are Albariño, Chardonnay, Sauvignon Blanc and Viognier for the whites, Cabernets Franc and Sauvignon, Merlot, Pinot Noir, Syrah and especially Tannat for the reds. Just as Argentina has re-introduced Malbec to wine drinkers, so Uruguay has taken Tannat to levels of elegance and power that the grape's home at Madiran in southwest France can rarely achieve.

At the end of January, I flew to Budapest to give a masterclass on wines from Fiona Morrison's *10 Great Wine Families* at the city's well-attended wine fair, having spent the whole of the previous day in Villány, three hours south of the city and home to some of Europe's finest Cabernet Franc. Villány Cabernet Franc now has its own appellation as Hungary's most highly regarded red wine. The three main producers, all located in or around the historic little town, are Bock, whose tasting took us back to a 1993; Malatinszky, whose wines are as aristocratic and elegant as their owner, and Gere, which produces some remarkable Merlot.

A quick turnaround found me once again in Washington DC for my fifth year as a judge of Virginia's Governor's Cup. This year the reds dominated – Cabernet Franc, Meritage, Petit Verdot and Tannat – with the exception of a superb 2018 Vermentino from Barboursville Vineyards. The winner emerged as 868 Estate Vineyards' Vidal Blanc 2017.

My second evening in the city coincided with the opening night of a band named Palace, whose songwriter and base-guitarist was my nephew. I took a long drive downtown to find standing room only at the venue. I managed to grab a beer and squeeze in about five rows from the front, where I was surrounded by a wildly expectant young crowd. After a warm-up act, Palace appeared to thunderous applause and I pushed myself towards the stage to wave at Rupert, who waved back. Two girls wheeled round exclaiming 'My God, you actually *know* Rupert!'

'Yes, I am his uncle,' I replied, proudly, later reflecting that it was good to be known in Washington DC for something other than the Judgement of Paris.

Late February found me in Alsace. This beautiful wine region is so sheltered from rain and cold winds by the Vosges Mountains that the historic centre, Colmar, has a climate as dry as Perpignan's on the Spanish border. The myriad soils on the mostly hillside vineyards are so different in each village that 51 grands crus have been identified, and there are 100 or so premiers crus awaiting classification. Alsace is becoming more and more like Burgundy, as is its Pinot Noir, which was made only as a rosé on my first visit in 1965.

Since the revivification of the Académie du Vin name in 2017, Marc Nadeau had been working on setting it up again as an education and tasting centre in Toronto, where in the 1980s it had been a part of his successful Wine Establishment venture. In March I arrived for the launch, which started with a walk-around tasting for sommeliers and members of the wine trade, followed by a dinner with a superb selection of wines, mostly from Marc's private cellar, in homage to Michael Broadbent. Future events will be held in partnership with the Vintage Conservatory, Toronto's answer to 67 Pall Mall, with whom they have a reciprocal members' arrangement. The following evening there was a dinner over rare sherries, the Académie du Vin Library's book *Sherry* much in evidence.

When I arrived back in Gatwick the morning of March 15th, the country – and soon much of Europe and the world – was heading for 'lockdown' in response to the Coronavirus pandemic. Commercial and social life were suspended, no one knowing how long lockdown would keep us confined. The extraordinary circumstances this brought about left me with time on my hands to make a thorough inventory of my cellar.

Our early-Victorian house doesn't have stone bins, but there is space for many wine racks and stacks of wooden cases behind. The temperature averages 10°C over the year, which is good for long maturity. I decided to go off-piste for evening reds, opening the odd bottle that had been forgotten for years. First off were three Douro 2001s, including the second vintage of the Prats-Symington Chryseia, still in its Médoc mode. Hearing of the death of Carlos Falcó, Marqués de Griñón, led me to open a 2000 Syrah from his Dominio de Valdepusa estate near Toledo, which was still full of velvety vigour. The Spanish rack revealed several old vintages of Marqués de Cáceres Rioja Gran Reserva, of which the 1998 and 1991 were classics in their mature warmth.

France could not be ignored and my last bottle of Dominique Lafon's Volnay-Santenots du Milieu 1999 was sumptuously worth waiting for. Château d'Angludet 1996, punching above its weight as usual, showed the vintage's staying power, while the Delas Côte-Rôtie Seigneur de Maugiron 1999 reminded me why I have followed this wine through most of the younger vintages. The 1999 Brunello di Montalcinos – from Tenute Silvio Nardi, La Gerla and especially Casanova di Neri – also showed superbly, and then it was time for the New World.

Rustenberg's Cabernet Sauvignon Peter Barlow recalled a fruity Latour, Andrew Pirie's Pipers Brook Opimian 1997 from Tasmania was very much in the claret style, and even better was Cullen Diana Madeline 2001, the first vintage released by Vanya Cullen in memory of her mother. From Chile Viñedo Chadwick 2005, planted by Eduardo on his late father's polo field, raised the Alto Maipo Valley Cabernet Sauvignon to new heights, while Seña 1996, only the second vintage made by Eduardo with Robert Mondavi, blossomed with warmth and depth. California's St-Supéry Private Reserve Cabernet Sauvignon 1989 proved that you can keep Napa Cabs and they won't disappoint.

Each of these wines and others had a story to tell of the place and the people, but, as the last bottles of Léoville Barton from the 1990s reminded me: 'One always comes back to claret.'

The wines in my cellar are 90 percent European, about 70 percent of which are French (with Italy on the rise), about 35 percent of those being claret.

I have always maintained that the bottles Hugh Johnson describes as being 'worth talking about' are simply represented by the three Ps – the Place and the People create the Product, which will tell its own story. Writing this I have recalled the theme of my speech at Kate's wedding in May 2004, taken from Annie Bingham, our great friend from Paris who was of course present. The secret to a happy life actually lies in the three Ss – Someone to love, Something to do and Something to look forward to. I have been most fortunate in my Ss (my initials giving me a head start). Meeting Bella and joining the wine trade in early 1964 has guaranteed the first two, and Kate's astute observation that 'your problem, Dad, is that you're bored by the present', recognizes that looking forward is a way of life.
July 2020

Our engagement photograph appeared in November 1967 in the *Daily Express'* 'William Hickey' society column, then written by Nigel Dempster. In a different time and different place (*right*), Bella and I strike a similar pose in August 2020.

283

INDEX

Page numbers in *italic* refer to the
illustrations.

Picture credits: p101 Alamy; p157 Alamy; p259 Catharine Lowe/*Decanter*.

Jancis Robinson's tribute to Steven Spurrier on page 36 is an extract from a longer piece written for the *Financial Times* May 27th 2006.

Excerpt from George Taber's *Judgment of Paris, California vs France and the Historic 1976 Paris Tasting that Revolutionized Wine* (Scribner 2005), pages 130–137, reprinted in Steven Spurrier's original memoirs and here with kind permission of the author.